Baseball's Funnymen

ALSO BY LEW FREEDMAN
AND FROM McFARLAND

The Boyer Brothers of Baseball (2015)

Joe Louis: The Life of a Heavyweight (2013)

*DiMaggio's Yankees: A History of
the 1936–1944 Dynasty* (2011)

*The Day All the Stars Came Out: Major League
Baseball's First All-Star Game, 1933* (2010)

*Hard-Luck Harvey Haddix and
the Greatest Game Ever Lost* (2009)

*Early Wynn, the Go-Go White Sox and
the 1959 World Series* (2009)

Baseball's Funnymen

Twenty-Four Jokers, Screwballs, Pranksters and Storytellers

LEW FREEDMAN

McFarland & Company, Inc., Publishers
Jefferson, North Carolina

All photographs are from the National Baseball
Hall of Fame Library, Cooperstown, New York

LIBRARY OF CONGRESS CATALOGUING-IN-PUBLICATION DATA

Names: Freedman, Lew, author.
Title: Baseball's Funnymen : Twenty-Four Jokers, Screwballs,
Pranksters and Storytellers / Lew Freedman.
Description: Jefferson, North Carolina : McFarland & Company, Inc.,
Publishers, 2017. | Includes bibliographical references and index.
Identifiers: LCCN 2016054829 | ISBN 9781476663586
(softcover : acid free paper) ∞
Subjects: LCSH: Baseball players—United States—Anecdotes. |
Baseball players—United States—Biography. | Baseball—
United States—Anecdotes. | Baseball—United States—Humor.
Classification: LCC GV873 .F72 2017 | DDC 796.3570922 [B]—dc23
LC record available at https://lccn.loc.gov/2016054829

BRITISH LIBRARY CATALOGUING DATA ARE AVAILABLE

ISBN (paper) 978-1-4766-6358-6
ISBN (ebook) 978-1-4766-2493-8

© 2017 Lew Freedman. All rights reserved

*No part of this book may be reproduced or transmitted in any form
or by any means, electronic or mechanical, including photocopying
or recording, or by any information storage and retrieval system,
without permission in writing from the publisher.*

Front cover: Washington Senators coach Nick Altrock (right)
and umpire Harry Geisel (National Baseball Hall of Fame Library,
Cooperstown, New York)

Printed in the United States of America

*McFarland & Company, Inc., Publishers
Box 611, Jefferson, North Carolina 28640
www.mcfarlandpub.com*

Table of Contents

Introduction 1

1. Nick Altrock	5		13. Lefty Gomez	96
2. Al Schacht	11		14. Bill Veeck	103
3. Waite Hoyt	19		15. Jim Bouton	111
4. Babe Herman	27		16. Bo Belinsky	118
5. Rabbit Maranville	35		17. Tug McGraw	126
6. Dizzy Dean	42		18. Harry Caray	134
7. Satchel Paige	51		19. Ron Luciano	141
8. Max Patkin	58		20. Jay Johnstone	148
9. Casey Stengel	65		21. Bill Lee	155
10. Joe Engel	73		22. Steve Lyons	164
11. Yogi Berra	80		23. Ozzie Guillen	172
12. Joe Garagiola	88		24. Bob Uecker	179

Epilogue 186
Chapter Notes 193
Bibliography 205
Index 209

Introduction

> "He's got power enough to hit home runs in any park, including Yellowstone."—*Cincinnati Reds manager Sparky Anderson on fellow Hall of Famer Pirates slugger Willie Stargell.*[1]

THERE ARE MORE LAUGHS in baseball than in football, basketball and hockey combined. That is not a mathematical surety, but it is an observation that feels true.

It's not as if funny stuff never happens in those sports, but football seems serious and the head coaches come off like the spokesmen in the White House briefing room. In hockey, it's all about stand-up guys. In basketball the players seem worried that if they make fun of something they will be ridiculed.

Over the years it has been suggested that more humorous things happen or are said in baseball because of the game's pace. There are short breaks between every pitch. There are longer breaks between each half-inning. There is pre-game clubhouse time leading up to the game. There is spring training, which lasts for weeks, an environment where the games don't count in standings.

There is plenty of time to kill, considerable time for a wit to express himself or a practical joker to dream up gags.

> "If I played there, they'd name a candy bar after me."—*Reggie Jackson on perhaps signing with New York as a free agent.*
>
> "When you unwrap one, it tells you how good it is."—*Jim "Catfish" Hunter, after the Reggie Bar was created when Jackson joined the Yankees.*[2]

Sometimes players do or say unintentionally funny things. They are captured on tape recorders or in video highlights. These may be one-offs or accidents. The true baseball funny man works at his craft. He is naturally witty or clever. Certain players, managers, owners, or broadcasters are funny men and they have built up repertoires over time.

With the exception of the Harlem Globetrotters, who lifted clowning around to an art form in basketball, it is difficult to identify many players, coaches or others involved in football, basketball or hockey as clowns. To them it would be an insult. In baseball, to be labeled a clown is more of a compliment. There are several individuals associated with professional baseball that were called clowns and reveled in the description, making a living, essentially a second career, out of being funny.

Some players have always been strongly identified with the lighter side of the game. Yet they were not intentionally funny. They just did things that came naturally that made people chuckle. Mark Fidrych, who took the country by storm as a rookie with the Detroit Tigers in 1976, was a joyful young man who gained renowned because he talked to the baseball before pitching. It helped that Fidrych won 19 games that season.

Fidrych was spontaneous, youthful, naïve, and a good pitcher whose actions tickled fans, and they loved him. He was the personification of entertainment within the game, but he was no stand-up comic.

> "They wanted me to play third base like Brooks, so I did play like Brooks—Mel Brooks."—*Andy Van Slyke, who did not compare favorably with Brooks Robinson as a glove man.*[3]

Clowns make people laugh, and going back to the early days of the 20th century, selected individuals recognized that there was a market for a baseball-oriented clown act. Whether coaching, managing, or broadcasting, there are those who love baseball with every fiber of their being, but do not have the talent to reach the majors as a player, or who wish to remain in the game after they retire as players.

They somehow find a niche, a way to stick around. Nick Altrock, Al Schacht and Max Patkin were baseball men through and through, but they did everything but dress like circus clowns when it came to perfecting humorous acts that could entertain the thousands sitting in the stands.

One word—flake—has long been used to describe a player by his teammates who seemed a bit off-kilter. Whether he said weird things or did weird things in the clubhouse or on the field, "flake" could be applied, and although the definition is vague, everyone knew what was meant when someone said, "He's a flake."

Given the benefit of hindsight, some early 20th-century players called flakes or summed up as unpredictable might well have been mentally ill. At least revisionist history tells us so in the case of Rube Waddell.

Introduction

A terrific pitcher when he was focused, Waddell did not hold his concentration well. He played by his own set of rules for the Philadelphia Athletics, St. Louis Browns, and other teams. That resulted in conflict with his managers. Once, Waddell walked off the mound in mid-game and went fishing. He drank excessively, blowing through his paychecks. Shiny objects flashed in his eyes seemed to hypnotize him. So did the sight of passing fire engines. Periodically, he ran out of a ballpark to chase them. Waddell wrestled alligators at times, though his won-loss record in that sport is hard to come by.

Waddell won 193 games, completed his career with a 2.16 earned run average, set strikeout records and ended up in the Hall of Fame, but was only 37 when he died in 1914. The independent observer laughed at Waddell's antics, but if he suffered from mental retardation, attention deficit disorder, or some other mental deficiency that went undiagnosed, it feels discomfiting to classify him as a funny man.

> "One percent of ball players are leaders of men. The other 99 percent are followers of women."—*New York Giants Hall of Fame manager John J. McGraw.*[4]
>
> "If diamonds are a girl's best friend, why do so many girls get mad when you want to go to the ball park?"—*Singer-songwriter Bob Dylan.*[5]
>
> "She wanted a big diamond."—*New York Mets player Mookie Wilson on why he got married at home plate.*[6]

There are players whose humor endures, and there are players who were transitory on the scene. One fellow who is little remembered today was a funny man in the 1930s and 1940s and then died tragically.

Jackie Price was born in 1912 and spent several years in the minors between the mid–1930s and mid–1940s (with time out for World War II) and reached the majors for seven games in 1946 as a shortstop with the Cleveland Indians.

He entertained crowds by hanging upside-down to hit. A Cadillac dealer lent Price a convertible, and he drove it around the outfield, leaning out the window to catch fly balls shot from a bazooka-type gun. Once, Price went too far in a practical joke by unleashing two boa constrictors on a train. Indians manager Lou Boudreau—generally a fan of Price's antics—ordered him thrown off the train. For a short time Price was called "The Clown Prince of Baseball," but he committed suicide by hanging in 1967.

Perhaps Price would best fit on a list of baseball tragedies, but choosing the funniest of the baseball funny men automatically opens the task to second-guessing. Humor is a subjective art, and what is funny to one person is obnoxious to another. One person may laugh hysterically over certain behavior, and another might want to see the perpetrator arrested for the same act.

The 24 funny men (plus bonus honorable mention guys) included here earned their reputations, some in press conferences, some on the air waves, some in their writings, several in more than one area. In some cases, it's possible that you had to be there to appreciate the full flower of the fun, but here's hoping all incidents cited translate to the printed page and stand the test of time.

> "With tears in my eyes."—*Pitcher Frank Sullivan on how he pitched against slugger Mickey Mantle.*[7]

1. Nick Altrock

"Since two screwballs seemed better than one, we decided to work together."—*Al Schacht on his partnership with Nick Altrock*[1]

HE COULD WIGGLE HIS EARS like an elephant, and some suggested that Nick Altrock's ears were about as big as a pachyderm's, too. He was a natural performer who became part of vaudeville.

Once a well-respected pitcher, Altrock was the first individual in baseball history to make a living by clowning or entertaining. Another player, Arlie Latham, who spent most of his playing days with St. Louis and Cincinnati in the late 1800s, clowned on the field, but his owners had no sense of humor and fined him rather than rewarded him. Altrock got paid for his comedy.

Born in Cincinnati in 1876, the same year the National League was founded, Altrock was a left-handed pitcher who broke into the majors with the Louisville Colonels in 1898. He seemed destined for a solid hurling career, but his pitching days were cut short by injury.

Altrock's best pitching occurred for the Chicago White Sox between 1904 and 1906, when he won 19, 23 and 20 games, respectively. In 1905, Altrock's earned run average was 1.88. In 1906, Altrock won a World Series game as the "Hitless Wonders" Sox upset the Chicago Cubs. However, he never won more than seven games in a season again, and by the time he was 32, Altrock was reduced to mostly a sideline role in baseball.

Occasionally, he dabbled on the field once more, but his lifetime pitching record was 83–75, the bulk of his success bunched into those three top-notch years.

By 1912, Altrock was a full-time coach for the Washington Senators. Periodically, he entered a game as a pinch-hitter over the years, the last time as a 57-year-old, becoming one of two players (Minnie Minoso is the other) to play in a Major League game for five decades. Altrock was a Senators coach for 42 years.

Altrock's humorous side emerged publicly for the first time shortly before his coaching days for the Senators began, when he was serving as a coach for Kansas City in the American Association. Altrock suddenly began shadow-boxing—with himself—before a crowd of 10,000 people. In the fourth inning, Altrock burst into fight. He pantomimed knocking himself out with a big right hand, falling to the ground as fans howled. Then he climbed to his feet, dusted himself off, and did it all over again.

The first reaction to Altrock's histrionics, appearing in the daily newspapers the next day, was to suggest that he was drunk. Actually, Altrock had dreamed up the scheme the night before the game while watching a film of a real boxer shadow boxing. The fighter was featherweight Johnny Kilbane, and Altrock said he chose a dull moment in the game to rev up his highly noticeable hand motions.

Altrock had a rubbery face, though not a handsome one, and when the Kansas City team cut him he told the manager, "Don't worry about me, with my face, I might break into the movies."[2]

Early in the 20th century, managers did not have the assistance of a gaggle of coaches. They did not have coaches at all. Altrock was hired by Senators owner Clark Griffith. Since Altrock couldn't pitch at a big-league level anymore, it was not clear just what his job description was. Trying to hang on to a paycheck, Altrock said, "I'm the king's jester."[3]

Washington decided to try out the novel position of first-base coach. Altrock returned to the field, but almost as soon as he got there, he went into a new act, wrestling with himself. That set off paroxysms of laughter amongst fans, players and umpires.

Naturally, some fuddyduddies expressed dismay that Altrock was disrespecting the game with his slapstick comedy routines. But he gained a powerful ally when American League president Ban Johnson sided with him. Johnson ruled that Altrock could perform his light-hearted joking as long as he did so between innings or when the ball was not in play.

Altrock was wildly popular with the Senators' fan base. The team itself, however, usually came up woefully short in the standings. Led by the inimitable Walter Johnson, Washington won a World Series title in 1924, but over the ensuing decades the Senators typically finished close to the bottom of the league standings. It was during this lengthy, dismal period that the phrase, "Washington, first in war, first in peace, and last in the American League" took hold to describe the fortunes of the team based in the nation's capital city.

1. Nick Altrock

Nick Altrock even enlisted umpires like Harry Geisel in his baseball clowning act. Like any good clown, Altrock would do just about anything to cajole a laugh out of the audience.

The fans' affinity for Altrock led management to insert him into the lineup near the end of lost seasons for the periodic pinch-hitting roles. That's why Altrock appeared in games in five decades. Mostly he was paid to make people laugh.

Later in life Altrock offered the intriguing observation that not even when he was in his heyday as a pitcher had he looked at throwing a baseball as a serious profession. "I never took but two things seriously in my life," Altrock said. "My clowning and my golf."[4] Altrock was a superior pitcher for the White Sox when he was healthy, but there is minor-league evidence to suggest he was goofy with the old Los Angeles Angels. In one game he walked a batter and subsequently picked him off first base. It was said he enjoyed eliminating the runner in that fashion so much that he promptly walked several more men on purpose and picked them off, too.

Altrock was a master of pantomime, acting out in exaggerated form to entertain a crowd by faking energetic boxing, tennis and golf matches. His big ears aided him, as did his bulbous nose. Altrock also had thick eyebrows, which he could arch dramatically.

Once a heckler got on Altrock's nerves and Altrock told him, "If I had your mouth full of dollar bills, I'd retire." But the heckler was not cowed. He shot back, "If I had your ears full of nickels, I'd retire."[5] Even Altrock admitted it was a snappy comeback, but he had the final word upon reflection. "Well, I guess the fan was right," he said, "but I wouldn't trade them ears for his mouth, not even with the world's greatest tenderloin steak thrown in. Why, them ears are my trademark."[6]

At times, mostly when he was still pitching, Altrock was referred to as "The Cincinnati Dutchman." Yet he was more often recognized as part of a comedy duo during his career. Once Altrock established that he could be funny, he was teamed with another Senators player, Germany Schaefer. That lasted until 1915, when Schaefer jumped to the Federal League, temporarily a third Major League. For two years Altrock worked with Senators backup Carl Sawyer.

Then Altrock paired with Al Schacht. The partnership became the most memorable double-play combination in baseball comedy history. That was an adventure story in itself since the men had a falling out, but continued to perform together. They were very much the odd couple due to the strained relations. Altrock and Schacht both coached for the Senators. They were so widely admired that they were invited to do their act at the World Series every year from 1921 to 1933.

Altrock's longevity in the role gave him broad appeal. Fans and sportswriters knew and appreciated his performances. "Nick is baseball's court jester," one sportswriter opined. "He's the fellow who provides the 'funny stuff' to an otherwise serious pastime, and the fact that King Fan, after years and years of his buffoonery hasn't as yet ordered his head chopped off testifies pretty conclusively to the effectiveness of this clown's wit."[7]

The writer, who referred to Schacht as Altrock's "assistant," as did many sportswriters, focused on Altrock as the bedrock of the act. "There is probably no greater practical joker in baseball than Nick Altrock, but we have yet to see one of his victims leave angry." Altrock's humor, it was noted, was "never offensive."[8]

Sometimes Altrock took things too far—away from the field. In 1940, when he was 63 and attending Senators spring training, Altrock spied an inviting grapefruit hanging from a tree. He began climbing the tree, took a slip, wedged his foot on a branch and broke an ankle. He stayed on the ground after that.

In 1944, working from memory, Altrock jotted down a poem that was attributed to the famed sportswriter Ring Lardner, harkening back to early in the hurler's career when his efforts helped carry the White Sox over the Cubs for a World Series crown in 1906.

1. Nick Altrock

The poem read in part:

> They called us the hitless wonders, yes,
> But what did we care for that?
> We used to travel a clip, I guess,
> We won even though we couldn't bat.
> Now they say I'm a clown and funny bloke,
> They laugh at my stunts and tricks,
> But the Cubs didn't think I was such a joke
> In Autumn of Nineteen O Six.
> My speed is all gone, my arm is all in,
> But I still have a lot of pride in
> The thought that Nick once helped to win
> A flag for the good old South Side.

The longer they worked together, the more creative acts Altrock and Schacht developed. At one point it was estimated that they had more than 150 skits in their repertoire. They kept adding routines based on current events in the sports world and the real world. Their partnership ceased after 1933 when Schacht moved to the Boston Red Sox as a coach.

Altrock and Schacht's reputation transcended baseball, and they spent their winters on the stage with vaudeville troupes. Even in the theatre the men played baseball coaches with a sense of humor, occasionally chewing tobacco the way they would on the field. As part of one shtick, Altrock complained that the joint they were in had furniture too nice to spit on.

Altrock was nationally famous for clowning for many years after he finished his pitching days, as noted by prominent columnist Joe Williams in a New York newspaper in 1938. "Baseball's court jester is known throughout the country for his comical antics on the coaching lines, but only a comparative handful remember him as the left-handed ace of the Chicago White Sox. Laughs, not skill, made Nick rich. Nick is worth $180,000 in cold, hard cash today, on the gold standard, but he didn't get it through his pitching ability."[9]

Altrock maintained some kind of affiliation with the Washington Senators until he was 80 years old. When he celebrated his birthday that year, in 1956, Altrock was inundated with telegrams of good wishes, including one from President Dwight D. Eisenhower. The telegram read, "The record book shows you have added another memorable statistic to your life. Greetings on this day. Over a great many years you have contributed much to the enjoyment and good sportsmanship of baseball. What's more, you also have added immeasurably to the fun of the game for millions of fans."[10]

Altrock suffered a stroke when he was 86 and died at 88 in 1965 in Washington, D.C.

One inquisitor asked Al Schacht at the time what prompted the falling-out between him and Altrock in 1927, but he remained mum on the subject. He admitted writing to Altrock's wife several times when his former partner was ill, but still did not talk to Altrock over the final 40 years of his life.

"We took separate cabs to the theatre and separate cabs to get home," Schacht said. "I can't tell you why we didn't speak. I have never told the story. But let's just say we got along better that way."[11]

However, Schacht did not hold back his praise for Altrock, gushing about how the other man achieved so much.

"Nick was a great comedian," Schacht said. "He had a great way of doing things. I have never seen anyone with better facial expressions. And we should all remember that he was a fine big-league pitcher, as well as an exceptional entertainer."[12]

2. Al Schacht

> "There is talk that I am Jewish—just because my father was Jewish, my mother was Jewish, I speak Yiddish and once studied to be a rabbi and a cantor. Well, that's how rumors get started."—*Al Schacht*[1]

As a Major League pitcher, Al Schacht was a great comedian. Born in New York in 1892, Schacht aspired to be a ballplayer and was just good enough to squeak into the top level of play.

Schacht made his big-league pitching debut at 26 in 1919 and went 2–0 for the Washington Senators. A right-hander, he pitched two more seasons, going 6–4 and 6–6, both for Washington.

It seemed as if Schacht's baseball career was over, but it was really just beginning, in a new discipline. In an era before television and before movies featured sound, live acts were always in demand. Schacht joined forces with Nick Altrock as a comedy duo, and they had tremendous success working together.

The Schacht-Altrock combo became as much of an institution at the World Series as the phrase "Fall Classic." Even after they had a falling-out personally they remained together professionally with their skits making fans laugh.

Later, when they went out on their own, it was Schacht who was crowned "The Clown Prince of Baseball." Although others have had the appellation affixed to their name, only a few stand out in Major League history.

Neither Schacht nor Altrock ever talked publicly about the reasons for their hostility away from the field, though insiders suggested that their irritation with one another was sparked by a gag that got out of hand.

Where once the two men shadow-boxed for fun, one day Schacht decided to put a little more realism into the act and cold-cocked Altrock.

Altrock didn't think that was very funny and retaliated with another gag, substituting a soft baseball thrown at Schacht with a real hard ball flung at him. And that was that.

Schacht said he was virtually born into baseball, growing up in the shadow of the Polo Grounds. He said the New York Giants' home field (shared by the Yankees from 1913–1922) was only "a stone's throw and a short swim from my house."[2]

Schacht would sneak into the park, stand in awe of the big figures of the game, and eventually work his way into the position of a go-fer for the Giants. Schacht was a runt as a kid, and while he grew to 5-foot-11 in height his big-league weight was only 142 pounds.

What Schacht knew was hustle. His family was poor and he helped out with a newspaper route. He discovered that if he shouted that Christy Mathewson won another game, it was better business than touting world events. The equivalent might still be true today if there were a pack of newsboys manning corners in big cities the way they used to.

Schacht was a kid on the make who cared only about making it as a ballplayer so he could suit up with his heroes. Good at self-promotion, Schacht got himself chances to be seen, but his innate talent on the mound was limited.

Most players think back on their careers and credit influences that helped them develop their hitting, pitching or fielding. Schacht was playing in Newark at age 17 when he came across a catcher named Harry Smith, who was the king of practical jokers. Maybe Schacht learned the wrong stuff when he hooked up with Smith. In less than a week of employment with the Newark franchise, Schacht had a bucket of water spilled on him, watched as a ghost ran through his room shouting, "He got me!" and more inventively watched agog as Smith turned Schacht's garments into puppets and made them dance on a string.

Schacht fell for the ages-old "snipe hunt" mission rookies got maneuvered into and headed off to a graveyard where he stood for a long while in the dark, holding the bag, literally, and a lantern. Eventually, scared of zombies arising to attack, Schacht ran five miles back to his hotel room, only to find a white-faced, baseball-uniform-clad, bloody person in his bed. He believed it was The Living Dead from the graveyard. The human form proved to be a dummy, and the blood proved to be ketchup.

If anyone asked how Schacht became such a silly clown, he could point to any number of episodes when in his youthful, naïve nature he fell for everything and anything.

Schacht soon enough graduated to pulling his own stunts. He was pitching in a game for Jersey City in the minors when rain began pelting the field. Trying to protect a one-run lead, Schacht angled for a cancellation, but the umpire refused to act. In the eighth inning, it was Schacht's turn at the plate. He approached carrying not one, but two bats. Then he sat down in a puddle and began making rowing motions with the bats. The scheme didn't work, and the other team hit a home run before the ump called the game.

For a long time it seemed as if Schacht was headed for the team he rooted for as a kid. The Giants signed him and had him in the minors. But at that time he weighed just 130 pounds and when he got sick with ulcers and malaria, he dropped more weight. He didn't seem strong enough to throw a ball to home plate. Adding in a sore arm turned Schacht from a hurler into a cheerleader for the Giants during the 1916 season.

Schacht worked out hard all winter, regained his strength, and actually gave himself another sore arm through the ill-advised activity of throwing dice. He shook and threw enough dice to lose too much money and too many articles of clothing.

Giants manager John McGraw believed in his troops running to stay fit. Schacht felt he didn't have any excess weight to lose. "One more day of this and they'll be picking me off the street with a shovel," he said.[3]

The team took salt baths, and shortstop Art Fletcher blasted Schacht with a bucket of cold water, which nearly gave him a heart attack. When he stopped shivering, Schacht stealthily approached Fletcher's cubicle with his own bucket of ice water. Only the compartment belonged to McGraw and Schacht drenched him. When the enraged manager appeared looking for someone to chew out, Schacht was standing there with an empty bucket in his hand.

Rather than berate Schacht, McGraw fooled him. "If you can throw a baseball like you can throw a bucket of water, you've got a job on this ball club," McGraw said. "There's nothing wrong with your arm."[4]

Schacht was the kind of guy stuff happened to, as well as initiating his own adventures. Pitching in the minors, he verbally lashed out at a nasty heckler, only to find out that a woman sitting in the stands swore out a complaint about him for using offensive language. His manager put off the sheriff, but when Schacht faltered in late-inning relief, the boss failed to shield him any longer. "You can have him and keep him," the manager said to the law. "I don't want him any longer."[5]

Schacht began earning his reputation as a funny man during his repeat visits to teams in the International League. He threw a slow ball, as he called it, and his arm just wasn't up to Major League standards for

BOSTON HOBOS
featuring "The Nit-Wits of the Diamond"
VS:
KINGSTON COLONIALS

TUESDAY
AUG. 27
Game Time 8:15 P. M.

AT 7:45 P. M.

featuring **AL SCHACHT**
"Clown Prince of Baseball"

Dietz Stadium, Kingston, N. Y.

Al Schacht made the rounds as the Clown Prince of Baseball, playing minor league diamonds as well as big-league stadiums. He traveled near and far to make baseball crowds laugh.

long. He pitched well in AAA, but never consistently well in the bigs, nor could he stay healthy.

Yet wherever he went, Schacht, who at various times referred to his own goofiness and even called himself "a mental case," did leave 'em laughing.

Schacht did not endure it silently when fans in ballparks heckled him. One instance was provoked by punishment. Schacht missed curfew and his manager said he was on his own that day to pitch the entire game, even if he surrendered a million runs. Schacht had the sense of humor in later years to admit that his chief did not miss by much.

He happened to be on the mound with his team trailing, 19–2, with the fans giving it to him when Schacht planned a retort. Trailing by 17 runs, Schacht allowed the opponents to fill the bases once more. The unhappiness in the crowd reached a high-decibel level. Schacht called time, walked to home plate, and yelled to the fans, pledging that despite the bases being loaded he would get the team out of danger.

On his next pitch, the batter smashed a grand slam for four more runs. With aplomb, Schacht announced, "Ladies and gentlemen, I kept my word. There are no runners on the bases to worry about now."[6]

Schacht wanted to be taken seriously as a pitcher, but it turned out this gift was not being taken seriously at all.

During World War II, Schacht made overseas trips to entertain soldiers. One trip took him to North Africa, where he gave a show in Casablanca. But even when Schacht was not on, he was "on" because the representatives of different branches of the service ferried him around, met him at meals, and teased him everywhere. He bantered with them all as they asked for news from major cities back home and what Schacht thought their favorite teams might do that season.

Sometimes Schacht did impromptu skits for guys traveling between towns when he ran into them. He had a near-sighted pitcher act that involved the moundsman trying to read the catcher's signs—with the aid of binoculars. Finally, the pitcher gave up the equipment and crawled to home plate to try to decipher the catcher's finger signals.

Schacht slept in tents like the enlisted men and shared food at the mess hall, including cold cereal in large barrels. It seemed, he joked, that too many of them saw him pitch because he faced remarks like, "Did you ever get anybody out?" or "Is it true you used to pray before each pitch?"[7]

Much of Schacht's performing life, with Nick Altrock and without, was at ballparks where the fans came for the game and got a bonus seeing the clowns clown. He noted that it was different going overseas, where young men were fighting a war and were not at the auditorium (indoor or out) to watch baseball, but to watch him.

Crowds topped 70,000 for the World Series at times when he and Altrock performed, and they were somewhat of a side show. With the military guys, Schacht was the main event. "If the crowd didn't like the act, they still had the ball game," Schacht said. "But here it was a little different. I was supposed to be the attraction and as I looked around the little stage, scanning the faces about me, faces had a certain look. "Go ahead, you bum," they seemed to say. "Make us laugh."[8]

Schacht did serve during World War I, and the GIs asked what he did during the war. "I was a secret weapon," he said. "They hid me in a hospital at Fort Slocum. I won the Battle of Influenza."[9]

Actually, one thing Schacht didn't need was soldiers making fun of his short big-league career. He had evolved from someone who didn't want to take grief from a fan in the stands into an ex-player who made fun of himself, even if his lifetime record was 14–10. "No matter how high or low a batter's average was, they were always hitting at least .700 against me," he said. "I have yet to meet a batter who didn't start a conversation with me by saying, 'Remember that triple I hit against, you, Al?'"[10]

Schacht made bigger headlines in military newsletters and newspapers than he did back home. He was greeted at one locale by a lead headline reading, "Al Schacht Here!" He was pleased to read on and see "Al Schacht, the Clown Prince of Baseball, who has evoked gales of hysterical laughter from millions of baseball fans, several American presidents, and countless crowned heads of Europe, will appear at our diamond at 1400, Saturday, Sept. 11, 1943, before, during and after a game between the 61st Regulars and the 26th General."[11]

That was a keeper of a review and Schacht hadn't even done anything yet! "What an imagination those kids had," he said. "I not only had never been to Europe, but the only crowned head I ever saw was the guy I beaned in Baltimore one afternoon when I was a little wild."[12]

As a clown, Schacht had moved on to the self-deprecating phase of his baseball career. Earlier he was proud of what he accomplished, and as he hustled to try to stay in the majors it was more important that he convince teams he had the goods. Long retired, he made fun of himself, along with just about everything else.

Schacht visited with many, many servicemen and he usually concluded with a comment that if they were ever in New York after the war they should look him up. Since he ate their food overseas, he said he would feed them. Once, he figured out that the steak house that he owned, held 150 people, and he wondered what would happen if what he estimated as a million soldiers he had performed for showed up at once. Schacht's restaurant was popular enough. His menus were round, shaped like baseballs, and many of the items were named after former players.

Overseas, Schacht noted that American soldiers posted the names of familiar streets in their camps, from Michigan Boulevard to West Palm Drive, and every town had a Broadway.

Schacht acted at more than 20 World Series, but said he got a bigger thrill out of performing at an Army ballgame in New Guinea in 1944. "I gave them my versions of the conceited and near-sighted pitchers, working my way into impersonations of the great stars of the past and present—Babe Ruth, Bob Feller, Walter Johnson and Mel Ott, among others," he said.

On his journey to North Africa and Italy, Schacht was close enough to the fighting to experience many blackouts intended to dissuade enemy planes from bombing the men he was with. Immediately after his return to New York, he went through a practice blackout. "My god," he said. "They're still after me."[13]

Before he was an official funny man and trying to stick in the majors, Schacht pulled off one of his better stunts. Stuck in the minors, he wrote a series of letters to Washington Senators owner Clark Griffith. Each was signed, "Just a fan." But each extolled the virtues of this pitcher Al Schacht. Griffith finally showed up in person to scout Schacht, who happened to throw his tenth shutout of the season for Jersey City. The scheme worked and won Schacht a job.

A man of countless skits evolved during a long career can be hard-pressed to identify his favorite, but Schacht always believed one of his all-time bests occurred when he was still in uniform in the minors, but not on a day he was scheduled to pitch against the Baltimore Orioles for the Reading club he served more as coach and showman.

He called it his golf skit and performed it between innings in the first game of a doubleheader. Schacht said he used a ten-cent baseball he termed a "rocket ball" for a golf ball, and a shovel for a club. He did his thing, stuffed the ball into his pocket and went to the bullpen for possible emergency use.

Sure enough, the Reading pitcher faltered mid-game and Schacht was called upon in relief with the bases loaded. After picking up the regulation, ball he reached into his pocket and remembered the other ball. He slipped the real ball into his shirt, called his catcher out and said, "Don't laugh if you value your life. And call for nothing but fastballs. I've got a phony ball here and I'm going to stop these birds."[14]

The first hitter got good wood on the ball, but it flew awkwardly and plopped into the glove of an infielder. Schacht said the ball was lopsided, but he straightened it out. The second batter hit the straight throw hard, but it only traveled to the third baseman. He taunted a rival hitter next and actually tossed the ball to the plate underhanded. The batter swung mightily, but only bounced oddly to first base for the third out.

Alas, the last hitter complained to the ump, who demanded to see the ball. Schacht immediately began lying about how it was the ball he inherited on the mound. A huge argument ensued and the ump made Schacht pitch over again to the third batter. Using a real ball, though taunting the hitter into an emotional state, Schacht struck him out. Furious, the batter screamed he wanted to see the ball again. He was wildly angry and threw the ball out of the park. That earned him an ejection and a $25 fine. Schacht couldn't have been more pleased.

In 1937, Schacht decided to switch from coaching and clowning to just clowning, as he put it, so not only the American League could watch him perform, but "to let the whole country see what a nut Schacht was and charge them for it at the same time. I assumed the title of 'Clown Prince of Baseball' and became the Vagabond Zany—a one-man circus—a traveling fool."[15]

One of the odd things Schacht did was sometimes speak in tongues. He actually used a made-up language to tease people. Moe Berg, the catcher who became a spy for the United States during World War II, said, "It is as nutty as he is and he's nuttier than a fruit cake."[16]

Schacht stayed in baseball much longer as a clown than he did as a pitcher. He lived till age 91, dying in Connecticut in 1984.

3. Waite Hoyt

On the scorching hot day of Babe Ruth's funeral, old teammate Waite Hoyt was a pallbearer. Joe Dugan, another ex-teammate, said, "Lord, I'd give my right arm for an ice-cold beer." Hoyt replied, "So would the Babe."[1]

HALL OF FAME PITCHER AND FAMED BROADCASTER Waite Hoyt tried an off-season career as a mortician because it was his wife's family business. A *New York Times* reporter, taking note of Hoyt's natural personality and his seemingly dour second profession, called him a "Merry Mortician." Hoyt's response was: "Shh, my second wife doesn't like that 'mortician' reference to my first marriage."[2]

One might have thought she would enjoy it a bit since she got the prize.

Hoyt, at 6 feet tall and 190 pounds, was a good right-handed pitcher who won 237 games in a 21-year career plus six World Series games. His best seasons were 1927 with the "Murderers' Row" New York Yankees, when he won a league-leading 22 games, and 1928, when Hoyt won 23 games. A glib, witty man, Hoyt was better-known later as a baseball broadcaster. He spent 24 years with the Cincinnati Reds and did national broadcasts as well.

After retiring, Hoyt's goal was to become the Yankees' broadcaster, but a sponsor vetoed his selection and the Reds won out. The reason Wheaties gave was that Hoyt did not have a wide-ranging enough vocabulary. The cereal-maker could not have been more wrong.

Once, as a player, Hoyt leveled perhaps the most articulate criticism of what he believed to be an umpire's missed call in the annals of the game. Hoyt thought George Moriarty missed a strike call and he let him know. "You're out of your element! You should be a traffic cop so you could stand in the middle of the street with a badge on your chest and insult people with impunity."[3] Take that.

Hoyt wanted the New York job and took it badly when he was turned down. When it was suggested he go after the Reds' broadcasting position, he almost didn't try for it. At the time he did have his own radio show, though he had designs on being a play-by-play guy.

> They [Wheaties] didn't think ball players had a vocabulary. I was thwarted and disappointed, naturally. Then an agency man [William Morris] came to me and asked if I'd consent to going out of town. I asked him where. He said Cincinnati. I laughed and told him that when I was playing Cincinnati was the only town in the majors where there was no place to go out after a game. But I went and I found a level of happiness in Cincinnati that I've never known anywhere else, young or old.[4]

Hoyt was born in Brooklyn in 1899 and was signed by the New York Giants when he was just 15. He made his Major League debut in 1918, his only season with the Giants, and while he played for seven teams in all, plus the Giants and Dodgers a second time around, his true success came with the Yankees as they blitzed the American League in the 1920s. Sometimes called the most handsome pitcher in baseball, Hoyt took great care with his appearance. Once, a newspaper jokingly commented on Hoyt's setting a world record for barbering when he sat for haircuts three days in a row in spring training of 1930.

One of the famous stories that followed Hall of Fame Pirates Paul and Lloyd Waner was that a Brooklyn fan referring to them as "big person" and "little person" accidentally bestowed their nicknames of "Big Poison" and "Little Poison" because of his accent. Long before he became president, Ronald Reagan was a sports announcer, and he said that Hoyt once confirmed a story for him. On a play where Hoyt slid into second base, a fan worried about injury said something that sounded like, "Gee, Hurt is hoit."[5] A Brooklyn paper wrote a headline reading, "Hert Hoit."

While it is commonplace for former athletes to move into the broadcast booth these days, that was not so when Hoyt retired from the mound in 1938 as a three-time World Series champion. In fact, it was basically unheard-of, and there were many fewer broadcast outlets and opportunities to go around during that era anyway.

Furman Bisher, the legendary Atlanta sports columnist, spoke up for Hoyt when it seemed his pioneering role had been overlooked. "He brought to the microphone of the Cincinnati Reds' broadcasts a strong voice of eloquence," Bisher said. "His father had been a vaudevillian of some stature, Ad Hoyt. Waite had played the old Palace Theater in New York between seasons."[6] Bisher made the point that Hoyt could talk. He did not spout clichés, and he performed with such famed stars as Jimmy Durante.

Hoyt also had a good memory. He told stories in the booth, which he manned solo for the Reds for his first 11 years on the job, stories that harkened back to his early days in baseball. One day, Hoyt recalled, he and battery mate Bill Dickey, another future Hall of Famer, were in Mobile for an exhibition game when Dickey was recognized.

Dickey was born in Bastrop, Louisiana, and grew up mostly in Arkansas. A woman saw him in the train station and said, "Bill Dickey! Bill Dickey! What ah you doing heah?" Dickey replied, "I'm playing with the Yankees." To the southern lady, "Yankees" was not a favorable description. "Why, Bill, couldn't you find some nice southern boys to play with?"[7]

Much later, while discussing the relationship between a pitcher and catcher, Hoyt said it was like a marriage and the catcher was the wife half of the partnership.

Hoyt was a fine pitcher at his best, but when he had lost some of the spin on his curveball and speed on his fastball, it was harder to succeed. Hoyt was well into his thirties in 1933 when he suited up for the Pittsburgh Pirates against the Chicago Cubs, who had been manhandled in the previous World Series by the Yankees. Cubs players teased Hoyt about his age and other things, but he wasn't about to let their ears go unscathed. He replied, "If you guys don't shut up I'll put on my old Yankee uniform and scare you to death."[8]

Hoyt was good enough with the Yankees in the 1920s to pull down a $20,000 salary from owner Jacob Ruppert, big bucks in those days, though not as much as Babe Ruth was earning. Amongst his many other accomplishments, Ruth, Hoyt's old friend, uplifted the salary structure for a while (at least until the Great Depression cut into all profits). Ruth made as much as $80,000 a year in that era.

"Hell, he wasn't always the pot-bellied, skinny-legged guy who didn't run or field well," Hoyt said. "He was a complete player—fast, sure-handed and, of course, strong—and every guy who ever played owed something to his popularity. I used to tell my kids, 'Thank God, thank Mommy, thank Daddy—and thank Babe Ruth.' His gargantuan paychecks helped us all get a little extra money. Series checks, too."[9]

In 1922, Hoyt spent Thanksgiving in Kobe, Japan, with a goodwill All-Star baseball tour that also carried players to Korea, China, Manila and Honolulu. He was a bit surprised that the Japanese had adopted the British custom of pausing at 4 p.m. for tea, finger sandwiches and cakes. Hoyt pitched a no-hitter at Waseda University in an era long before the best Japanese players were of Major League caliber.

A turkey was presented to the players by the hotel. Hoyt theorized it was purchased off an American boat. "Bullet" Joe Bush's birthday coincided with the American holiday, and the players gave him a surprise party (which the Yankees hurler most assuredly deserved after going 26–7 during the regular season), actually dressing in clown hats.

Hoyt was a man of many parts. He was grossly underestimated when he sought to make the shift from the field to the broadcast booth. He could describe action, tell stories, and do comedy on the stage, became interested in art and painted, and spent 24 years telling Reds fans all about it. "Our trips then were made by train and I read a great deal while going from city to city," Hoyt said. "Sure we played some cards, but mostly hearts, bridge and pinochle. There were poker games, but Miller Huggins [the Yankees' manager] put a 50-cent limit on them."[10]

Hoyt drank and partied like other ball players, but then realized he was drinking too much, joined Alcoholics Anonymous and stuck with teetotaling. But that wasn't until the early 1930s, after he married (though he was married three times).

Hoyt's father was a singer, and some of the father's show biz acumen rubbed off on him. In the 1920s, ballplayers were only just beginning to obtain product endorsements. If they were well-known, especially in New York, and they had any talent at all (and sometimes not), they were frequently invited to make stage appearances.

Hoyt was gifted enough to hold his own in vaudeville. In an undated advertisement in the Baseball Hall of Fame Library archives, Hoyt received top billing for a show Thursday, Friday and Saturday at Poli's Theater. His name in large letters, Hoyt was pictured in baseball garb throwing a pitch. The ad read, "WAITE HOYT IN PERSON, The Famous Pitcher of the New York Yankees and Hero of the World Series. With TOMMY GORDON the clown, in a comedy skit entitled 'A BATTERY OF FUN.'"

On another occasion, the *New York Times* printed the headline, "Waite Hoyt, Pitcher, Sings At The Palace." A review said of Hoyt, "as a singer Mr. Hoyt is not strictly a pitcher. He sings very acceptably, and as they say has 'an easy delivery.'"[11]

A sportswriter made sure to take in a Hoyt performance in a different show and came away rather impressed by Hoyt's all-around skills. In his account he made Hoyt sound like "The Most Interesting Man In The World."

> Waite Hoyt is, indeed, a fantastic combination of baseball pitcher, undertaker, vaudeville star, writer and golfer, and nearly every one of these activities of Master Hoyt, which go to comprise his wondrous versatility, is nationally identified with him. Hoyt's father, Addison, shed jests from behind his burnt cork for more than 20 years in variety and so Waite perhaps inherited some of the traits and mannerisms of his actor father and one or two vintage gags.[12]

Hoyt considered himself fortunate to be a big-name player in New York when he competed and the Yankees were on top of the baseball world.

3. WAITE HOYT 23

Don't forget this. When the Yankees first became a dynasty, it was in the middle of the Roarin' Twenties. It was the birth of something new and everybody from the Astors to gangsters wanted to meet baseball players. It was fashionable to say, "I met so and so last night at such and such night club." Maybe you only shook hands or signed an autograph for a particular person, but once you did you were branded in the public's thinking.[13]

Hoyt was renowned for being able to fill on-air dead time during Reds' rain delays during his broadcasting days. Many a listener said they did not change that dial, but settled in to hear what he might say or tell them about the good old days. Sometimes, Hoyt was part of the old stories. Once, he was warming up, but when he reached into the ball bag he found a worn-out baseball instead of a new one. He stashed it in his shirt. Later in the game, when future Hall of Famer, Zack Wheat, came to the plate, Hoyt turned his back to the plate and switched the game ball with the old ball. When they use the expression "old horsehide," they must have been referring to this ball as the model. The cover was half peeled off. But in the game's critical situation Hoyt heaved it to the plate. The ball wobbled like a knuckleball. Wheat swung and missed, then turned to the umpire, furiously protesting. Pants Rowland, the ump, responded and checked over the ball. "Mr. Hoyt," Rowland said, "you can't do a thing like that in baseball. Not to me. I am an official." Hoyt replied testily, "Then call 'em like an official. Like the baseball, you're only half right."[14]

Hoyt did not practice his acquired skill of embalming and other mortuary work for very long, but one time he got a call to pick up a corpse for delivery to the funeral home when he was scheduled to pitch that same day. Hoyt drove by, lowered the body into his trunk, drove to Yankee Stadium, pitched the game, and then dropped off the cadaver where it belonged.

Once established in Cincinnati, Hoyt developed a legion of fans, not only amongst the listening public, but also fellow broadcasters. Russ Hodges, who handled Giants games, made the famous call, "The Giants win the pennant! The Giants win the pennant!" in 1951 when Bobby Thomson slugged the playoff home run that topped the Brooklyn Dodgers and sent the club to the World Series.

Hodges became pals with Hoyt and spoke glowingly of sharing time with him in Cincinnati when the National League teams met. Hodges called Hoyt "now a terrific baseball broadcaster and the idol of Cincy fans. As a baseball announcer he must be rated with the very best. His solid 'down-the-middle style' is well loved by the 'good burghers' of the Ohio Valley. There is nothing hysterical about his style. He is authoritative."[15]

He was also philosophical, including about his own performances, especially near the end of his pitching career when the off-days occurred more frequently than during his prime days. Once, after being thrashed by Boston of the National League and giving up three late-inning runs, Hoyt said, "I think that I shall plead insanity."[16]

Probably more than one pitcher could benefit from such a defense.

Hoyt recognized the difference in his skills in the late 1920s and 1930s and verbalized it when he signed on with the Pirates in 1933. "I see some of these fellows, who never saw me pitch when I was at the top of my form, looking at me in amazement," he said. "They are too polite to say anything, but I know what they're thinking. They're thinking that the American League must be a pretty soft league if I could get by in it as long as I did with as little as I've got." When someone (though probably a sportswriter) had the temerity to ask, "Waite, what became of your fastball?" he had a ready answer. "If you'd really like to find it, look in the upper tier in left field at Shibe Park. I threw it to [Al] Simmons this afternoon."[17]

Back when the starting pitcher was always expected to be the finishing pitcher unless his style was seriously cramped by the opposing team's bats, Hoyt made an intriguing connection between his roles as actor and vaudeville player and as a baseball player. Figuring he still must have something left in the tank for the eighth or ninth innings, Hoyt compared pitching to delivering a punch line.

> The vaudeville actor saves his greatest thriller until the end of his act. The public speaker holds his real message until the climax of his address. The serial writer winds up his chapters in such a way as to cause the reader to all but count the minutes until the next chapter is printed. So the pitcher should save his best bet until what the baseball writers term "the crucial moment" arrives.[18]

The Yankees, especially by the 1940s, 1950s, and beyond, were viewed as a buttoned-down entity. Even back in the 1920s, management wanted the team to be perceived as a class outfit that did not goof around. But Hoyt said the team was always fun-loving, though the players kept the laughs under the radar (except perhaps in the case of Ruth).

When Hoyt was still drinking and staying out late during those Roaring Twenties, it was an epidemic amongst players who knew where the right doors to the speakeasies opened. Manager Miller Huggins grew concerned with the level of boozing and, instead of having the team gather for midnight train rides for road trips, began booking the Yankees with earlier departure times. Instead of rolling out at midnight, the team left town at 9 p.m. Didn't matter.

"What happened was that we just drank that much faster," Hoyt said. "We stayed up most of the night fighting, believe it or not, with pillows. Next day we beat the Red Sox, 19–2, or something like that."[19]

The Yankees having pillow fights? Imagine that.

New York sportswriter Joe Williams, who came along too late to cover Murderers' Row, took Hoyt's and other ex-players' word for the inside story. "They were, for the most part, men of light hearts and high spirits," Williams wrote, "happy warriors, indeed. Only on the field were they deadly serious."[20]

Another example of the off-the-field games the old Yankees played, as part of a longer article Hoyt once wrote, was the story of how Ruth made a bet with weak-hitting pitcher Wilcy Moore. Moore, who was a 30-year-old rookie in 1927 when he won 19 games for the Yankees, was a horrible hitter, with a lifetime .102 average. "Wilcy, you couldn't hit a bull in the rump with a barrel stave," Ruth said. Ruth bet Moore that if he got even one hit all season, the Sultan of Swat would give him $100, but if he went hitless he owed Ruth $100. Hoyt said that Moore went hitless until the last weekend of the season, but managed three safeties on an infield hit, a bunt that stayed fair, and a swing-away single in one game. Ruth owed Moore $300. "The Babe with great fanfare and hilarity paid off immediately after the game."[21]

It's clear that this incident didn't really happen, or at least not as Hoyt described it. He said that the opponent was the Detroit Tigers, but Moore did not play in a season-ending series versus Detroit while with the Yankees between 1927 and 1933. Only twice, in 1927 and 1931, did he amass more than three hits in an entire season, six and nine, so he could not have obtained his entire output of three hits in a season in either of those years.

But it's a good story and maybe something similar occurred. Moore did come into a season-ending series game against the Washington Senators on September 28, 1933, did get the win in relief, and did come to the plate three times, though he cranked out just one hit. Of course, for Moore that was a hot streak at the plate.

Late in the two men's careers, Hoyt surrendered two home runs to Ruth, after Hoyt took divergent paths to other teams. The pitcher was with the Red Sox for one of them and another came while Hoyt was throwing for the Philadelphia A's. In Philadelphia, Ruth worked the count to three-and-two and Hoyt tried to fool him inside. Ruth slaughtered the pitch. "After he hit it, I forgot for a moment that I was the pitcher as I watched the ball go," Hoyt said. "Then I remembered I was the one who threw it. And then I got mad."[22]

Hoyt broadcast Reds games for nearly a quarter of a century and retired to Cincinnati, where he lived the remainder of his life. He passed away from a heart ailment at 85 in 1984, but not before being enshrined in Cooperstown in the Baseball Hall of Fame by the Veterans Committee in 1969.

Hoyt was reflective when he was elected to the Hall of Fame.

> You start out as a child and you wonder whether you're going to make it to the neighborhood team. Then you wonder whether you're going to make the high school team and then whether you're going to make it into the big leagues and then whether you're good enough to stay there. And when you get out, you wonder whether you did as well as you should have.[23]

By all measurements, Waite Hoyt was good enough.

4. Babe Herman

"Are you going to buy your children an encyclopedia?" a sportswriter once asked Babe Herman. "No," he said, "they can walk to school just like I did."[1]

When Babe Herman played for the Brooklyn Dodgers, they were called "the Daffiness Boys," and he was a card-carrying member.

Herman could be funny, hah-hah, with words, and he could be funny with deeds, sometimes accidentally. One of those times was when he played the outfield and a ball landed on his head instead of in his glove. Another time occurred when he smacked a deep fair ball when the Dodgers had the bases loaded. Mostly due to the base-running blunders of teammates, Herman ended up on third base, but it was already occupied by two other Dodgers.

Herman, whose real name was Floyd, was a secondary "Babe," of course, to Babe Ruth, but one of the best of all others called Babe. He batted .324 lifetime and in 1930 hit .393, but did not win the National League batting title because Bill Terry hit .401 that year. Herman also hit for the cycle three times during his 13-year big-league career.

The .393 was a career peak, but Herman also hit .381 in 1929. Brooklyn had rabid fans, but little success on the field beyond individual play. "To tell you the truth," Herman said, "they were called 'The Daffiness Boys' before I got there. Of course, I helped carry the name on."[2]

Goofy guys like Casey Stengel and future Hall of Fame pitcher Dazzy Vance contributed as well. Herman insisted that the St. Louis Cardinals' "Gashouse Gang" was far screwier man-to-man and pound for pound than the Dodgers. Still, some tales of Dodgers' ineptitude in the field and running the bases lived on in lore, even if Herman suggested the baseball writers exaggerated the Dodgers oddities. "The three guys on third really did happen," Herman said of an August 15, 1926, game. "Only it wasn't the way they wrote it. They said I tripled into a triple play, except there was one out at the time."[3]

Although the legend grew that Herman's miss of a fly resulted in being conked on the head, in an era before night-time baseball highlights shows, there was no proof. He said he lost a ball in the sun because he left his sunglasses in the dugout one day at Ebbets Field. The ball that handcuffed him, Herman said, bounced off his chest, not his noggin.

Other stories followed Herman around for years—that he carried lighted cigars around in his uniform pockets on the field. He did not deny that one.

> That wasn't no big thing. That came up when a newspaperman started to interview me one day and I took this stogie out of my pocket and started to puff right off. His eyes liked to pop out, I tell ya. But I knew it was lit all the time, see? It was only in my pocket a few minutes because I had just come out of a room where there was a "No Smoking" sign.[4]

Maybe. Others say that Herman delighted in refusing the offer of a light when he said he was going to take a smoke, then pulled the lighted cigar out of his pocket.

Herman did not start out in baseball as a "Babe." He collected the nickname along the way from a Major League coach who knew of a heavyweight boxer in Canada named Babe Herman. Herman was born in Buffalo in 1903 and as a major leaguer with five teams, most memorably with the Robins, he hit from the left side of the plate. Herman was 6-foot-4 and weighed 190 pounds during his playing days, between 1926 and 1937 (plus 37 games in 1945).

Brooklyn fans were almost hysterically supportive of their players, and in 1926, when Herman became one of the Robins, they referred to him as "Our Babe." That was to differentiate him from the better-known Ruth in the other league.

Herman and Casey Stengel, who lived in Glendale, California, in the same neighborhood for decades, were more of a duo. They both had a good sense of humor and liked a good prank while being serious about their contributions to the game. Yet not everyone was kind in describing Herman's glove work, one early scribe writing, "Floyd Caves Herman did not always catch fly balls on the top of his head, but he could do it in a pinch."[5]

It might be said that most of the time Herman provided unintentional laughs, but was good-natured about it. And although Herman was one of several memorable players who passed through Brooklyn before the Dodgers fled to Los Angeles decades later, he was always the most popular.

Herman was tremendously talented as a hitter and, for a time, base stealer, but not always as a base runner. One game Herman smacked three doubles, and when he blasted another ball deep in his fourth at-bat, he was a sure thing for what would have been a record four doubles in a game. Herman tripped rounding first base on what seemed likely to be a sure double and had to settle for a single. Enough of those kinds of things happened to Herman that fans got used to them.

One future writer said his father wanted to name him Babe on his birth certificate because he was told that both Babe Herman and Babe Ruth had big hitting days on the date of his birth. Turned out it was a mild fib. But the youngster's mother wouldn't tolerate it anyway. He said his family did have a dog named Babe, after Herman. Many years into adulthood, the fan convinced his mother to attend a Brooklyn game with him, and on the night before their planned excursion he said he prayed that the game would be fun and enjoyable for his mom and "don't let Babe Herman make a fool of himself."[6]

Some sportswriters hinted that Herman was dumb, but Stengel always took exception to that suggestion. "They called him dumb?" Stengel said. "In the late Thirties he started a turkey farm near Glendale and he sold his birds to the Brown Derby and other restaurants. The first year he had the farm President [Franklin D.] Roosevelt proclaimed TWO Thanksgivings."[7]

Herman was known to brag about the smarts of his son Bobby as a five-year-old, and he once showed him off to teammates by giving him a bit of a quiz to prove his stuff. Herman asked how much six times two equaled. Bobby answered, "Ten." Herman said, "See that? He only missed it by one."[8]

Later, when Bobby was grown up and preparing to represent his country in World War II, Babe Herman noted that he was a major in the intelligence service who had mastered speaking Japanese. "After Bobby got to know Japanese well, they shipped him to Italy," Herman said.[9] It sounded like something that might have happened to dad.

Herman stumbled over malapropisms at times and was witty as the quickest standup comic at other times. Once, Herman showed up at a fancy eatery dressed in a white linen suit. A young woman appraised him and said, "My, you look cool." His response? "You don't look so hot yourself."[10] How to make friends and influence people.

Better yet, Herman, indulging in the long-gone fine art of hotel lobby sitting with teammates, heard two other players discussing a man who walked past. They said, "He used to be rich, but he lost all his money in the war [World War I]." Herman said, "Why, did he bet on the Kaiser?"[11]

Back in the day when Americans devoured sardines as a more regular staple of their diet, Herman was in a restaurant inquiring about a sardine sandwich. The waitress asked if he preferred domestic or imported sardines, and Herman asked what was the difference. She told him that the imported ones cost 50 cents extra. "I'll take the domestic," he said. "Darned if I'm going to pay passage money to America for some lousy sardines."[12]

Despite some highly publicized mishaps in the field, which stuck to Herman like leeches, all evidence indicates he was a very good player. He hit over .300 nine times. He scored as many as 143 runs in a season and knocked in as many as 130 runs. His single-season home-run high was 35. He just didn't have big numbers every year. Some believe that Herman should be in the Baseball Hall of Fame, but his overall career numbers do not match those of most outfielders and first basemen enshrined in Cooperstown.

Babe Herman was a good enough player to hit for the cycle three times and retire with a lifetime batting average of .324. But he was known in Brooklyn (before moving on to other teams) just as much for his sense of humor.

Although Herman was born in upstate New York in Buffalo, by the time he was two his parents had relocated the family to California. By 1917, they were living in Glendale, and that became Herman's lifetime home. He was a superb high school athlete, lettering each year in baseball, football, basketball and track. In those days Floyd's nickname was "Lefty."

Herman's father was a home builder, and he wanted his son to follow him as a contractor. Herman liked the idea of playing sports for money better and signed a minor league deal to play in Edmonton for $175 a month. His unsympathetic father said he would run out of cash and beg him for money to return. Supposedly, Her-

4. Babe Herman

man replied, "I'll come home in a boxcar first."[13] So he went out on his own at 17.

Herman's dad was right to worry about finances. It wasn't as if baseball players made huge salaries in 1921 when his boy went off to Canada.

Sometimes what may have been blamed on Herman as ill-advised base-running was not his fault at all. One game his rookie year Herman slashed a ball deep to the outfield at Ebbets Field, and as he dug around the bases he saw the outfielder bobbling the ball. But when he chugged into third base the coach was holding his arms up—a stop sign. Herman asked coach Joe Kelly what the heck he was doing by halting him because he saw the outfielder boot the ball around. "Babe, without my glasses I can't even see who's pitching," Kelly said. "And I won't wear my glasses on the field."[14] Herman came up short of a snappy comeback to that explanation.

The Dodgers, who did not win a World Series while representing Brooklyn until 1955, did not win many pennants in that borough either until after World War II. They captured National League flags in 1916 and 1920 (just too soon for Herman), but during the 1920s the best they could do was tease their fans. The team had many colorful players and a revered manager in Wilbert Robinson, but could do no better than second in 1924 before becoming annual also-rans.

In a pre-season exhibition doubleheader against the Washington Senators in 1928, Herman had some shaky moments in the field, making two errors in one game and catching a popup only after circling under it as if he did not truly have it in his sights. Senators coach and clown Nick Altrock stung Herman with the comment, "Safety first, Babe. Don't get wounded."[15] But Herman apparently just told Altrock to go chase himself around the bases. He also drove in six runs in one of the games. That was a foreshadowing of Herman's break-out season at-bat in 1929 when he batted .381 with 21 home runs and 113 RBI.

Although Herman stole as many as 21 bases in a season, he was not exactly Rickey Henderson on the base paths. Twice during his career he was on base when a teammate belted a ball out of the park that should have counted as a home run, but Herman slowed down so much to watch them that he was passed by the hitter, nullifying the swats and transforming them into singles.

"Uncle Robbie," as Wilbert Robinson was affectionately known, defended Herman's outfield play at Ebbets Field, even though he led the National League in errors twice in the outfield (and once at first base). "A right fielder at Ebbets Field must be a combination of civil engineer and mountain goat," the manager observed. "It is one of the hardest 'sun fields' I have ever seen and it is bounded by a slanting wall off which batted balls carom at all sorts of weird angles. A Brooklyn right fielder is more to be pitied than scorned."[16]

Some events followed Herman forever. The actual analysis of what happened on that three-men-on-third base tale showed that Herman technically doubled into a double play rather than tripling into a triple play. However, it became a story too irresistible not to tell and poke fun at. One story, perhaps real, perhaps not, has a taxi driver pulling up outside Ebbets Field and hollering for an update to a patron overhanging the top row. He yelled back that the Dodgers had three men on base. The cabbie shouted, "Which base?"[17]

The longer Herman served as high-profile fodder in the majors, the more sportswriters brought up that they knew him when he was in the minors. One sportswriter stated that he was out for a walk with Herman in Macon, Georgia, when the Babe inserted a penny into a scale to obtain his weight and fortune. The return message said that he weighed 184 pounds and was "a student of history." The sportswriter promptly decided to test Herman's knowledge and asked, "What do you think about the Napoleonic era?" Herman said, "It should have been scored as a hit."[18]

For all of those critics of Herman's fielding, he did answer with a powerful arm, one time throwing out a base runner at home plate from a distant corner of Ebbets Field's right field. No one could believe the perfect strike from hundreds of feet away, least of all teammate and future Hall of Fame pitcher Dazzy Vance. "I have trouble throwing strikes from 60 feet," Vance said later that night when the team was riding a train out of town to its next series. "That guy does it from 280."[19]

Herman's son Bob later in life became the artistic administrator and assistant manager of the Metropolitan Opera. Babe was asked how that came to be. "Opera, baseball, what's the difference?" he said. "It's all show business, ain't it?"[20]

Herman had his own ups and downs with show business. It was once reported that when a baseball movie was being cast, Herman was turned away and told, "You're not the type."[21] Sounds more like a Rodney Dangerfield self-deprecating joke than anything else. Herman should have waved his lifetime batting average in the casting director's face. Actually, he did appear in *The Pride of the Yankees*, the movie about Lou Gehrig that starred Gary Cooper. Herman was the stand-in at the plate for Cooper. "Gary Cooper was the star, but he didn't know a thing about baseball," Herman said. "They tried one take with him at the plate, but he looked awkward. They called me and I did all the hitting scenes without close-ups."[22]

Even while still active, Herman insured his retirement when he started that turkey farm Casey Stengel mentioned in passing. It was 18½ acres in size and Herman raised 1,500 turkeys at a time. He also invested wisely in real estate and owned 14 rental properties. This was in addition to staying in baseball in different capacities, as a Pittsburgh Pirates coach and as a Bakersfield minor-league manager. He also scouted extensively for different Major League teams, including his Dodgers and then the Yankees. For a brief time Herman was also employed by the New York Mets. Brooklyn's National League successor.

Decades after Herman left the playing fields and the Dodgers left Brooklyn, the team is still beloved in some quarters. It must be a generational thing because Herman, Stengel, Vance and the others are long gone, even if the stories live on. Once, also many years ago, Dodgers owner Walter O'Malley made the comment, "Not all the lies they tell about the Dodgers are true."[23] Most of the ones about Herman are. The others are just as blurred slightly by reality and as fanciful in the telling now as they were way back when.

Herman took the story about his being hit on the head by a fly ball personally, but most of the other jokes at his expense he let slide, saying that sportswriters had to make a living, too. He also couldn't help his own clever answers, so what did he expect?

Herman was out of the majors after 1937, when he was 34, following a 17-game fling with the Detroit Tigers. But eight years later, after he had stayed active in the minors, during World War II when teams were short-handed and looking for help in all kinds of creative places, Herman fielded a request from his old Dodgers to wear the uniform again in 1945.

Herman said he was feeding turkeys when Branch Rickey called with the offer. Herman had dabbled with the Hollywood minor-league team the year before, so he wasn't completely rusty in the batter's box.

Herman got into 37 games that season at age 42. Near the end of the season he was solely a pinch-hitter, but batted a respectable .265 before retiring again. Contacted in 1979 by a sportswriter, Herman was asked if he could still hit. "I don't know," he said. "The last six times I was up at the plate I got hits."[24]

Herman was 76 when he made the comment. (He was 84 when he passed away).

Babe Herman could always hit and some of the best baseball men of his era knew how dangerous he could be in the batter's box. "Herman was the stylist of them all," said Hall of Fame catcher Al López, who was a Brooklyn teammate of Herman's. "Babe swung a bat with more ease and grace than any man I ever saw. You could fool him on a pitch and at the last second he'd reach out with one hand and knock it over or against the fence."[25]

Hall of Famer Grover Cleveland Alexander added, "Herman is bad medicine for a pitcher. I fooled him three times on a ball and every time he hit the ball safe."[26]

The sportswriter who posed the question to Herman about his old-age-hitting capability was Pulitzer Prize–winning columnist Red Smith, who also wrote of Herman at that time, "He is an institution like the (Brooklyn) bridge itself and legends have grown around him like ivy."[27]

One truth that no doubt satisfied Babe Herman was that he never did have to make that humiliating phone call to his father asking for car fare home. He used baseball to set himself up for life.

5. Rabbit Maranville

"Nobody gets any fun out of baseball anymore. I guess a kid's crazy not to be serious about it when he's drawing down $20,000 or $30,000 a year and any smart-aleck gag you try might be your last. But what's life without a laugh?"—*Rabbit Maranville*[1]

ALTHOUGH THIS ACT DID NOT OCCUR in front of a baseball audience, Rabbit Maranville's character and reputation in the sport was firmly established on the long-ago day in St. Louis when he jumped into the fountain in front of the Buckingham Hotel and swallowed some of the goldfish attempting to swim past.

When it came to climbing, Maranville did not pretend to be a mountaineer, but on another occasion, after being shut out of a poker game being played on the day of a rain out, he made a daring ascent and entrance. The location was the Majestic Hotel in Philadelphia, and Maranville climbed out a window onto a ledge ten stories off the ground to enter the poker game site via another window.

If Maranville wanted something it was hard to deny him. He had proven that in his youth as an undersized competitor in boxing, football and basketball, as well as baseball.

Walter James Vincent Maranville, born in Springfield, Massachusetts, in 1891 (in the same community in the same year when the sport of basketball was invented) and was neither big nor strong. He was short at 5-foot-5 and weighed just 145 pounds, but was a speedy enough runner to earn the nickname Rabbit. Even Maranville's wife called him Rabbit. It should be added that Maranville's large ears might have had something to do with the moniker.

Mostly a shortstop, Maranville managed 23 years in the big leagues, and while he hit just .258 lifetime, he was a good enough fielder and base runner to gain Hall of Fame election in 1954, the same year he died at 62.

Between his debut in 1912 with the Boston Braves, and his demise, Maranville made sure he had a good time.

Alas for Maranville, his selection as a Hall of Famer came only a couple of weeks after he passed away. His death was a sudden one, and over the preceding summer he spoke about his desire to be enshrined in Cooperstown. "I know I'm close to making the Hall of Fame," Maranville said. "I'd like to be alive if it does happen."[2] It did happen, but he missed the show in person.

Maranville's value to teams was mostly in the field and in the clubhouse, not the batter's box, and he spent the majority of his career with the Boston National League team with time out in the middle for stops with a few other franchises, most notably the Pittsburgh Pirates.

One time, Maranville lost an argument to future Hall of Fame umpire Bill Klem and was ejected from the premises. Soon after, fans looking for an explanation were rewarded by the sight of Maranville parading in front of the exits, still in uniform, waving newspapers and shouting, "Extra! Extra! Read all about Maranville and that big baboon Klem."[3]

Tomfoolery came naturally to Maranville, and while management was occasionally fooled into giving him positions of responsibility, he had difficulty suppressing his innate wish to have a good time. Late in the 1925 season, the Chicago Cubs made him manager and Maranville did not outline a long list of rules for his charges. One policy could be defined as the anti-curfew. As a get-acquainted method, Maranville prowled through the train cars taking his club to its next game and poured ice water on the sleeping fellows with the admonition that there would be no sleeping after midnight on his watch.

When he was affiliated with the Braves as a player, Maranville once had the misfortune of being nabbed by a police officer for reckless driving under the influence. He spent the night in jail before being hauled before the judge. The officer of the court fined him $100, which Maranville considered grossly unfair. His attorney cited his nine error-free chances in the field and two hits at bat to show that a man could not perform so well and be intoxicated. "Maranville can," the judge said.[4] It seemed as if the Rabbit was getting too well-known in Boston.

Maranville did eventually acknowledge that he drank too much, and from 1927 on he stayed on the wagon.

Maranville did play to win at all times, but he also sometimes employed the shortest distance between two points if it included a touch of the offbeat. Sometimes, due to his diminutive stature, he crawled between the legs of tall umpires to get the crowd on his side. He was brash enough as a young player to whip out a pair of glasses, polish the lenses, and hand them to an ump. Long before Willie Mays made the basket catch popular, Maranville gathered in pop-ups in such a manner.

When he tagged an opposing runner around second base, Maranville made sure to emphasize that the visitor was out by sitting atop of him following the tag. Yes, Maranville pointedly was a showboat. If he made a good play in the field—his bread and butter—he stood up straight and strutted back to his position, a look-at-me gesture that likely was none too popular with opponents.

Maranville was even more demonstrative between innings when he was warming up at short. He danced around, made quirky gestures and wasn't satisfied unless he made the crowd laugh. Once, near the end of his career, Maranville's 18-year-old daughter was in the stands and stunned him by saying she wished she was married and had a baby. The reason? So she could show the infant grandpa's antics on the field.

In 1914, the Boston NL team became known as "The Miracle Braves." Following a 4–18 start and without picking up steam until well into summer, the Braves somehow won the pennant and advanced to the World Series. Boston defeated the Athletics in four straight games for a world title, and Maranville was part of it. About 40 years later, Maranville was asked his biggest thrill in baseball. "That's easy," he said, citing that year's crown.[5]

Sometimes Maranville was the victim of a prank as well. Usually, though, he had an answer to turn lemons into lemonade. In the middle of his career (during Prohibition in the 1920s), when he was representing the Pirates, he was hanging out in his hotel room imbibing something much stronger than a soft drink. While he was occupied, a teammate swiped his pants. For whatever reason other than to demonstrate he would not be easily cowed, Maranville picked up a hat, plunked it on his head, borrowed a teammate's trombone and imitated a one-man band. He marched through the hotel lobby playing tunes while wearing a shirt and shorts.

Before he gave up drinking, prodded by an unceremonious demotion to the minors, Maranville was always armed and dangerous. A close friend on the Pirates was a pitcher named Moses Yellow Horse, who in mid-game declared that he would not throw another pitch until he had a drink. While first baseman Charlie Grimm urged him to trot into the dugout for a sip from the water cooler as long as there was time out, Yellow Horse said he wasn't talking about water, but fire water.

This sudden boycott perplexed the Pirates, who did not see a ready solution, believing there was not a drop of whiskey to be had in Forbes Field.

Maranville, who had also dashed to the mound, did bring the answer with him, however. He reached into his pocket and produced a miniature bottle of whiskey. Yellow Horse drank from it and the game resumed.

Maranville enjoyed a good cigar as much as he did a good alcoholic beverage. During one game Maranville seemed likely to be safe at third base if he slid, but chose to come in standing up and was tagged out. The third base coach cussed him, saying, "Why didn't you slide, you so-and-so?" Maranville replied, "What, slide and break a 50-cent cigar?"[6] A friend had presented him with the then-high-priced model before the game, and he stashed it in his uniform.

It took a bit of sleight-of-hand, very good hands handling the ball indeed, for a .258 hitter to be voted into the Hall of Fame. From his earliest days in the game, in the Deadball Era, Maranville impressed onlookers with his fielding skills. As far back as 1919, one sportswriter spent many column inches dissecting Maranville's throwing style.

> Maranville seems to get the ball away without making half of the usual motions. He can shoot under or over handed, but his best trick is in shooting from a sort of side-arm overhand. Maranville's throw has always been a puzzle, even to players on the field with him. He seems to push, rather than throw, the ball. Another pecularity is that the players on the same team say he has a "light" throw, that is, it hits the receiver's hands without jarring them.[7]

It seemed that hardly anyone could figure out Maranville. Maranville kept goading Braves teammate Jack Scott into wrestling with him. This went on for weeks before the pitcher accepted the challenge. They faced off in a hotel room with other Braves as witnesses. When Scott threw Maranville and he landed hard on the floor, the shortstop lay still. He could not be cajoled awake. A distressed Scott left the hotel and was on his way to the police to turn himself in for murder when a teammate stopped him. They turned back to the hotel room, where they found Maranville laid out and looking mighty pale (which was due to the application of talcum powder). As Scott moaned his sorrow, Maranville rallied and the entire room laughed. Scott nearly killed Maranville on the spot for real.

The kooky Maranville pulled off another stunt with the Brooklyn Robins that angered others more than it tickled their funny bones. Alone in his hotel room, Maranville fired a shot from a pistol and then moaned loudly. Others came rushing to the door and, hearing nothing on the other side, they broke it down. When they fought through the wood, there was Maranville, sitting in a chair, laughing.

Then, as now, anyone who let loose a sense of humor gained attention. New York Yankees owner Jacob Ruppert called Maranville the funniest man he ever met. Sportswriters routinely referred to his pranks and how he always joked around, and often called him baseball's funny man. In 1930, when Maranville was back with Boston for a second tour and he was 38 years old, one article referred to him as "the Peter Pan of baseball."[8] Generally, the name fit. He didn't want to grow up and do anything besides play baseball.

Neither Maranville's mouth, nor mind, slowed down, even if his legs dropped a notch or two in speed. He fondly recalled his efforts ducking between the legs of umpire Hank O'Day, going from first to second with the crawl. "I guess my best stunt was when I crawled between the legs…. O'Day stopped the game while he consulted the rules to find a way to punish me," Maranville said. "But it wasn't in the book and I got away with it."[9]

Maranville was living in Rochester, New York, in the upstate snowbelt, as he prepared for his 20th season in 1931 when a sportswriter visited and made much of the wintry weather and how it must affect the old bones of a veteran of 39. His line of questioning was deflected with ease by Maranville. Asked if he had any broken bones, Maranville said, "Haven't been in a crap game for years." How was his wind? "Still can holler pretty good."[10]

Before his brief sojourn as a manager in the majors, Maranville did give it a whirl running a team in Montreal in the minors. There was no evidence he had tempered his behavior. When one of his batters made a hit, Maranville would dance along the foul lines, playing an imaginary violin. He would raise his cap and make a curtsey when one of his own blasted a home run.

Maranville, who became a popular banquet speaker in Montreal, could also tell jokes on himself. Enough time had passed since the beginning of his big-league career that no one quite recalled if they were true or embellished. He said the great Jim Thorpe once held his feet and dangled him out a 16th-floor window of a hotel, and he rather daringly challenged Thorpe from his position of weakness. "Let go, you big bum, you haven't got the guts to drop me," he said he said. Since Thorpe was not arrested for murder and Maranville told the tale, it appears his life was spared.[11]

Maranville offered insights into the changes in big-league baseball from when he began during the Deadball Era, and the sport in 1935 when he was 44 and just leaving it.

> In those days, baseball was played for a run at a time. Now it's played for an inning of slaughter. The tricks which used to win games don't pay any more. In the old days,

if you weren't up to all the tricks, you might miss a run and a run often meant a game. Nowadays a fellow might spend his spare time thinking up a trick that's good for one run, only to have somebody like Jimmie Foxx, who'd been spending his spare time in batting practice, come along with a home run good for four runs.[12]

Civility is a much bigger part of the game in the 2000s than it was a century ago, and Maranville, who possessed a tart tongue, said the bench jockeying was fierce and personal. When he broke in with Boston in 1912, the king of taunting was New York Giants manager John McGraw.

Maranville said McGraw could be vicious, but he was no shy youngster and when he heard the way big-leaguers bashed one another with insults, with McGraw as the ringleader with New York, he fired back. Others may have feared McGraw, but Maranville did not.

> I had a sharp tongue myself. It was the best defense against a man like McGraw, who shared the weakness common to most dishers-out; he couldn't take it. Underneath an apparent armor-plate of callous disregard, McGraw really was sensitive. There were two nicknames that hurt his feelings. You could call him anything else and it was like dropping medicine into the ocean, but you couldn't call him "Jawn" or "Muggsy" without shocking him right down to the marrow. I had no more sense of reverence than a cat.[13]

Maranville's was a winning strategy. He was told by another player, Hank Gowdy, that McGraw adopted new rules for dealing with the Rabbit since he clearly only had rabbit ears physically, not in the form of sensitivity. "Presently the Giants stopped riding me and McGraw would go out of his way to avoid speaking to me at all," Maranville reported. "(McGraw), after a year or so of trying to get my goat, instructed his team not to ride me at all. 'Lay off that brat Maranville. He's poison.'"[14]

Maranville did cotton to the old tricks that might catch a player off-guard. Once, he and second base partner Eddie Fitzpatrick of the Braves discovered that the great Honus Wagner, who heretofore could never be distracted by conversation, owned a chicken farm. Fitzpatrick, claiming he also owned one, peppered Wagner with questions on the topic as Maranville sneaked behind the Pirates star and picked him off second base.

When he was in his 40s and sportswriters kept asking how he kept hanging on to a big-league job, Maranville admitted that after seeing it all, experiencing it all and having his body banged up and bruised, he did feel a bit elderly. But he still loved the game.

> I've broken both my legs. I've sprained everything I've got between my ankles and my disposition. I've dislocated joints and I've fractured my pride. I've spent more time in hospitals than some fellows ever spend in church. I've ridden on railroad trains until a steam shovel couldn't lift the cinders I've combed out of my hair. I've eaten lousy food and slept on literally lousy beds. I've been socked with fists and pop bottles and

insults. I've been broken out of bed in the middle of the night by fat-headed bums who only wanted to know what Pop Anson's all-time batting average was. I've lost a lot of teeth and square yards of hide. But I've never lost my self-respect—and I've kept what I find in few men of my age—my enthusiasm.[15]

That key word might be why a sportswriter would say, "Pound for pound he [Rabbit Maranville] outclassed them all in the fine art of revelry."[16]

Although Rabbit managed several teams in the minors, his stint running the Cubs as manager in 1925 lasted only 55 games. One day he did not show up for work. He was strangely absent from the clubhouse.

It turned out that Maranville had reprised one of his old standby routines. He was outside the ball park hawking newspapers, going through that same "Extra! Extra!" call. "Maranville Fired As Manager! Maranville Ousted!"[17] Perhaps that would be the equivalent of tweeting the news flash today. In any case, Maranville's actions became a self-fulfilling prophecy and he was fired the next day.

A heart attack ended Rabbit Maranville's life in January of 1954. When Maranville passed away, a legion of sportswriters told the story. One called him an imp. Others liberally employed the word colorful.

The *New York Times*' commentary was a bit more eloquent, reading in part, "Rabbit Maranville was as big as a leprechaun and had all of a leprechaun's elfin instincts. And he added a few refinements of his own, those which no self-respecting leprechaun ever would countenance."[18]

6. Dizzy Dean

"I think he's going to be a great one, but I'm afraid we'll never know from one minute to the next what he's going to do or say."—St. Louis Cardinals manager Gabby Street[1]

THE RIGHT-HANDED PITCHER WHO "SLUD" into America's consciousness could baffle hitters with his fastball and baffle listeners with his syntax.

The hitters walked away in tears after trying to best Dizzy Dean. The listeners walked away chuckling.

Lesser used now, but quite popular as a phrase in the 1930s when Jay Hanna Dean was entertaining baseball fans on the mound, were the words "an American original." If the words were not coined for Dean, they were ideally applied.

Born in 1910 in Lucas, Arkansas, Dizzy did leave them dizzy with his fantastic pitching, clever comments, and supreme confidence. It was tough to figure out whether his baseball ability, or trying to follow the logic of his general commentary, was more fun to observe.

Athletes were supposed to be humble—it was practically written into their contracts—but Dean was one of the first to embrace the great big stage by boasting about just how great he was. While brother Paul, nicknamed Daffy, was not quite as flamboyant, Dizzy more than covered for both of them.

Once Dizzy predicted that he and Daffy would pitch back-to-back no-hitters in a doubleheader for the Cards, and they produced a no-hitter and a one-hitter.

Dean parlayed the ability inherent in his 6-foot-2, 180-pound body, along with a rough-hewn professed Southern innocence, into fame as an All-Star ballplayer and a nationally renowned broadcaster whose charm

6. Dizzy Dean

was the likelihood he would say anything that popped into his head—and bruise the English language, nearly fatally, as he did so.

Dean made it through 12 years in the majors with a 150–83 mark, mostly with the Cardinals and also with the Chicago Cubs, but he was better than that. Although worthy for the Hall of Fame, Dean's was a career of what-ifs.

His 30–7 record in 1934 remains the last time a National League hurler won 30 games in a season. Dean also won 28 games the next year. His downfall was injuries, chiefly a broken toe in the 1937 All-Star Game and then a sore arm that he threw out of joint by trying to compensate with an altered motion.

At his best, Dean was magnificent, but the unfortunate series of injuries ruined his pitching by the time he turned 30 in 1940. He sadly went from untouchable to washed-up faster than the rinse cycle in a washing machine.

Once, Dean, who always referred to himself as "Ol' Diz," as if he was an invented character (and maybe he was), bet a friend that he could strike out Vince DiMaggio four times in a game the next day. Vince may not have been the equal of his Hall of Fame brother Joe, or his All-Star brother Dom, but he was a major leaguer. Such things did occur where a batter might whiff four times in a game, but this was a brash prediction.

Sure enough, Dean fanned DiMaggio three times in a row. He also put two strikes on him immediately in his fourth at-bat. But DiMaggio got wood on the next pitch and popped it up in foul ground. Dean's catcher appeared ready to grab the soft hit, but Dean came running towards him shouting, "Drop it! Drop it! Damn it, if you ever want to catch me again, drop it!" So the backstop dropped it. Cardinals manager Frank Frisch nearly had a heart attack over the goings-on, jumped up from his seat in the dugout, and hit his head on the roof.[2]

Dean won his bet.

Dean was the son of a cotton-picking sharecropper, and he earned his nickname while in the Army, not on the baseball diamond. It is difficult to picture Dean following orders too closely.

Ol' Diz not only oozed confidence and charisma (his version—"Crizzma"), he was talented. In the 1934 World Series, when the Dean brothers were at the top of their games and before both careers were truncated by injury, Dizzy was forever mesmerizing the press with comments about "Me and Paul." St. Louis won the championship over the Detroit Tigers that year when each Dean won two Series games.

Once, in a game against the New York Giants, Dean was following through with his pitching motion and was hit in the head by a line drive. Everyone knows that is no trifling matter and that it is a miracle no pitcher has been killed by such a shot in the history of the majors. The liner was struck by Burgess Whitehead and at least one eyewitness wrote that the ball bounced off Dean's head and landed in the bullpen in left field in the air, scored as a double. On another occasion, in the 1934 World Series, Dean was hit in the head by a throw while he was running the base path. Knocked unconscious by the blow, Dean was taken to a hospital for an examination, just in case he had a skull fracture. It was probably no accident that a newspaper headline read, "Xrays of Dean's Head Show Nothing."[3] It seemed as if Dean might have written that one himself, with a smirk.

Dean infuriated the opposition by sometimes noting what his pitching repertoire would do to them—and making good on it. Then he would be gleeful about his success, almost childlike in the way he reveled in the game of baseball. He was good at what he did, not shy about dispensing that fact to the world, but had such a good time playing the game that it was hard to stay mad at him.

Early in his career, especially, Dean made a show of his Li'l Abner–type innocence, the barefoot boy from the country who ate poorly, worked hard, and succeeded. There was truth to it all, but behind that exterior Dean was a savvy man whose homespun commentary often included wisdom.

Much later in life Dean ballooned up in weight, and once, while playing golf with President Dwight D. Eisenhower, he was asked how he had gained so many pounds while being an avid golfer. "Mr. President," he said, "I was on a diet for 25 years. Now that I'm makin' some money I'm makin' sure I eat good to make up for the lean years."[4]

Dean wielded a knife and fork with enthusiasm when given the chance, bulking up to about 300 pounds during his TV days.

It was part of Dean's charm, and his back story, that he had made good in the National Pastime by overcoming childhood deprivation. He was just a good ol' boy whose admirable skills on the pitching mound carried him a great distance from his roots. Probably not even Dean would have pictured himself as a broadcaster on national television, if only because there wasn't any TV when he was a youth. Dean did have the gift of gab, though, so if he could have envisioned moving pictures on a little screen in a living room he might well have thought, "I can do that." He played upon a hillbilly image and sang songs on the air, especially "The Wabash Cannonball."

6. Dizzy Dean

Sometimes Dean spoke up to newspaper reporters in a humorous manner, and other times he offended opposing players. In one game Dean did not appreciate the way the arbiters handled a brawl between his Cardinals and the New York Giants, and that included National League President Ford Frick. "Frick and Umpire Barr are among the biggest crooks in baseball," Dean said.[5] That did not go over well and he was suspended. Dean was cajoled into denying he said that, but then he refused to sign a document saying he rescinded the comment. "I ain't signin' nothin'," the pitcher said.[6]

Going back to the origin of the nickname Dizzy, it is ironic that it did not stem from participation in baseball, but Dean was not a good fit for the U.S. Army. In 1929, peacetime in the country, it was possible for a soldier to pay the government to release him from service. It cost $120, which Dizzy did not have. Brother Paul raised the money from wages for picking cotton and sent the cash to his brother.

Dizzy lost $80 in a craps game before he could use the money for what it was intended. Paul told him there was no more cash where that came from and "he might as well try to win it back."[7] Dean raised his bank account to $140 and exited the Army.

Dean was 19 at the time, and it would take a few years of baseball success before he picked up another nickname solely based on ability. Ol' Diz and Dizzy were fine, but he was so good he was also called "The Great Man." Dean may not have been sophisticated coming off the farm, but he did have an innate sense of self-promotion. The story goes that at one point syndicated sports columnist Bob Considine was filling out a crossword puzzle asking for a three-letter answer pertaining to Dean and that he penned in "ego."[8]

Dean's formal schooling ended in the second grade and he once added, "I wasn't so good in the first grade, either."[9] For a guy who was not much associated with the written word, Dean's popularity led him to write a column called "Poppin' Off," though it was ghost-written. It made sense since Dean said anything off the top of his head to sportswriters and later on CBS on-air.

Of two-time All-Star shortstop Dick Bartell, then with the New York Giants, Dean wrote in dismissal, "He pays himself a compliment in the fourth game of the series, supposin' that I'd throw a bean ball at him. For pity's sake, why should anybody throw at him? Pitchers never use a duster, except on the good hitters."[10]

Of future Detroit Tigers Hall of Famer Hank Greenberg, Dean opined, "They tell me Old Hank knocked in his 100th run of the season the other day, and as anybody which can knock in 100 runs by early July must be pretty good in the old pincherino, which is when men is on the bases and a base hit is needed to cash him in."[11]

Dean occasionally was criticized for his bragging and showmanship, but others were jealous that he pitched for St. Louis. Charlie Dressen, who was managing the Cincinnati Reds, a perennially losing team of the 1930s, said in his mind Dean was not "swell-headed." If Dean joined him in Cincinnati and kept winning as often as he did for the Cardinals, Dressen would think of a way to reward him. "I'd be willing to give him a whole rubdown," Dressen said.[12]

There was the rare time when Dean clammed up and refused to talk, yet the stock market did not crash and the trains kept running. Dean was property of the Chicago Cubs in 1939 when he showed up in his hotel bleeding profusely from his left, non-pitching arm, and manager Gabby Hartnett wanted an explanation. Dean spun a yarn, and Hartnett gazed at him suspiciously and replied, "That's out of a book called the Arabian Nights." After a second try, Harnett replied, "Right from Baron Munchausen." Dean took just two stitches, a bit of an anti-climax. "Will he live?" Hartnett asked the doctor. "Yes," said the medical man. "Aw shucks," retorted Hartnett. Soon Hartnett concluded that Dean's condition was so at risk that "You can't afford to take any chance of putting on a sweaty old uniform." Some interpreted that as a suspension. Ultimately, a *New York Times* reporter on the scene suggested the mystery was solved and Dean was injured when "a glass fell off the table [in a restaurant] and just then the taxi cab door flew open, causing Ol' Diz to put his arm through the cigar case while the telephone was ringing by his bedside and the Bronx directory jumped up and bit him the length of two stitches. It was pitch dark at the time."[13]

Anyone who believed Ol' Diz was dumb pretty much flunked his own SAT test. Textbook learning aside, Dean understood human nature and knew the image he was crafting. "He was Dizzy Dean, with enormous charm, color and appeal," said famed broadcaster Red Barber. "He was smarter than a fox. I think he always knew what he was doing and what he was saying and I wish I had the money he has made and saved. He has it buried in tomato cans all over."[14]

Dean was also very much a good-hearted soul, chatting with strangers, making jokes with baseball fans, and giving to charitable causes. "His philosophy was doing a fellow right," said Daffy Dean. "He never saw a man he didn't like or respect and I never saw anyone who didn't respect or like Dizzy."[15]

6. Dizzy Dean

Of course, some with a different perspective might suggest that at times Dean could be too helpful. He once told a succession of three sportswriters different versions of the same story, namely where he was born. "I was helping the writers out," Dean said later. "They ain't lies. Them's scoops."[16]

At his finest, there was no better pitcher than Dean, and some believed he had the goods to become the greatest ever. Instead, his career was cut short because of a lame arm, although he kept trying to revive it for a few years. Dean's career hung by a thread in 1938 after specialists examined his arm and walked out of the room shaking their heads. Another doctor, who some suggested was more of a voodoo specialist, arrived on the scene and began rubbing Dean's arms with special potions. He felt better and threw better. "That's what did it," Dean said, "old goose grease." The doctor said it was olive oil and turpentine, which may have been the generic product. "That oil and turpentine keeps the sweat right there on the muscle," Dean added.[17]

Whatever it was, the cure enabled Dean to go 7–1 with a 1.81 earned run average in 1938. But it didn't have staying power and Dean floundered again.

Given that Dean was in good shape as an athlete and that he was later proven to be a pretty smart fellow, one must wonder if his exploits in the Army that earned him his enduring nickname were really done on purpose, from lack of effort, or simply because, as he put it, "I was the worst soldier in God's livin' world." There was back-up for that opinion coming from his

They didn't call Jay Hanna Dean "Dizzy" for nothing. He earned the nickname, first in the Army and then on the field, where he fractured the English language in an endearing manner.

sergeant, William Barnett, who had every reason to call Jay Hanna "Dizzy." Barnett said, "That boy couldn't pour piss out of a boot with instructions on the heel."[18]

At one point Dean took a tongue-lashing from a squad leader for making his bunk poorly, a no-no in the Army, and a task everyone is expected to master easily. "I like wrinkles," Dean said.[19]

Dean did not like discipline and saw the world in a way different from authority figures. Guys like that do not thrive in the Army, or sometimes in team sports if the manager or coach is a disciplinarian.

In 1931, while playing for Houston in the Texas League against Birmingham of the Southern League in the Dixie Series, Dean established one of his trademarks—belittling enemy batters' capability of scoring runs off him. "If I don't beat them Barons, I'll join the House of David," Dean said of the famous touring team known for its facial hair, "grow a beard and never, ever shave it off. It would hide my shame."[20]

Dean stayed out late to party and slept late, until mid-afternoon, to recuperate, driving maids in hotels batty. If they tried to clean his room before he was ready, Dean shouted through the door at them: "I ain't here!"[21]

The brash young pitcher was an acquired taste. Other pitchers did not enjoy it when Dean made fun of opposing batting orders or shirked work in practice, and teammates did not like the way he riled other teams either.

After one particularly exasperating run of behavior that stretched the bounds of appropriateness, manager Gabby Street made like a drill sergeant all over again, reading a baseball-related riot act to Dean. The short version of the reaming included comments calling Dean "lazy and unreliable, always trying to dodge work, and a god-damned crybaby."[22] Dean wasn't going to take the insult and was preparing to jump the team when general manager Branch Rickey brought him down to earth.

Despite high hopes that one day he would awake and miraculously discover the old magic in his arm, Dean's pitching career was over by the early 1940s. He was moving into coaching, which he did briefly for the Cubs, but then came a life-changing offer. The Falstaff Brewing Corporation, which sponsored St. Louis Cardinals and St. Louis Browns games, offered Dean a three-year radio broadcasting contract in 1941. A star was born—in another field.

"I'm just gonna speak plain ol' ordinary, pinto bean English," Dean announced when he took the job.[23] That was one way to describe Dean's manner of speech, but in his description of Dean's radio manner, biographer Robert Gregory noted that he also spoke "with contempt for grammar."[24] Fans who already considered him more or less a folk hero loved him for that, too. This was not sixth-grade English class.

One of Dean's most popular words was "slud" to describe sliding into a base. He employed "can of corn," the old expression, for pop flies easy to catch, "throwed" for threw and "blue darters" for line drives. No matter that an interpretive manual would have come in handy, the fans ate up Ol' Diz's style.

Dean was so beloved that a Hollywood studio offered him a four-picture movie contract to make westerns, apparently much on the strength of the fact that he wore ten-gallon hats. Dean said no. He was a straight shooter with his vocabulary, not a six-gun.

A smash, Dean was given a longer and richer contract and in the last year of World War II the beer company sent him to Army bases and hospitals as a morale builder.

Teachers who were slaves to the prim aspects of the language organized a protest against Dean's grammar and urged that he be taken off the air. Dean weathered that little storm quite easily, but noted, "I know what's a ball and what's a strike and vice-uh-veeda."[25]

He certainly did.

Eventually, Sam Breadon, the Cardinals' owner with no sense of humor and sympathy for the teachers, did Dean in because of his syntax. He exiled his radio efforts to the Browns only. After a few years of that, in an unlikely pairing with the most stiff-necked team of all, Dean began handling pre-game and post-game shows for the New York Yankees. "I'm gonna talk like I've always talked," Dean said. Indeed, no one was going to alter his speech patterns. He did note that he had trouble understanding New York accents, too.[26]

Dean's broadcasting renown spread from there. Between 1953 and 1966 he became a household name to a new generation of fans through the growth and expansion of television and by handling the "Game of the Week."

When he teamed with ex–Dodger Pee Wee Reese in the booth, Dean was apt to take a walkabout during a dull game. He once headed out to buy a hamburger at the concession stand and took Reese's order on the air.

A few years into his broadcasting career, Dean proved how sage he really was. "The thing I've got to guard against is improvement," he said. "If I start talking better, they'll throw me out."[27]

The world can only wonder just what kind of fabulous statistics Ol'

Diz might have put up if he had stayed healthy as a pitcher for longer. Yes, he did drive his player-manager Frankie Frisch nuts at times despite his Hall of Fame talent. One time Frisch visited the mound and Dean looked at him levelly and said, "Frankie, you're the greatest second-baseman in the game, but don't tell the greatest pitcher how to throw."[28]

Probably the only time in his life when Dizzy Dean wasn't funny to his audience, or having fun himself, was in 1974 when he died of a heart attack at age 64.

7. Satchel Paige

> "How would you like it if you were the world's greatest tenor, but had to stand outside the opera house with an organ grinder selling pencils, while a guy who couldn't come within two octaves of you stood on stage receiving curtain calls and showers of money?"—*Pulitzer Prize–winning sports columnist Jim Murray*[1]

ON THE EXTERIOR, SATCHEL PAIGE, perhaps the greatest pitcher of all time, wore a slight smile, sometimes turning into a smirk. He could be sharp-tongued and witty, but inside he was burning up.

That's because for most of his lengthy and legendary career, Leroy "Satchel" Paige was banned from Major League Baseball because of his skin color. The sport's unwritten rule kept African Americans on the sidelines until Paige was in his 40s.

But the unfairness of life did not prohibit Paige from gaining a national reputation and ultimately being squired into the Hall of Fame. He negotiated a treacherous path with supreme confidence, ironic commentary, and a wicked fastball, as well as guile and smarts, blazing a unique trail across a prejudiced country.

Humor, as well as a rubber arm, was part of the repertoire of the man born in Mobile, Alabama, maybe in 1906, maybe not. The mystery surrounding Paige, essentially classifying him as ageless, regarded when he was born and he fed the curiosity with jokes and offbeat tales.

What a journey it was for the Negro Leagues star, the barnstorming genius, the 42-year-old Cleveland Indians big-league rookie in 1948. "There never was a man on earth who pitched as much as me," Paige said of a career that with only one sore arm lasted from the 1920s to the 1960s. "But the more I pitched, the stronger my arm got."[2]

Never was there a man who concocted his own code of living in such vivid fashion. His teams may have traveled by bus, but Paige followed in a Cadillac. His teammates may have been bound by strict salary caps, but Paige was paid bonuses in advance, or with percentages of the house.

No one could believe how effectively Paige pitched for so long. He was a marvel and a miracle, but he fed adoring reporters his own propaganda when they were around to listen, after his prime years when he rode the back roads of America, in exile from the limelight.

Appropriately, Paige was involved in penning an autobiography called, "Maybe I'll Pitch Forever." He crafted six rules for staying young and staying happy that were essentially his Gettysburg Address, a speech that followed him to his grave.

> 1) "Don't Look Back, Something Might Be Gaining on You"; 2) If Your Stomach Disputes You, Lie Down and Pacify It with Cool Thoughts; 3) Go Very Light on the Vices, Such as Carrying on in Society, the Social Ramble Ain't Restful; 4) Avoid Fried Meats Which Angry up the Blood; 5) Keep the Juices Flowing by Jangling Around Gently as you Move; 6) Avoid Running at all Times."[3]

Paige was gangly, kicked his foot in the air as he delivered, and had the type of control, exhibited more than once, that could direct a thrown ball over a gum wrapper on the corner of home plate, and mixed in strange blooper pitches that flummoxed batters. He frequently toyed with hitters. "I never threw an illegal pitch," Paige said. "The trouble is, once in a while I tossed one that ain't been seen by this generation."[4]

Paige was almost terminally laid back and he knew that his behavior sometimes irked managers, umpires or others in a hurry. His ace up his sleeve was being the starting pitcher. "I never rush myself," he said. "See, they can't start the game without me."[5]

Paige usually knew what he was saying and sometimes there was a specific purpose

Satchel Paige was a legend in the Negro Leagues before becoming a 42-year-old rookie for the 1948 world champion Cleveland Indians. Paige slayed listeners with his wit wherever he went.

behind his comments. He mostly stayed clear of coming off as an angry man, but he could be sarcastic and plaintive, even while he was funny. "Mother always told me, if you tell a lie always rehearse it," Paige said. "If it don't sound good to you, it won't sound good to nobody else."[6]

Playing to appreciative audiences, Paige named many of his pitches with unorthodox monikers that baffled listeners as much as clarified things. He was able to throw pitches called hesitation, trouble ball, alley oop, wobbly ball, blooper, and midnight creeper, among others.

"Just take the ball and throw it where you want to," Paige said. "Home plate don't move."[7] For him that was easy, but for others the ball didn't always elude the bat.

Statistics were not always kept in great detail in Negro Leagues games and certainly not in barnstorming games. Paige starred wherever he went. He was a huge drawing card on the highways and byways of America, in big cities and little towns. Decade after decade he rolled along, throwing bullets to make men with big sticks flail at his pitches. He estimated he pitched in 2,600 games, won 2,100 of them and threw 55 no-hitters. Or maybe it was 100, which Paige also claimed.

Tighter rein on his numbers occurred when at last baseball's color barrier was shattered by Jackie Robinson and Paige was hired by the Cleveland Indians as a relief pitcher. As a rookie turning 42, he helped the club win its only world championship since 1920. Paige finished 6–1 with a 2.48 earned run average that year. Before he retired at 46, he was a two-time All-Star.

That was just a glimpse of what Paige was in his early years, when he so dominated most of the games he pitched that he jumped from team to team for the highest paycheck, usually without penalty. He was too valuable not to have in the league, and he was so valuable every team wanted him on its roster.

Before Major League Baseball was on television more often than soap operas, large segments of the country never saw the biggest stars play. After the end of the regular season, many of the underpaid stars put together touring teams. Dizzy Dean and Satchel Paige linked up and barnstormed, pitching against one another regularly. This was a proving ground for Paige, striking out big leaguers whom he believed he would never otherwise face. Later, Paige and Bob Feller, who became teammates on the Indians in 1948, worked out similar tours. "Paige was the best pitcher I ever saw," Feller said. "He's a better pitcher'n I ever hope to be," Dean said.[8]

At 6-foot-3 and 180 pounds, Paige was deceptively long-limbed rather than sculpted. He possessed a mix of deliveries so the hitter didn't know from what angle Paige's next pitch would come at him.

In one of his most redoubtable moves, sometimes performed just for show, or sometimes pulled out of his trick bag because he felt insulted by an opposing team, Paige would wave his fielders to the bench and remain on the field with only his catcher. The bold statement was that he needed no help to pile up three outs against these weak challengers. Paige proposed to strike everyone out and not even permit them a pop-up or weak ground ball. Somehow he made that outrageous stunt work for him.

"Of course the stories about Satchel are legendary, and some of them are even true," said Buck O'Neil, who teamed with Paige on the Kansas City Monarchs and was a lifelong friend. "For Satchel, making believers out of doubters was sweeter than winning any ballgame. It was as sweet as life itself."[9] Naturally, transforming those foolish beliefs usually meant that Paige won the game.

The numbers in the official record books will never show it, but Paige might have been the greatest of all, possibly better than Cy Young, Walter Johnson, Christy Mathewson, Dean or Feller, but with the possible exception of Dean he could surely out-talk them.

O'Neil, who for more than two decades after Paige died became the keeper of the flame of his legacy, once said the odds were probably 1,000,000-to-1 that Paige would ever become as famous as he did. Part of the reason was growing up in poverty in Alabama at a time when discrimination ruled the state, the region, and the United States. Part of the reason was that he excelled in a sporting field where black men were not welcome.

O'Neil said that Paige was "one of the first ball players to realize that sports is show business.... Satchel discovered he could get laughs. He perfected his act shuffling to the mound as if he had all day. He enjoyed clowning, but not at the expense of winning."[10]

Paige had a long-running rivalry with the powerful catcher Josh Gibson, the greatest hitter in the Negro Leagues, and they teased one another constantly about who would get the best of whom in a showdown. Leading 3–2 versus Gibson's squad with a man on third base after tripling, and two out on strikeouts, Paige informed O'Neil of a stunt he had in mind. O'Neil called it "Crazy, even for Paige." Paige walked the next two hitters on purpose to challenge Gibson with the bases loaded. He even told Gibson what was coming, fastballs, for the first two pitches, and still got an 0–2 count on him. He told Gibson he was going to get a third fastball, "a pea at your knee." The ball came in knee-high for called strike three.[11]

Paige threw so many thousand pitches in games later in life when he kept on truckin' that he sometimes didn't bother to throw a full complement of warm-up pitches. As his cited rules for living explained, he was not much for running to get a sweat going. He thought his effort would be better preserved for game action. "I pitch with my arm, not my feet," he said.[12]

Paige liked to travel in style, even when he did not have much money. While he did not haul in a big-league salary, big-league salaries in the 1930s, 1940s and into the 1950s were not usually munificent. Paige cut private deals with owners and even made $40,000 in a year when other top players were earning under $10,000.

He was also very good at spending money. Paige loved fishing, and when he was out of town and caught fish, especially catfish, he wanted to fry it up. Sometimes he turned his hotel room into a kitchen, doing his own cooking. Not all of his roommates appreciated the smell.

No one, whether it was Mae West or any other secretive Hollywood actress, ever had more fun lying about his age, or at least avoiding admitting the accuracy of numbers thrown out at him, than Paige. For the longest time, wild guesses were attached to his name in newspapers. When Indians owner Bill Veeck signed Paige, he urged him to stick with the gag because it would be good publicity. Veeck even offered a $500 reward to anyone who could prove a different age for Paige than was being talked about. Paige said people were stopping him in the street looking for clues to determine his age. "Look all you want, ain't no clews here," Paige said. 'Open your mouth,' a boy said. No evidence there. Another fellow said, 'Let me see your eyes.' A couple of boys asked me, 'Bend down. Let's see your hair.' Imagine, Satch ain't got a gray hair.' As they left I heard one of the boys remark, 'Maybe that Satch was a Leap Year baby.'"[13]

Paige reveled in the mystery. Eventually, the story got around that Paige's birth certificate could be found in the family Bible in Alabama. In the mid–1970s, Paige was confronted by Pulitzer Prize–winning columnist Dave Anderson of the *New York Times* with this question: "If you were called into court and had to take an oath on your age, what would you tell the judge?" It was a game try.

The pitcher replied, "The goat ate the Bible with my birth certificate in it. My grandfather got up from the chair to talk to the lady next door and he forgot about the Bible and the goat ate the Bible with the birth certificate in it." The exchange continued. "They couldn't follow that goat around all the time." The goat, Paige said, ate the Bible in 1926 or 1927, and he was ten or 12 at the time. "But you said you were 16 or 17 in '26," Anderson said. "I said I did which?" Paige answered.[14]

Paige was wise enough to keep the ball low and away against most batters, and he was proud enough of his control to zip it past them high if a batter thought he had him figured out and leaned across the plate to swing at the outside throw. "Hah, that's when I take that button off their shirt under their chin," Paige said. "I got a basket full of buttons at home." Once, a player retorted that Paige took the second button off his shirt. Paige replied, "My control is a little off. I was aiming at your top button."[15]

Paige, who threw three shutout innings for the Kansas City Athletics in 1965, presumably at age 59, was peppered with age questions wherever he went in his later years. At that time Paige said he was at the end of his "100-year career in baseball."[16] Still, he signed on with the Atlanta Braves as a player-coach (he did not play) in 1968, and the reporters hoped they had him surrounded on the age issue. Paige was not easily trapped in conversation. "They've done a lot of investigating," Paige said, "and to tell the truth it's got where it puzzles me myself. They couldn't find my record in Mobile because the jail had moved and the judge had died. They did a lot of checking on my family and found I had some relatives 200 years old."[17]

So take that.

Actually, the Braves hired Paige as a courtesy to allow him to obtain the last 158 days he needed in the majors to qualify for a pension. It was a kindness granted by an organization that had once treated him cruelly. There was a full intent to get Paige into a game on the mound, but it never occurred. When Paige announced his retirement, supposedly for good, a bit later, he said he was doing it to spare the younger generation the chagrin of being out-pitched by an old man. "I can still throw faster than most of 'em, but I don't want to embarrass them," Paige said. "It might have a bad effect on 'em." Hank Aaron, who swatted 755 home runs and is one of baseball's greats, teased Paige, saying, "I hear you didn't even have a curve." Paige fired back, "I didn't need one."[18]

Even during his retirement press conference in 1969, there was no let-up about Paige's age, and as usual he did not give an inch on the facts. The Atlanta media guide listed his birth date as July of 1906 (which has come to be accepted as the real one). When Paige said he had been pitching for 52 years in a row, someone pointed out that meant he pitched his first game at age ten. "I was the best pitcher in my grade-school class," Paige said.[19]

He was the best pitcher anywhere, many may argue.

Periodically, after he attained legendary status, mainstream America discovered Satchel Paige. In 1941, at a time when African American players were still prohibited from playing in the majors because of the specious argument that they weren't good enough, *LIFE* magazine published a profile of him.

In 1948, Paige moved into the majors, albeit too late to demonstrate his true gifts. In 1971, when Paige became the first Negro Leagues star to be chosen for the Baseball Hall of Fame, it was announced that he was going to be honored in an auxiliary wing. That plan didn't last long, but it was out there long enough for Paige to say, "Baseball has turned me from a second-class citizen to a second-class immortal."[20]

Paige lived better than most of his contemporaries, but he liked to live in luxury and he spent more lavishly than they did as well. He could be aloof and looked out for No. 1 in his contract negotiations, but also made sure he had fun along the way. He insisted that the players of his early days had more fun than the players of the 1980s. "It was more fun playing in the Negro Leagues," Paige said. "Today's majors are too stiff. In the Negro Leagues we'd fish or go catch rattlesnakes before putting on the uniform. That's fun."[21]

After being elected to the Hall of Fame, Paige was in more demand as a sports banquet speaker than ever, and he lit up rooms. In fact, he was so sought after that he might almost have admitted that age was catching up with him whether he looked back or not. "When I was a younger man," Paige said in 1976, "I could go two or three months without sleeping. But now I need a little snooze time between cities."[22]

In his latter days, Paige, who outlived many of the stars of the Negro Leagues, such as Josh Gibson and others who would later be elected to the Hall of Fame, did talk about their capabilities at those dinners. One of his most famous lines was informing the world that "Cool Papa" Bell was so fast he could turn off the light and be in bed before the room darkened. There has probably never been a more descriptive way of talking about a player being a fast runner.

When Paige died in 1982, Bill Veeck, the man who gave him the big-league job he had long coveted, was effusive in his praise of the pitcher who had become a friend. "He would have broken every pitching record in the book," Veeck said. "He was unlettered, but not unlearned. He was a remarkable man, a character you don't find. I think 'colorful' is a trite term to define Satchel. Satchel was a showman, one of the very few in baseball."[23]

8. Max Patkin

"Therein lies the power of the clown—he makes us laugh to remind us where we hurt, and somehow the pain is lessened."—*Ron Shelton, director of "Bull Durham," who used the real-life Max Patkin as himself in the movie*[1]

MAX PATKIN OWNED A RUBBERY FACE that he could contort into any form in the service of comedy. He knew slapstick like it was his hometown, and he had a sharp sense of comedic timing and an innate sense of what thousands of people would laugh at as they gathered in a ballpark.

Patkin wanted to be a pitcher, but instead he made pitchers (and all other position players) laugh along with his gags for a half-century. He played the big houses in the big towns and the small houses in the small towns. He earned the title "The Clown Prince of Baseball," not through inheritance like other royalty, but through effort, through hard work, and by showing up year after year wherever baseball was played across the United States.

Patkin turned to clowning when he was 26 when his right arm ran out of steam, and he retired from ballpark clowning after an estimated 4,200 shows when the rest of his body wore out in 1995. By then *The Sporting News* had been writing about Patkin since the 1940s.

Patkin could stretch his neck in ostrich-like fashion and turn his face into putty to exaggerate his looks. Once, when he was perfectly serious after his car broke down on a highway in Illinois, he knocked on the window of a car, seeking help. The woman screamed and zipped away. "I smiled and shrugged my shoulders," Patkin said. "'So what?' I said to myself. 'You've frightened other folks with that face.'"[2]

Born in 1920 in Philadelphia, Patkin used to say that he was so old that the first family car was a Model T—and he might have been telling the truth. Patkin was stationed in Hawaii during World War II and was on the mound for a game in 1944 when New York Yankees star Joe DiMaggio nicked him for a home run. Patkin indulged in some mock outrage following the blast and closely followed DiMaggio as he circled the bases. Spectators laughed. That was Patkin's first on-field gag.

After the war, when Bill Veeck bought the Cleveland Indians, he hired Patkin to entertain fans. He gave him a personal services contract for $650 and a baseball contract for $1. Once, requesting a favor from Detroit Tigers first baseman Hank Greenberg, Patkin appealed to him on the basis of both of them being Jewish. He asked Greenberg to fake a hot foot and Greenberg obliged him. Greenberg, a man of great strength, picked up Patkin and shook him. Patkin loved it. Another time, Patkin used Ted Williams, perhaps the greatest hitter who ever lived, as a fall guy to show off to some old friends from home. He bribed some kids to surround Williams for autographs until Patkin appeared, and then all shift to Patkin for his autograph, just so his Philadelphia pals would go back home and tell everyone what a big star Patkin was.

Actually, since Al Schacht had been called "The Clown Prince of Baseball," Patkin did not use that moniker until after his predecessor bowed out of the picture.

Although Veeck called Patkin a coach, he was almost exclusively a clown. The only one who did not like having Patkin around was Cleveland manager Lou Boudreau. Boudreau challenged Veeck with the famous words, "What are we running, a circus or a ball club?"[3]

Veeck counted on Patkin to coach first base and throw some batting practice, and as the best friend the fan ever had, Veeck also turned Patkin loose to make the paying customers chuckle. Not satisfied with one clown, Veeck hired two for a little while, the other being Jackie Price, who as part of his shtick pursued fly balls as he drove around the field in a car.

Veeck bowed to the wishes of his manager. He fired Price, and Patkin was banished to the minors. That's where he thrived.

In the movie "Bull Durham," about a minor-league baseball team, Patkin plays himself. When he spotted the Kevin Costner character, longtime player Crash Davis, Patkin said, "He's played in more towns than I have."[4] That couldn't be literally true because Davis was hitched to individual teams while Patkin was a freelancer on the go, a master of one-night stands in parks across the land.

Blessed with double-jointed flexibility and a remarkable talent for flapping his elbows to resemble a bird in flight, Patkin was a whiz at physical comedy. He was a brilliant mimic. If a manager lost his temper and began screaming, the errant knight might look up and find the entire park laughing at his ways because Patkin so energetically imitated him. Patkin pantomimed giving signs to players and he danced to one of the great, original rock and roll songs, "Rock Around The Clock" by Bill Haley and the Comets.

Patkin was no different from most people who enter baseball in any capacity, though especially players. He dreamed of making it in the majors. But like many of them, he had to be content with most of a career spent in the minors. In 1941 he even posted a 13–10 pitching record for Wisconsin Rapids; or maybe it was 10–8, depending on the source. He also pitched for Green Bay and briefly in Wilkes-Barre, Pennsylvania. Unlike most of those other minor-league individuals, Patkin became a legend.

Veeck did his best to help out, bringing in Patkin to perform wherever the owner ran a team. The largest crowd Patkin played in front of was Cleveland's Municipal Stadium on a night the Indians drew 70,000 people. The smallest crowd to watch Patkin at a park was in Great Falls, Montana, when only four fans showed up. The other residents were busy that night of July 20, 1969, when astronaut Neil Armstrong walked on the moon. Perhaps Patkin should have been sent with him. Somehow he would have made a good fit visiting outer space.

Long after Patkin retired as a baseball player, he frequented baseball stadiums in uniform. His was not the tight-fitting style of the day in the second half of the 20th century. Rather, Patkin's standard garb was ridiculously roomy and rather than a number on the back, his forever-insignia was a question mark.

There is no underestimating Patkin's physical appearance as a connection to his role as a clown. He described himself as "built like a lollipop stick with a nose."[5]

Patkin was light on his feet while performing his acts, and that was logical since he was a renowned dancer. His life on the road was hard on wives, and he saw two marriages go kaput. The travel could be brutal, and when he passed away it was estimated that Patkin had traveled seven million miles during his years of clowning.

For the most part Patkin came across as an old-timer even before he was old—and he did clown at baseball games until he was 75. That's because he was straight out of vaudeville, straight out of moving pictures before sound. He often set up in the coaching box, and it helped a great deal if an umpire he was about to make fun of was in on the gag. In that way his performances resembled the Harlem Globetrotters—you could see his actions from the rafters. Actually, at times Patkin did make appearances with the Globetrotters. They were definitely kindred spirits. Like those

8. Max Patkin

Globetrotters humorists, Patkin played with audience members. He tried to swipe women's purses and didn't let the players escape unmolested between innings either.

Patkin made faces, sticking out his tongue. He spat out sodas he sipped from. One of his props was infield dirt. His mind-bending facial maneuvers seemed cartoonish, but he had terrific command of his muscles. Patkin always wore a baseball cap turned sideways, or sometimes backwards, long before anyone but a catcher twirled his cap around to fit it under the mask ever did so while walking through a mall. He employed a children's-sized baseball glove to good effect as well. When coaching, Patkin would remove one shoe, smell it, and pretend to faint. Players in on the gag threw water on him.

For those who expected Patkin to shape his features into the equivalent of a male model's in *GQ*, he had a ready answer. "What did you expect, girls, Robert Redford?"[6]

Besides his reputation as a funny man, Patkin earned another kind for reliability. Hot or cold, dry or rainy, in the middle of nowhere or in the big city, if Patkin had an appointment to play your park he would be there. Sometimes he overcame bad travel connections or injuries, but for 35 straight years Patkin never missed a single date he had scheduled.

As the years passed and Patkin became a single man not once, but twice, he tired of the road. The grind of transportation and the sameness of hotel rooms wearied him, and he sometimes admitted to being lonely or depressed. But like the Broadway star who sucks it up to play before the live audience even when he does not feel well, Patkin always came through with his act. "I can do my best routines when I'm feeling down," he said. "I'm a performer. I can turn comedy on and off like a faucet."[7]

If Patkin tired of his lifestyle, he never tired of his life entertaining in baseball parks. He could flip a switch and he did so. Generations of fans saw the Max Show, and he did not shortchange them. Patkin embraced the youngsters of the 1990s the way he had the first audiences of the 1940s.

When "Bull Durham" appeared in theatres in 1988—and was a hit— it not only gained positive reviews, it served as a vehicle to rejuvenate Patkin's career for fresh fans who may not have known about his history or existence. He was not on screen very long, a scene in a bar with Kevin Costner and Susan Sarandon, but it was a choice and memorable part. And Patkin didn't even play out his entire routine, just in snatches. Mostly, all he had to do was talk.

Occasionally, although he mostly played to family audiences at minor league games, Patkin could tend to the risqué. "I once mooned the crowd in Lethbridge, Canada," he said. "There was snow on the ground and maybe 50 people in the stands. I was never invited back."[8]

Right up until he chose to stay in one place for his summers rather than building up the frequent-traveler miles, Patkin served as his own booking agent. At his peak Patkin played up to 100 stadiums a year. In his older age he cut back to 50. Typically, he was paid between $500 and $1,500 for his appearances. In the off-season, in Philadelphia, he sold shoes for years.

Besides the movie "Bull Durham," of all things the San Diego Chicken, later called the Chicken, and other anthropormophic, creature-like mascots led to a resurgence of interest in Patkin's career. Compared to them he was the genuine article. But after a while the younger fans warmed up to the growing numbers of mascots and business dropped off some. "I'm the last of the breed," Patkin said. "They've got the Chicken now. I'm not jealous, but I am envious of the money he makes. Me, I'm no duck. I'm 100 percent baseball."[9]

At another time he did credit the Chicken and the colorful mascots for helping him. In early April of 1986, Patkin and the Chicken performed on the same bill in Louisville. That was a first. "This is probably the most unusual booking of all time," Patkin said, crediting the Louisville Cardinals' owner's innovative approach. "He is booking both the present and the past."[10]

Depending on which day someone asked Patkin, he expressed appreciation for the new trend in mascots for helping gain him fresh attention, or distress for overshadowing him. "Those barnyard animals have brought me back into baseball," he said. "I'm not making as much money as I should be after 35 years, but it's a great living. And I like being the Clown Prince of Baseball. It has a nice ring to it."[11]

That title was sometimes tossed around loosely, but there was little doubt that Patkin deserved it. "It was a corny act, but the fans liked it," Patkin admitted after he retired.[12] He touched something in them. They did not come to the ballpark to watch Shakespeare but to have a good time, and Patkin tickled their funny bones.

One thing Patkin showed was consistency. He rarely changed his act, but he pulled it off game after game, year after year, despite performing through injuries like sprained ankles and broken bones. Patkin had bad knees and a bad back at the end. But he played with pain.

When news broke in the 1990s, after his brother died and his second wife divorced him, that Patkin was undergoing treatment for depression, he received 5,000 letters of support.

Late in life, when he was off the road, Patkin often visited Veterans Stadium in Philadelphia to watch the Phillies. He was welcomed in the home and visitors' locker room, where many of the players greeted him with tales of watching him perform when they were playing in the minors. Patkin liked to think of himself as a good-luck charm of sorts. He told one Phillies pitcher that Steve Carlton, who ended up in the Hall of Fame, once rubbed "my nose for luck and he won six straight." Coaches Mike Cubbage and Frank Howard said Patkin kissed them for luck and each hit a home run.[13]

Patkin passed out his own baseball card. Some of those ex–minor leaguers already had them from past meetings. It's an unknown, gargantuan number, how many players Patkin met during his grand tours of the minors. Bill Pulsipher, then with the New York Mets, reminded Patkin that once in Binghampton, Patkin threw a brush-back pitch at him, but Pulsipher tried to hit it even though he wasn't supposed to do that in his routine. "Lots of guys did that," Patkin said. Added Pulsipher, "I knew you wouldn't remember, even though we sat in the clubhouse for a whole game and drank beer together." Patkin replied, "A lot of guys did that, too."[14]

He tried to stay true to the game, his comedy an offshoot of what was happening on the field. Patkin was rooted in baseball and he never strayed from those roots. When pushed and given the opportunity, Patkin could be witty, too. Kansas City Royals owner Ewing Kaufman was known for wearing loud sports coats. Patkin took a gander at one of them and produced a strong reaction. "I was gonna try and buy it from him, but it would've made me look like a clown," Patkin said.[15]

Patkin, of course, always made himself look like a clown, and he sold himself as a clown when he was serving as his own agent. He personally made advertisements for himself, and included such selling points as, "Max (he's wacky) Patkin" and "Hail to the new Clown Prince of Baseball."

Furthermore, "From Maine to Frisco, from Miami to the Great Northwest, millions of baseball fans have rocked to Max Patkin's antics. The 'Funny Man' of baseball has exploded the laughter-producing dynamite in packed ballyards from Podunk to Philly—to the financial delight of scores of happy owners. Maxie is real boffo. He jitterbugs and double-joints his way through hundreds of side-splitting routines."[16]

Patkin, who grew to be 6-foot-2, with long arms and long legs, dreamed of becoming a Major League pitcher, but had to settle for becoming a legendary Major League clown. "I would rather have been a big-league player than a clown, but I've always liked to clown around, too," Patkin said near the end of his career.[17]

Joe Garagiola, who made his own outsized reputation (a far bigger one than he did playing the game) for being funny about baseball, once said Patkin had "a high-stepping strut" that made him look like "a flamingo on hot coals." More than that, though, Garagiola saw Patkin once on the veranda of a Cooperstown, New York, hotel charm both his grandchildren and nearby senior citizens. "At that moment I said, 'That's why Max Patkin's so great,'" Garagiola said.[18]

A nude male model Patkin was never going to be. One sportswriter, in comparing him to the Chicken, said he was a whole zoo, with the neck of a giraffe, the wings of a penguin, and the snout and slope of an aardvark. Bill Veeck, who was a friend, also said Patkin's body looked as if had been put together by someone who misread the instructions. But Patkin was also proud of his career, what he put into it and what he got out of it. "I am baseball," he said. "I know that I've made a lot of kids laugh. How many? God, who knows? Better than five million people have seen the show. I can't tell you how many people. Just pick a number."[19]

Patkin made that comment in 1982. He stayed on the road clowning through 1995. So many more games and many more laughs lay in his future.

Patkin said his parents never thought he was ugly. He and his brother Eddie were entered in a baby contest on the boardwalk in New Jersey, though he admitted that neither won any prizes. "It's a great thing when you can go through life not just being homely," Patkin said. "You look out at those kids and you know you're not ugly in their eyes. You're a lovely, beautiful person."[20]

Max Patkin died in 1999 and that might have been his epitaph, verbalized 17 years earlier. No one could have summed up his life any better than that.

9. Casey Stengel

"There was never a day around Casey that I didn't laugh."—*Hall of Fame outfielder Zack Wheat of the Brooklyn Dodgers*[1]

SOME THOUGHT OF MANAGER CASEY STENGEL as simply a clown who diverted attention from his weak ball clubs with his humor. But they had no response later when he took over the New York Yankees—was just as funny—and won ten pennants in 12 seasons.

There is no doubt that Stengel was one of a kind, a brilliant manager who kept the sportswriters and crowds laughing as he piled up Hall of Fame credentials by capturing World Series. It was a later-in-life recovery from bad teams that had stained his reputation when he first took a seat as a leader in the dugout.

What a wild ride it was for Stengel, from the time he broke into the majors as a player until the time he walked away from baseball after being saddled with a New York Mets expansion team that was the equivalent of a AAA team.

Stengel was born in Kansas City in 1890 and died in Glendale, California, at 85. He broke into the majors as a player in 1912 and he didn't leave the baseball stage until he was in his 70s.

A Stengel image was established when he was young. Always clever, always devoted to studying the finer points of the game, Stengel was disappointed one game when he was having an off-day and his home Brooklyn fans booed him. In the sixth inning, as he headed back to his right field position, he paused at the Dodgers' bullpen and noticed a pitcher holding a small animal. It was a sparrow. When he next came to bat, Stengel approached the plate with the bird under his cap. When he was booed, he doffed his hat and the bird flew out. The gesture turned the fans back in his favor. Manager Wilbert Robinson said, "Hell, he always did have birds in his garret."[2]

No one enjoyed Stengel's company more than sportswriters. He understood their needs and was a constant source of entertainment. Sometimes he gave one story to one writer and a different story to another. He also was magnificent in a crowd, sometimes speaking double-talk and avoiding answering a question he did not want to answer.

Any opponent or any player of his own who underestimated Stengel did so at his own risk. Stengel cared about winning, not about fellows' feelings. He became a most active practitioner of platooning with the Yankees. Fortunately for him, his team had more talent than anyone else, so he could afford to bench a player another team wished it had in the lineup. He swapped out guys at the same position, but not indiscriminately. He played the lefty-righty percentages, and if it left some players steaming, so be it. The Stengel method won games.

Despite his apparent easy-going manner, Stengel was stern on selected occasions. When he came to the mound to lift a pitcher, his mind was made up and he could not be talked out of the move. Once, a pitcher who wanted to stay in the game said, "I'm not tired." Stengel said, "Well, I'm tired of you."[3]

Mostly, Stengel cared if his players performed on the field. Good thing, because many of his Yankees stars were known to party into the wee hours, drinking liberally, and sometimes finding themselves in public trouble. Stengel was not going to ground future Hall of Famers like Mickey Mantle and Whitey Ford.

The story goes that Don Larsen, who pitched the only perfect game in World Series history against the Dodgers in 1956, was out until 5 a.m. in spring training and crashed his car into a utility pole. Stengel explained that he got up early to mail a letter.

Pitchers did not have to stay sober away from the park, but to stay in Stengel's good graces they had to win. Right-hander Bob Turley won 21 games for the Yankees in 1958, but then slid into virtually a career-long slump for the rest of his 12-year career. "Look at him," Stengel said of Turley. "He don't smoke, he don't drink, he don't chase women and he don't win."[4]

Stengel did not spare his players embarrassment, usually speaking of foibles or mistakes with a tart tongue. He was very direct and sometimes players felt the old man (he was always the old man to the Yankees since he was 58 when he took over the team), threw them under the bus. Stengel could watch his words when he chose to, but he was not naturally a diplomat when it came to evaluations and analysis about player problems, slumps or errors.

9. Casey Stengel

Stengel had seen everything in the big leagues, the good, the bad and the ugly. He knew players sneaked out of their hotels to drink. Heck, he drank plenty, too, though not staying out nearly as late for adventures as he did when he was a much younger man. He also knew that one of the reasons they spent so much time in saloons was to meet women. This included the married players. Stengel could definitely be politically incorrect by today's standards. In the 1950s, writers mostly looked the other way when they learned of players' late-night carousing and peccadillos.

Stengel became grumpy if he thought the party life interfered with on-field production. "It ain't getting it that hurts them," he said of extracurricular sex lives. "It's staying up all night looking for it. They gotta learn if they don't get it by midnight, you ain't gonna get it, and if you do it ain't worth it."[5] Could Dr. Phil put it any better? Or more bluntly?

Stengel had originally intended to become a dentist and spent three years studying that specialty. Becoming a chatterbox instead was as close as he came to pulling teeth afterwards. He played in the minors from 1910 to 1912, when the Dodgers purchased him and played him in 17 games. His .316 start got their attention and while he was never a superstar, Stengel did bat .284 lifetime in 14 seasons, all in the National League.

In 1934 Stengel took over as manager of the Dodgers, an assignment which lasted only until 1936. He managed the Boston Braves from 1938 to 1943. Those teams were so weak that it took more than a decade of extraordinary success with the Yankees later for him to move his career won-lost mark over .500.

Although between the Braves and the Yankees Stengel enjoyed minor league success, the reception to the announcement that he was going to take over the perennial world champs for the 1949 season was met with a lukewarm response at best. Some dismissed Stengel as a buffoon, confusing his levity with a lack of smarts. He was a witty man with a sense of humor, but remarkably perceptive on the nuances of baseball. For the first time, with the Yankees, he had the material to apply his thinking, and the talent prevailed. Still, there was great skepticism when Stengel showed up for spring training in 1949 and instituted position training by veteran players, carefully massaging Joe DiMaggio's ego.

In comparison with those other failed big-league stints, Stengel surveyed his Yankees roster and said, "I never had so many good players before. I'm with a lot of real pros. When I think of some of those other teams I had, I was wondering whether I was managing a baseball team or a golf course. You know what I mean—one pro to a club."[6]

There were so many pros on the Yankees that it could have overwhelmed Stengel. But he knew what to do with them. New York won the World Series in Stengel's inaugural season as boss and kept on winning pennants and more Series for the rest of his tenure.

As he rolled along as the most successful manager of his time, Stengel molded a persona with the public. He was aging and sometimes walked with a hitch. He had large ears and a rubbery face that enabled him to create memorable photographic impressions. He made his wink famous and was not averse to bantering with anyone who appeared in front of him in the dugout, or in other public settings.

Stengel's results were genius-like, including his public relations abilities similar, his inner workings, and his ability to out-smart others also in that category.

It was no wonder that Stengel was soft-hearted towards players who stayed out late and engaged in their own sketch comedy, for he was the same way as a young ball player, occasionally participating in pranks that outdid the latter players. In one spring training game, as strange as it seems, Stengel actually climbed down into an on-field plumbing box, disappeared from sight, and yet while peeking out from his hole recognized when a fly ball was hit his way. He lifted the covering, something akin to a manhole cover, leapt out, and caught the ball after alarming the audience, which thought there was no one playing left field. Wacky stuff.

Such performances came naturally to Casey Stengel. At 1916 spring training in Daytona Beach, Florida, inspired by a story of another player catching a baseball dropped from the Washington Monument, the Dodgers set up manager Wilbert Robinson for a similar stunt. A female pilot guided her plane over Robinson, and a round object was dropped. It splattered over Robinson and Robinson declared, "Help! I'm dying!" because he thought the wet stuff on him was his own blood. Rather, it was smashed grapefruit. For years Stengel was blamed for tossing the grapefruit.[7]

As a manager, Stengel provided players with sliding lessons—in a hotel lobby. One time when he came out to protest a call to umpire Bill Klem, the arbiter showed him little patience, threatening to throw him out of the game in 30 seconds. Klem even displayed his watch to time Stengel. Stengel commented, "Gee, Bill, you're crazy to show that watch in front of this crowd. Its owner may recognize it."[8]

Proof that Stengel had plenty of smarts came in the way he invested in the stock market. He became rich through that endeavor, not from baseball. Frustrated with the play of his minor league Toledo Mud Hens, Stengel cleverly integrated his stock market experience into a dressing-down following a stretch of poor play. He came into the locker room, looked over his last-place team, and said, "Fellas, buy Pennsylvania Railroad." When quizzed about whether he was telling them the truth, Stengel added at a much higher decibel level, "Sure thing. I'm going to ship so many of you birds on the Pennsy tonight the 'road will be able to declare an extra dividend."[9]

Although it was originally his life's ambition, Stengel never really missed not becoming a dentist, though he once said with the usual twinkle in his eye that he could see how to apply one profession to the other. "Once in a while I think I'd like to become a dentist and have some of these umpires come in for treatment," he said. "I'd make a plate for them that would keep them from talking back."[10]

An all-time epic Casey Stengel performance came in testimony before Congress and was recorded in the Congressional Record. On July 8, 1958, Stengel was called to testify before the U.S. Senate Anti-Trust and Monopoly Subcommittee. It was quickly clear that any politician who was skilled in double-talk had met his match. Stengel was just being Stengel, providing the type of answer to questions that baseball writers for the *New York Times*, *New York Daily News*, *New York Post* and others were used to, but which mesmerized elected officials.

Asked about pay television and its possible impact on baseball, he said,

> Well, to tell you the truth, if I were starting in it myself I would like to be in that line of business as I did not think they would ever have television and so forth, but they have got it here now. I am thinking myself of anybody that is hospitalized and anybody who cannot go to a ball park, I should think if they could pass that they should try to pass it. But I don't think they will be able to do it because they have gone in television so far that they reach so many outside people, you have to have a sponsor for everything else you do, go pay television and that is going to run all the big theatres out of business where you have to use pay television.[11]

Nobody changed Stengel's channel and he kept right on rolling. A senator lightheartedly asked, in terms of monopoly, if he planned to keep on winning the world championship.

> Well, I will tell you, I got a little concerned yesterday in the first three innings when I say the three players I had gotten rid off and I said when I lost nine what am I going to be able to do and when I had a couple of my players. I thought so great of that did not do so good up to the sixth inning I was more confused, but I finally had to go and call on a young man in Baltimore that we don't own and the Yankees don't own him, and he is doing pretty good, and I would actually have to tell you that I think we are more the Greta Garbo type now from success.[12]

At which point one senator exhaled and another made a game try to obtain information from Stengel. On and on it went. There was much laughter in the chamber, but it was unclear what the esteemed senators learned about baseball and anti-trust. Mickey Mantle, by then a superstar, followed Stengel on the witness stand. As his answer to the first question posed by a senator, Mantle said: "My views are about the same as Casey's."[13] That produced the loudest laughter of all.

Stengel may have known how to befuddle listeners and how to make people laugh, but he was very serious about winning and losing. Winning was what he hungered for with the Yankees between 1949 and 1960, and he understood that was how he would be measured and rated by his bosses. "The most important part of his game comes when he sits down and figures out his lineup before the game," said player Jerry Coleman. "They've laughed about the way he keeps shuffling his batting order, but his lineup always is thoroughly researched and calculated. Little is left to chance."[14]

The Yankees won seven World Series, including five in a row starting in 1949, under Stengel's tutelage. Yet when the team was upset by the Pittsburgh Pirates in an epic seven-game Series in 1960, management ousted him. In a way only he could respond, Stengel said he would never make the mistake of turning 70 again.

But those who wrote finis to Stengel's managerial career were surprised to learn that the "Old Perfessor" had one more chapter left in the leadership limelight. The departure of the New York Giants and Brooklyn Dodgers for California was still a gaping wound in National League–less New York in the early 1960s.

In 1962, the New York Mets were created to fill the void, and the owners decided there was no better man to lead the expansion team (as a start-up one likely to be doomed to poor finishes in the standings) than Casey Stengel. He was back in charge of a team in 1962 and

Casey Stengel was a genius managing the New York Yankees, but had to rely more on his entertainment skills while managing the lowly New York Mets expansion team.

9. Casey Stengel

was dealing with the same writers in New York he had known with the Yankees. He was also wearing the same No. 37 uniform top. There was one major difference, however. The Yankees were at the top of the baseball world, still winners. The Mets were at the bottom, their first season of play registering the worst record of the 20th century at 40–120.

Stengel could talk only so much to cover up his team's weaknesses. He was lucky to have several big-name ball players on the roster, but they were past their primes. Stengel saw things occur on the field that not even he believed, and he believed he had seen it all. During the depths of horrific play Stengel asked aloud in astonishment, "Can't anybody here play this game?" Seizing upon the phrase, Jimmy Breslin, soon to become one of the greatest city columnists in American journalism history, wrote a book about the sad-sack Mets, employing that line as the title.

Bizarrely, with Stengel at the helm providing amusement for all as usual, there was a kind of backlash against the buttoned-down Yankees even though they continued to win for a few more years, and Mets attendance was disproportionately high for a losing franchise.

It was some roller-coaster with the Mets. The team was awful on the field, pretty popular at the box office, and often the author of the most stunningly creative ways to lose. Swings and misses and errors with the bouncing ball were routine with the early Mets.

Right from the start, from his introduction as the first manager of the Mets, Stengel was in vintage form. He thanked owners for hiring him. "It's a great honor for me to be joining the Knickerbockers," he said.[15] Of course, then and now, the Knickerbockers are the NBA team. Stengel was not switching sports, merely mixing names.

The Mets did not fare very well in the expansion draft for the 1962 season, a realm in which they competed with the then–Houston Colt .45s (later the Astros). The first pick was Hobie Landrith, a catcher. Stengel thought this was a completely logical selection since "You have to have a catcher, or you'll have a lot of passed balls."[16]

Who could argue with that?

Among the best-known players who suited up for the Mets in 1962 were pitchers Roger Craig, Clem Labine, and two guys named Bob Miller. Craig and Labine were holdovers from Dodgers glory days.

Landrith was one of seven catchers employed in 1962. There were still a lot of passed balls.

Gil Hodges, Charlie Neal, and Don Zimmer, other ex–Dodgers with a good name in New York from their Brooklyn days, also played that season. Richie Ashburn, Gus Bell and Frank Thomas (a generation or so before the Hall of Famer of the same name with the White Sox) looked good on paper for the outfield, but were aging out of the majors.

Marv Throneberry gained legendary status for making miscues at first base and earned the nickname "Marvelous Marv." He later starred in a series of beer commercials with other athletes. He too was at the tail end of his career. Throneberry's mistakes always seemed monumental, never subtle. Once he smacked a triple, but an umpire called him out for missing first base on his tour of the infield. Stengel came out to protest and another ump said, "I hate to tell you this, Casey, but he missed second base, too." Stengel drank that all in and said, "Well, I know he touched third base because he's standing on it."[17]

Stengel stuck around with the Mets into August of the 1965 season. Then he fell and broke his hip and needed surgery. That was the event that pushed him into retirement at 75. Appearing at a farewell press conference using a cane, Stengel said he had to give up the reins because he would be slow going out to the mound to talk to a pitcher or remove him from the game. "I want it understood that nobody put pressure on me to resign," he said. "I couldn't strut out there to take out a pitcher. There's no time for me to run the club freely. I didn't want to delay the game."[18]

Casey Stengel was elected to the Hall of Fame in 1966 and he died in 1975. It was probably too bad he wasn't available to give his own eulogy. No doubt he would have left them laughing again.

10. Joe Engel

> A minor league shortstop seeking a $5,000 raise approached team owner Joe Engel and demanded to receive the money or "count me out." With the aplomb of a boxing referee Engel said, "One, two, three, four, five, six, seven, eight, nine, ten."[1]

JOE ENGEL WAS THE BILL VEECK of the minors, a creative, inventive team owner who believed in fun at the ballpark and who dreamed up crazy stunts to entertain fans. His nickname was "The Barnum of the Bushes," and he was a man with a sense of humor.

Those who recall Engel, who passed away at age 76 in 1969, may be unlikely to realize that he was actually a Major League pitcher, mostly with the Washington Senators and briefly with the Cincinnati Reds and Cleveland Indians. A teammate of the legendary Walter Johnson, Engel's lifetime record was just 17–23, but his earned run average was a solid 3.38.

Even though Engel did his time in Ohio, his heart belonged to D.C., where he grew up playing with President Teddy Roosevelt's children and where he served as a Senators batboy and later team mascot before winning a roster spot with his left arm. His family happened to own a bar next door to the *Washington Post*.

Admitting that he was a hell-raiser, Engel was the unlikely roommate of the more subdued Johnson for several seasons. In all, Engel's Major League stay encompassed seven seasons from 1912–1920.

His overall baseball career, however, lasted decades longer, mostly as a minor-league team owner. Engel was an astute scout as well, but his niche was running the show in smaller towns, and a show it was once he took over leadership of the Chattanooga Lookouts in 1929. Over the ensuing decades he switched roles in Chattanooga and Washington at different times, always returning to Tennessee.

Political correctness was not in Engel's vocabulary, but in the first half of the 20th century few thought about such niceties. Among the skits Engel staged for his baseball fans were virtual theatrical events in the outfield, where Indians would lose battles and be scalped, and where elephants would be "hunted" as if during a safari.

Like Veeck, who became known as the Major League fan's best friend, Engel thrived on prize giveaways to those in attendance in the ballpark. Engel thought big. Twice, he gave away houses that came fully furnished and had cars waiting for them in the garage, too, once the winners obtained the keys. His ballpark's capacity was 16,000, and on one of those free-house nights more than 24,000 people showed up.

"The first giveaway was won by a $12-a-week grocery clerk," Engel said. "He sold the house and car and bought out his boss."[2]

More than once, Engel advertised a "cash and carry" event. One fan in attendance was picked at random to run down on the field and scoop up as many coins dropped there by armored car as he could. Under a time limit, one individual scooped up $384, a second $930. "There were some quarters and silver dollars in the pile," Engel said. "But you can bet most coins were nickels."[3]

Apparently Lincoln pennies were not included, perhaps because they didn't blend in color.

Wait, there's more. Hounds chased rabbits across the outfield, and Engel staged beauty pageants at the park based on the theory that all guys want to look at pretty girls.

Engel was at heart a generous man and described himself as "a soft touch."[4] During World War II, he planned a stunt to sell war bonds by jumping into the Tennessee River. The Coast Guard halted the scheme, claiming it was too risky. However, one Christmas season he heard that many in Chattanooga were having very tough times. Engel announced on the radio that anybody who was hungry could come to his ball park for dinner. Some 7,500 people came, a respectable crowd for a game during the season. Turkey, cranberry sauce and other fixings were served. Engel also gave clothing to those in need and provided toys for children. He was the Santa Claus of Chattanooga for sure that winter.

Like so many sports figures biased to the point of blindness by their association with a team, Engel was hard on umpires. Engel also owned a radio station and did not flinch when his sportscaster ended up in a street brawl with a future National League umpire. He rewarded the man with a three-day vacation. "If he had won the fight I'd have given him a week," Engel said.[5]

Engel was actually a very good all-around athlete as a young man. He

10. Joe Engel

attended Mount St. Mary's College in Maryland and earned letters in four sports. But it must be said that as swift as he might be in track or throwing a fastball, he was at least as nimble in his thinking.

Among Engel's peculiar credits were leading an elephant down Pennsylvania Avenue in D.C. in a parade, performing in vaudeville, importing bullfrogs from Louisiana so he could listen to their full-throated singing at sunset, and tying cocoanuts on palm trees to make the scenery more inviting in Palm Beach, Florida, so buyers would jump at real estate deals. He also once owned a horse that competed in the Kentucky Derby. Not all of his minor-league players were thoroughbreds, but that three-year-old definitely was.

From the 1920s on, Engel was the stand-up owner of the Chattanooga Lookouts, chieftain of the ball club, as well as the city's No. 1 promoter. Engel also managed the team when it suited him, and he was known as a superior scout. Before the Senators became the joke of the American League, Engel was just about the best talent spy that owner Clark Griffith had on the payroll. He could ferret out stars based on potential better than just about anyone else. The Engel connection to the finest players in franchise history is no accident. Engel's sharp eyes spotted Joe Judge, Bucky Harris, Goose Goslin, Cecil Travis and Ossie Bluege for the big club, among others.

The biggest find was Joe Cronin. Cronin was a Hall of Fame shortstop who married into Griffith's family and later became president of the American League. Cronin was actually in a hitting slump, batting just .221 for Kansas City in the minors, when Engel signed him for $7,500—he thought for the Senators. Griffith took one look at that batting average and he had Engel looking out. That was a lot of money in the 1920s. "When I told Clark Griffith what I had done," Engel said, "he screamed, 'You paid $7,500 for that bum? Well, you didn't buy him for me, you bought him for yourself.'"[6]

Cronin actually broke into the majors with Pittsburgh, playing briefly for the Pirates, and did eventually make a mark with Washington, four times batting more than .300 for the Senators before Griffith shipped him to the Boston Red Sox for $250,000.

One thing a trip to the Lookouts' home park offered was a bit of adventure. Couldn't afford to take a safari to Africa or go to the zoo? Combine baseball and wildlife in one place. At various times Engel had elephants and lions running around the park, and he regularly had canaries around to sing to the masses. "If we cannot give you good baseball, at least we can give you music," he said.[7]

Somehow it should not be terribly surprising that Engel once made a trade involving a pitcher straight-up for a bird dog. However, it was noted that was not the end of the dealing. "He traded the bird dog for a turkey squab. He cooked up the squab and served it to the Tennessee baseball writers. He recalled the pitcher was tough, the bird dog was tougher, the turkey squab must have been made of solid concrete—but the writers were tougher than the whole bunch of them."[8] The turkey weighed in at 25 pounds. Neither the pitcher's nor the dog's weights were recorded.

Another time Engel got wind that an old-timer who was a long-time fan of the Lookouts was in a bad way. He stopped by, got a fire going in the fellow's house as he lay in bed, fetched a doctor and fed him soup. But when Engel was wrapping up his charitable stay, believing the man would soon pass away, the Lookouts' supporter urged him not to forget his season pass the next season. Engel was a big man with a big heart.

When the old Murderers' Row New York Yankees stopped by Chattanooga to play a pre-season exhibition game against the Southern Association team, as a gimmick Engel hired a local 17-year-old female named Jackie Mitchell to pitch. She faced Babe Ruth, Lou Gehrig and Tony Lazzeri, and the three future Hall of Famers struck out. They did so as a stunt favor. It wasn't as if Engel thought the young lass had big-league prospects. "She couldn't pitch hay to a cow," he said.[9]

Such gimmicks garnered nationwide attention for the minor-league team. The sportswriters covering other franchises in the Southern Association gushed about Engel and marveled about his promotions, in general with an attitude of "What will he do next?"

A 1932 Alabama report on Engel featured a picture of him wearing a top hat tilted at a jaunty angle and a tuxedo. The article read, "The clever Mr. Engel, who comes from that vanishing breed of sportsmen who would sell a fellow a bathing suit in a tidal wave and give him a life-belt for a premium, is making the slightly matter-of-fact old league an eight-ring circus, much to everybody's delight, especially his own."[10]

Engel claimed to stem from a royal German family, flush with barons and was nicknamed "The Baron of Bonhomie." He probably enjoyed that phrase in a newspaper article more than he would have liked the genuine title.

At one time, long before the Atlanta Braves came along, transferring from Milwaukee, Atlanta had the Crackers. The club was in decline and was threatening to go out of business when 14 local men of wealth banded together to rescue the team. At one game, to obtain their due from fans, they rode into the ballpark in a row of fancy cars. The Crackers were playing Chattanooga, and Engel followed the suits into the park in an old Model T with the inscription, "Chattanooga's Only Millionaire" inscribed on the side.[11]

While Engel did have big-league credentials as a pitcher, he was never confused with his pal Walter Johnson when it came to production. Typically, a sportswriter penning tales of Engel's ballpark gimmicks delved into a few questions about his playing career in the bigs. Engel had a sense of humor about that, too. After all, he walked as many as 17 men in a game for the Senators. So when quizzed about his best year, Engel said, "Hell, I never had one."[12]

Actually that was not quite true. At age 21 in 1914, Engel went 7–5 for the Senators with a 2.97 earned average.

Engel was around baseball, mostly in Chattanooga, through the 1960s, but the Southern Association fell on hard times in 1962 and had to be reconstituted. His old sportswriter friends did not forget him and often called upon him to reminisce. Engel retained his old antipathy to umpires, caustically analyzing the state of umpiring as always. "They were lousy 120 years ago when the game started and they're lousy today," he said.

While not denigrating their skills, Engel did question whether ball players with dollar signs in their eyes were worth it. "In the old days boys played for love of the game. Now they're getting muscles in their legs walking back and forth to the bank," he said.[13] Imagine what Engel would think about baseball in the 2000s when every other player on a Major League roster is a millionaire.

Nicknames were more prevalent in baseball in the early part of the 20th century, and while Engel may have occasionally been called other names, the most appealing attachment and the nickname that permanently stuck was "The Barnum Of The Bushes." Still, others periodically referred to him as "The Baron of Baloney."

Engel was such terrific copy and such a lure for sportswriters that in 1952 *The Sporting News*, the bible of baseball, splashed a humongous three-part series about his life across its pages, written by the famed Frederick Lieb.

For starters, Lieb called Engel "the game's master showman."[14] That was the synopsis of the entire multi-page, thousands-of-words-long treatise. "There never was a time when Chattanooga fans knew what to expect when they entered Engel Stadium, Joe's own edifice," Lieb wrote. "Nor do his friends and associates in baseball know today what to expect of the game's Barnum. The guy is absolutely unpredictable." For one thing, Engel ran around telling people on the occasion of his 60th birthday that he had already lived 180 years. Not much explanation was offered or needed, and Lieb didn't disagree, saying, "That's no exaggeration, as the man already has crowded three lifetimes into his three-score years on the planet."[15]

Engel liked to be loud and colorful not only in his speech, but also in his wardrobe. The brightest colors and the most garish combinations never fazed him when it came to sartorial splendor. Others might have blinked or needed sunglasses upon viewing his attire, but the suits suited him.

Earl Mann, who operated the public address system at the park for Engel, discovered a piece of cloth so stunning he wondered if even Engel would find a way to make something of it.

> It was one of the loudest pieces of fabric I ever saw in my life. I know even the most daring among our sportive colored population would have hesitated to wear it. So I sent it to Joe Engel. He sent me an appreciative thank-you note. "It sure was nice of you, Earl, to send me the cloth. It will make me a swell sports coat." And sure enough, he had his tailor make it into a jacket.[16]

Engel said he operated his team and for the most part his daily life, as well, based on the theory that he couldn't go wrong with the philosophy of "Make 'em laugh." It was a reasonable assumption.[17]

Engel was not above playing pranks on his friends, carrying them out to the nth degree before admitting they were hoaxes. Selma team owner Maurice Bloch was a pal, and the two ate, drank and joked together. One time when Bloch's team was visiting Engel's park, Engel staged an elaborate joke in the form of a fake radio broadcast that announced that a major fire raged in Selma. Bloch immediately put down his drink, ran to his car and sped off at high speed. When he stopped laughing, Engel chased after him, but didn't catch Bloch for 20 miles. Even then, Bloch was difficult to convince the entire story was false. "But Joe, you wouldn't do that to me," Bloch said.[18] Yes he would.

Engel and Bloch once had a serious disagreement over a player. Engel had sent the pitcher to Selma and he was tearing up the opposition. Every time he threw, the crowds turned out. But suffering from an unexpected pitching shortage, Engel telephoned Bloch and told him he needed the thrower back pronto. At first Bloch thought Engel was joking, and when he realized he wasn't he was infuriated. He informed "Mr. Engel" that they were no longer friends. A couple of hours later, three tons of ice showed up on Bloch's back porch. Bloch was baffled because he hadn't ordered it, but accompanying the ice was a note from Engel reading, "Just a little something to cool you off."[19]

Engel had big dreams for life as a player, but he got the message in 1915 when Griffith sent him to Minneapolis and allowed him to participate in a trade for himself. Griffith asked for two players in return—picked out by Engel. That helped turn him into a scout. That role morphed into minor-league baron.

In 1936, Engel sweet-talked Dizzy Dean into appearing as part of an exhibition game in Chattanooga. The plan was to give the proceeds to charity for Christmas goods. But Dean arrived early, didn't think there would be much of a crowd, and took off, leaving Engel in the lurch. Engel was forever furious at Dean for that and issued a serious challenge to fight him at Engel Stadium. Dean demurred. Engel, who actually trained and lost weight in anticipation of a possible bout, said if Dean committed to it the event would attract 50,000 spectators. Later, Dean got into a baseball fight in Tampa that was reported on by writers. Engel fired off a telegram to Dean, saying, "You're just as dumb as I thought, fighting for nothing. I offer you $10,000 cash to fight me at the home plate at Chattanooga any day you set."[20]

There never was such a fight. A feud, yes.

In 1954, Southern Association owners, officials and sportswriters honored the fun-loving owner with "Joe Engel Day." The occasion was the 25th year of Engel's operation of the Lookouts. It was a multi-part celebration, including a luncheon, a ballgame, and a banquet.

Over the decades, Engel actually came to be seen as Mr. Chattanooga, indulging heavily in community service. At one time he was so beloved by Chattanooga baseball fans that they sought to buy him a house. Engel declined that honor, but kept giving to the fans.

There were several incarnations of Chattanooga Lookouts baseball, but in 1965 the Southern Association imploded. There were only four teams prepared to play, Chattanooga, of course, was one of them. But the league went belly up.

That left Engel the senior citizen with an empty stadium, except for local amateur play (something he enjoyed watching), although he still maintained an office there until 1969, when he died from a stroke.

A year later, in 1970, most of Joe Engel's baseball memorabilia, acquired during 57 years in the sport, was donated to the Baseball Hall of Fame in Cooperstown, New York. There were trophies and vintage photographs, all of them special to Engel. But they were just symbols of the spirit of the man who always made sure a trip to the ballpark was a joyful outing.

11. Yogi Berra

"Even when we were little kids in St. Loo, the quality was there. I talked all the time and Yogi talked hardly at all. But whenever he spoke, he made sense—which is more than anyone could say about me."—Lifelong friend and fellow major leaguer Joe Garagiola about Yogi Berra[1]

No one would ever suggest that Yogi Berra was not a funny man. Many have suggested that he was always funny unintentionally, that his wit was accidental. In reality, it was probably somewhere between planned and in the mind of the beholder.

Berra always said what he meant, but what he meant was not always clear to the listener. At least his intent was not always immediately apparent, without a pause for analysis. What Berra did was fracture the language. He was no Shakespeare, but just a guy who said what he thought in his own special way.

It just so happened that the way Lawrence Peter Berra, born in 1925, expressed himself was unique and slightly off-kilter in comparison to other Americans. That style, in conjunction with his exceptional baseball skills, helped make him beloved.

Berra was not a learned man in the sense of someone who went to college and stacked up degrees. He left high school before he earned a diploma, but he was sagacious about baseball, a supreme catcher, an extraordinary hitter, and someone who understood his sport inside-out.

Berra grew up in St. Louis across the street from best friend Joe Garagiola, who also reached the majors, but attained his greatest fame later as a broadcaster. Berra's on-field exploits earned him a spot in the Hall of Fame. Berra was a three-time American League Most Valuable Player, an 18-time All-Star, and a nine-time World Series champion. After retiring as a player, Berra became an outstanding, winning big-league coach and manager.

The 5-foot-7, 185-pound Berra had a squat build, a powerful swing, and a running style on the bases that did not inspire comparisons to Olympic 100-meter champions. He was never complimented as handsome by the sportswriters who covered his career, but had a lovely wife named Carmen for half a century, and like one of his mentors, Casey Stengel, Berra could make memorable faces for the camera.

Mostly, Berra spoke with his bat—358 home runs—and in off-hand comments that made their way to Bartlett's Quotations as if he were an oracle. Maybe he was in some ways. The highway to stardom is littered with the bodies of stand-up comedians who tried their hardest, but who could never gather as many laughs as Berra, who didn't try a tenth as hard for the appreciative audience.

"I really didn't say everything I said," Berra once protested in regard to all of the off-beat comments attributed to him by Garagiola and sportswriters. "This was a comment I made when someone asked me about quotes I didn't think I said. Then again, I might have said 'em, but you never know."[2]

What do you say to that? You just go with the flow.

There was plenty of flow, too, with Berra. Bob Broeg, a St. Louis sportswriter of great longevity, once wrote, "It's hard to separate the myth from the man in the saga" of Berra.[3] That was a perceptive comment. Berra was always well-liked throughout his life. He was an exemplary teammate, a clutch hitter, and entertained the writers, whether he planned to or not.

Berra became such a personality that his identity transcended the game. In 1958, a cartoon hit the airwaves featuring a character named Yogi Bear. The catcher inspired the cartoon animal. When he was a youth, Berra was hanging out with friends and an image came on the TV screen of an Indian yogi. A friend thought the man sat just the way his friend Lawrence sat cross-legged. That was how the baseball player got his nickname.

For a while Berra just didn't get the fact that people thought he was funny. He wasn't a Milton Berle (one of his contemporaries) and he wasn't going out of his way to make people laugh. It just happened. He had the New York writers in his corner, and they helped with the buildup. It was not as if Yogi didn't say what he said, but some made fun of the way he said it and characterized him as funny.

Most of the time there were pearls of wisdom hiding in Berra's phrasing. One just had to pause and think over the words for a little while.

Once, when Berra was a coach with the New York Mets, outfielder Ron Swoboda was having a tough time fighting off inside tosses. The pitchers were getting the better of him. "Then move back from the plate," Berra said. "But Frank Robinson crowds the plate," Swoboda said. "If you can't imitate him, don't copy him," Berra said.[4] It might sound awkward, but that was not only a witty remark, but was packed with solid advice.

Growing up in a hard-working, ethnic neighborhood of Italians called "The Hill," in St. Louis, Berra was neither born with a silver spoon in his mouth nor anointed as the local most likely to succeed. When he struck it big with the Yankees, he was honored with a special night back home. At the end of his thank-you speech Berra said, "I want to thank all the baseball fans and everyone else who made this night necessary."[5] That was one Yogi-ism that stuck to him.

The New York writers gravitated to Berra's locker as often as they could, for good reason since they were likely to be rewarded with fresh copy, a good story, or yes, a new Yogi-ism.

"Always go to other people's funerals, otherwise they won't go to yours," Berra once said. He later explained that he was talking to Mickey Mantle about going to a lot of funerals that year and they wondered if anyone would be left to come to theirs.[6]

Berra always enjoyed movies and he was actually asked to be a film critic for a little while. Once, commenting on a flick, he said, "Steve McQueen looks good in this movie. He must have made it before he died."[7]

In his leadership role in the dugout, Berra often dispensed advice to young players trying to make it. One of his favorite instructional tidbits was, "Ninety percent of the game is half mental."[8] While many used this example to cast aspersions on Berra's mathematical abilities, he said he used the line many times when talking to players.

Berra had three sons with wife Carmen, with whom he was married for 65 years until her death in 2014. One son, Dale, also played Major League baseball. For most of his professional life Berra lived in New Jersey, not far from New York City. It should not be a surprise that there was much laughter in the Berra household.

Carmen Berra was of the mind that Yogi did not say everything attributed to him over the years. "Many of the funny quotes attributed to Yogi aren't quite true and some were complete fabrications," she said. "But he does say a lot of very funny things, intentionally and unintentionally. He really breaks us up sometimes … believe me, he gets off some very humorous lines."[9]

It's unlikely the real Yogi lines will ever be sorted out from the other Yogi lines. At this point nobody wants them to be, and Berra himself didn't even always remember which were which.

The hits kept on coming.

11. Yogi Berra

Once, when he was managing Berra, Casey Stengel asked him what he would do if he found a million dollars. Berra said, "If the fellow who lost it was poor, I'd return it." At one time Berra roomed on the road with third baseman Bobby Brown, who later became a doctor and then president of the American League. Brown was reading a medical textbook and Berra was reading a comic book. When Brown closed the cover, Berra asked, "How did yours come out?"[10] He wasn't talking about the appendix.

Another time Berra was negotiating his contract with the Yankees' front office and the debater on the other side of the desk was assistant general manager Roy Hamey. As is usual amongst professional athletes, Berra wanted more money than the team wanted to pay. Hamey stood up, signaling the end of the discussion, and said, "Well, Yogi, I guess we've reached a stalemate." Berra replied, "Never mind the budget stuff, let's talk money."[11]

One of many Yogi-isms was recorded in his early days with the Yankees before he made it big. The manager was Bucky Harris, who preceded Stengel. When Harris saw Berra struggling at the plate, he proffered some hitting advice. Berra was notorious for hitting bad balls, pitches out of the strike zone, but only a small percentage of batters succeed that way. And if they are not going well, their swings and stance can look pretty lousy. "When you're up there hitting, don't swing at everything they throw you," Harris said. "Stop and think." That struck Berra as the wrong way to go about things. "Show me a guy who can think and hit at the same time," he said.[12]

When Berra broke in with the Yankees in the late 1940s, it was a less politically correct time. Since he did not resemble an Adonis, Berra's body was frequently made the butt of jokes. He was described as lumpy and stumpy, short and lacking musculature. He was ridiculed as a monkey or a gorilla, described as being fire hydrant-like or looking like a professional wrestler. Hecklers—and that included players in the opposition dugout—were noticeably meaner. It was a good thing Yogi had a sense of humor and reasonably thick skin.

"It don't matter if you're ugly in this racket," he said. "All you gotta do is hit the ball and I never saw nobody hit one with his face."[13]

It was no wonder that Berra became a film critic for a while. He made it a habit to see at least one movie every day. Not only did he read tons of comic books, but over time he upgraded. Teammate and roommate Frank Shea observed Berra's literary shopping choices and came to a conclusion. "I think Yogi's going high brow," Shea said. "The other day he brought four paperback mystery novels and only two comic books."[14]

Many of the newspaper anecdotes and settings portrayed Berra as someone who was not very smart, but that may have been more in book learning than anything else. He was savvy about baseball, and he was pretty savvy in the business world whenever he dipped his toe in, such as owning a restaurant or bowling alley. So it did not seem to be a matter of intelligence per se. It was just the way those one-liners sounded.

For one thing, Berra benefited greatly from the image in terms of fan appreciation, likeability, and even endorsements. By the time Berra had been in the majors as backstop of the world champion Yankees for a decade, those in the know recognized the differences between the easy-going persona and a well-rounded Berra. "The wise man in the mask" is how one sportswriter characterized Berra, an "assistant manager (who) not only knew more than he let on in public, but that he knew as much about the game of baseball as anyone around."[15]

One of the secrets of Berra's success—and it was a secret for quite some time—was the caliber of his memory. It was not exactly photographic, but it was pretty close. He catalogued pitcher and hitter tendencies, watched how batters planted their feet in the box, had exact recall of the scores of games, and was able to explain it all to teammates and managers. He was a human scouting report. In fact, his wife Carmen said that ability went beyond baseball. "I can't think of anything he doesn't know about sports," she said. "No matter what the question. It can be about any sport, about any result. But he is as unaware as can be about other things. What he has to know, he learns."[16]

A sportswriter got a look at the Detroit Tigers' scouting report on what their pitchers should do when Berra came to the plate. The summary was revealing, indicating that deep down they did not quite know what to do when Berra took his turn at bat.

> Berra is the most dangerous hitter on the Yanks because of his maddening ability to hit any pitch. No one way to pitch to him. He can switch his stance quickly and hit the high pitch with level power. Becomes increasingly dangerous as game goes on and as opposing pitcher begins to lose his fine edge. Best way to pitch to him is to throw a couple inside and hope he will pull the ball toward first base.[17]

There was not as much laughing about Berra when he was in there swinging.

He was a different kind of guy. Some things that would have deeply annoyed other players didn't bother him at all, and much of that was due to his sense of humor. "Funny thing about those jokes," he said, meaning others'. "When the fans do it, I like it. When the newspaper fellows do it, I like it. I like when they get on me. Makes me wanna do better. Know what

I mean? If I get a hit like, it's that much better a hit. I figure if they didn't like me, they wouldn't holler. It's when they stop joking with me that I'm in trouble."[18]

One of Berra's most famous sayings—another that has stuck for a lifetime—is "It ain't over 'til it's over."[19] He said that in 1973 when he was managing the New York Mets, and it referred to the Mets' place in the standings as they tried to catch teams and win a pennant. That one resonated with people and has been applied to myriad situations ever since. In fact, it has become something of a cliché.

This was a case where Yogi really did say it, but he wasn't sure he said it first. He was pretty sure that other baseball people, from long-time infielder Rocky Bridges to catcher Clint Courtney, said it somewhere along the way. "Sometimes it is over before it begins," Berra said. "If I fought Joe Louis in his prime, it would be over before it began. But in 1973, what I said made sense."[20]

Berra won one pennant at the helm of the Yankees in 1964 and one pennant with the Mets in 1973. He managed the Yankees a second time in the 1980s, but that stint ended with bitterness after owner George Steinbrenner fired him, and Berra was estranged from the Yankees for years. Baseball people recognized Berra's way with a club, but "The Boss" didn't. Still, likely forever, despite his brilliant success as a player and solid success as a manager, Berra will be best remembered for his Yogi-isms.

Another famous turn of phrase stemmed from shooting the breeze with Hall of Fame outfielder Stan Musial, who spent his whole career with the St. Louis Cardinals, Berra's hometown team. They were talking about restaurants and Berra noted that the well-known Ruggeri's was a place he hadn't been in a while. "Nobody goes there anymore," Yogi said. "It's too crowded."[21] Which was one way of saying that it was so popular it was a deterrent because he didn't want to wait for a table. Whether or not Yogi Berra would have had to wait for a table in that part of St. Louis was another discussion altogether.

Witness to the 1961 legendary home run race between Mickey Mantle and Roger Maris, when Maris broke Babe Ruth's single-season homer mark with 61, and other seasons when the outfield duo played together, Berra described them going back-to-back in the No. 3 and No. 4 spots in the batting order. "It's déjà vu all over again," Berra said of that one-two homer punch coming through.[22]

Once, Berra was giving his old pal Joe Garagiola directions to his home in New Jersey, and since this was before the GPS, he tried to be explicit. "When you come to a fork in the road, take it," Yogi said.[23] Berra's house was at the end of a circular road, so whichever fork Garagiola took, he would get there.

Once, George H. W. Bush, then vice president and running for president, visited the ballpark, and he and Berra had a chat. When the two men were parting, Bush mentioned the upcoming election and singled out Texas as crucial. Berra said he knew because of "the electrical votes."[24] Berra said that the future president didn't even smile because he knew exactly what Yogi meant.

Berra spent much of his retirement from baseball being asked if he really said something. Sometimes he says he did. Sometimes he says he didn't. Sometimes he says he doesn't remember if he did or not. For posterity, the sayings will blend. Sometimes Berra's explanations are as humorous as the original comments.

One came up in a discussion about Mt. Sinai Hospital in New York. Supposedly, Berra referred to it as "Mt. Sinus Hospital." "I didn't say about a sick friend that he was in Mt. Sinus Hospital," Yogi said. "But I could have. I could also have said, 'We've had enough trowels and tribulations,' if I knew what it meant. I don't, but it has been written that I said it."[25]

Another Berra classic in the baseball sense spouted from his mouth when he was playing left field in the 1961 World Series against the Cincinnati Reds. In those days, all Series games were played in the afternoon. Sometimes the sun was in a fielder's eyes before the October shadows began moving in. Yogi's famous line: "It gets late out there early."[26] The comment was made after Berra missed catching a fly ball because of the sun in his eyes.

One other thing that was consistent about Berra's game behind the plate that fans would never have known about if sportswriters failed to write about it was his incessant habit of chattering to the batter and the umpire the entire time they loomed near him. Berra blathered constantly with the hope that it would interrupt the hitter's concentration so his Yankees pitcher would get the best of him. He asked hitters how they were. He asked about their families. That strategy often drove them nuts. They had been hoping for peace and quiet, and Berra was white noise.

Vic Wertz, a power-hitting first baseman from the 1950s and 1960s, was one of Berra's favorite foils. He said that Wertz was sensitive about going bald, so when he came to the plate Yogi ragged on him. "The batter I rib most is Vic Wertz," Berra said. "'Hey, Vic, how come you don't take off your cap and bow to the fans?' Wertz answered: 'Aw, come on, Yogi, let me hit. I don't want to talk now.'"[27]

The Yogi Berra Museum and Learning Center opened in 1998 to commemorate Berra's career and house some of his memorabilia. It is located on the campus of Montclair State University in New Jersey.

On the occasion of his 80th birthday, Berra reflected on some of the pleasures of his life, from the creation of the museum to his playing days with the Yankees, to managing both the Yankees and Mets to the seventh game of the World Series. He joked that he wanted to count backwards on his birthdays, not add years.

Berra kept an office in the museum, which was visited by 20,000 children annually. Often he greeted them personally. "I got a face they can't forget," Berra said. "Wherever I go, people say, 'You're not Yogi Berra, are you?' And I'll say, 'No, I just look like him.'"[28]

Of course Berra could not issue such denials when he began making frequent television appearances in commercials. At the height of his fame, Berra endorsed Miller Lite Beer, Puss'n Boots cat food and Yoo-Hoo chocolate drink. When a woman asked Yogi if the name was hyphenated, he said, "No, ma'am, it isn't even carbonated."[29]

By the time he died at 90 in September of 2015, it was clear that Yogi Berra said a lot of things that nobody will forget—whether or not he really said them.

12. Joe Garagiola

"Joe is no funnier now and no snappier with his comebacks than he used to be as a kid around here. The difference now is more people hear him."—*Mickey Garagiola, Joe Garagiola's older brother in St. Louis*[1]

THERE MUST HAVE BEEN SOMETHING IN THE WATER in The Hill neighborhood of St. Louis where Joe Garagiola and Yogi Berra grew up across the street from one another, something that tapped into the funny bone.

Both boys were catchers and both are amongst the funniest people ever to slip on a baseball uniform. Berra was the better player, but Garagiola enjoyed a much longer career in the public eye as a banquet speaker, game-show host, broadcaster and wit.

Although future generations may not have been aware of it, Garagiola, born in 1926, was a big-leaguer first. He broke into the majors with his hometown St. Louis Cardinals as a 20-year-old and spent nine years in the big leagues while batting .257. He may have been born with an innate sense of levity, but he gathered material while playing for the dismal Pittsburgh Pirates from 1951–1953.

It helped to have a sense of humor if you were a Pirate during that era. At 42–112, some (including Garagiola) have suggested that Pittsburgh club was the worst of all time. "I feel we made genuine contributions to baseball, not only in Pittsburgh, but elsewhere," said Garagiola, warming up.[2] He found it effortless to list ways in which the Pirates were terrible. Some were factual. Some were insults.

> We were the first big league team to wear them [batting helmets]. But with hitters like we had pitchers never felt the need to throw at us. Last-place clubs sometimes have one area where they do better than other clubs. Not us. No matter what the category, we had an iron grip on last place. As Branch Rickey, our general manager said, "This team finished last on merit." We had the worst home record in the National League, and the worst record on the road. We were last in batting. Our hitters struck

out more than those on any other team. We had the lowest fielding average. We also led the league in errors. Our pitchers carried their part of the load. We had the worst team earned-run average in the league, gave up the most bases on balls and struck out the fewest opponents.[3]

Move over, '62 Mets.

Even if Garagiola did not strike the ball more often than other journeyman players, he did strike it rich as a broadcaster and in-demand speaker who also branched out into regular TV Land to host game shows and appear on the *Today Show.* During a six-decade career, he shifted from overlapping in the NL with Bucky Walters to sitting next to Barbara Walters. That made him at least as versatile as a utility infielder—with a higher profile.

The early 1950s Pirates provided endless material when Garagiola was making the shift from on-field regular to after-dinner speaker and broadcaster. He wowed them at sports banquets and formed a delightful broadcast combination with Harry Caray on Cardinals games before going on to do the "Game of the Week" in an era before cable TV.

As any baseball fan knows, by the end of the 1950s the Pirates were amongst the best teams in baseball and in 1960 won the World Series. Garagiola had every indication that he would be part of Pittsburgh's rebuilding, especially when Rickey informed him that he would be. "Joe," Garagiola recalled Rickey saying, "'We're turning a corner and going places. You fit into my plans.' Three days later I was traded to the Cubs.

"You know, when they read my baseball record it sounds like an obituary. I hate to be called a former star. Let's just say that I'm a finished player."[4]

The prematurely balding Garagiola never hit for high average. Nor did he hit the ball hard very often (42 homers lifetime with 255 RBI). He never made an All-Star team either. But he was a man of many parts. He was clever and could tell stories. He became friends with President Gerald Ford and tried to help him win his own full term of office. Garagiola helped found and gave selflessly to the B.A.T. (Baseball Assistance Team), which aids members of the baseball community in need, and he was a strong campaigner against smokeless tobacco use.

So he did have a serious side, but it's just that people who heard Garagiola speak remembered his funny side more. He could also be self-deprecating about his own baseball accomplishments and his other skills. It was difficult to find a situation Garagiola could not make light of.

Actually, the high point of Garagiola's playing career was his rookie year, when he hit .316 in the World Series against the Boston Red Sox. He could even make fun of his own broadcasting. "Sales went up immediately," Garagiola said. "Everybody sold their radios. My name means something to people. When you say 'there's Garagiola,' they think it's a new kind of flu."[5]

In 1960, Garagiola co-wrote a book with Martin Quigley that became a best-seller and further cemented his name with fans who enjoyed a good laugh about baseball. It was called *Baseball Is A Funny Game*, and it took off because it was a funny read.

Those hapless Pirates did not escape unscathed in Garagiola's first literary pursuit (he wrote two more books) either. Retelling an incident that featured Pirates manager Fred Haney, Brooklyn Dodgers star catcher Roy Campanella, and a Pittsburgh base-runner who remained nameless to protect the guilty, Garagiola said both Campanella and the Pirates were fairly convinced that he had deciphered the team's steal sign.

Haney flashed the steal sign to his man on first. Campanella called for a pitch-out and was ready to gun down the player at second. The player did not run. Haney sent out the steal sign again. Campanella called for another pitch-out. But the player did not run.

"By this time, Campanella was convinced he didn't have our steal sign," Garagiola said. "Even Haney wasn't sure he was giving the right steal sign, so he checked with our man. 'Did you get the steal sign?' 'Yeah, I got it.' 'I gave it three times. Why didn't you run?' 'I didn't think you meant it.'"[6]

Strange things happen during games, the unpredictable often breaking out when least expected. For decades, one part of baseball was bench-jockeying, with the aim of disrupting the concentration of the hitter or pitcher. But sometimes it was cruel and unnecessary. Insults were common. It was often a matter of getting on the umpire, as well, although that could be risky business. A thin-skinned ump, or one in a bad mood, might not have much tolerance for smack talking.

Once, umpire Tom Gorman was fed up with all of the harassment from the Brooklyn Dodgers' bench. He marched over to the dugout and yelled that Chris Van Cuyk, who may have had more skill as a needler than a player, was gone. "All right, Van Cuyk, get out! You're through," Gorman said. Only nobody moved to the locker room. "C'mon, get going! Van Cuyk, you're through." Gorman felt he was quite justified in tossing the motormouth. When there was no movement, Gorman followed up with manager Chuck Dressen. Dressen replied, "If you want to run Van Cuyk, you better go to St. Paul because that's where I sent him yesterday."[7]

Garagiola was a good listener during his playing career and remembered things heard in the dugout, especially the things that made him laugh. He was skilled at recalling and retelling the anecdotes to crowds or on the air.

One of those stories was particularly apt for a guy who became a broadcaster. Pirates outfielder George Metkovich was called upon to pinch-hit, but struck out.

"He threw me that radio ball," Metkovich said. Dick Groat, who later helped lead the Pirates to a World Series title, was sitting next to him in the dugout and asked what a radio ball was. "You can hear it, but you can't see it," Metkovich said of his creative way of labeling a fastball.[8]

Although Garagiola was a hot prospect as a teenager just after World War II, he

Joe Garagiola played on some of the worst Pittsburgh Pirates teams of all, then parlayed his material into a lengthy career as a humorous after-dinner speaker, author, and broadcaster.

never made it big. He never played in more than 118 games in one season and played in as many as 100 in only two. He was the type of guy who absorbed the game and its nuances from observing during his bench time. More often those kinds of players become coaches and managers. Garagiola used the knowledge gained in another profession.

One thing baseball fans have long wondered about is just what gets talked about on the mound when the catcher runs out to talk to the pitcher, or when the catcher, the manager and the rest of the infield show up on the mound when a pitcher is struggling. The all-time parody of what may take place in these mystery meetings was the comedy perpetrated in "Bull Durham." In that scene the participants in the clubby mound session discuss appropriate wedding gifts for a teammate.

For all the fan knows, that's all baseball people have ever talked about on the mound over the years. Garagiola, however, lent a little insight into those confabs.

What goes on out there? Sometimes the pitcher stands accused because the catcher said he let up on a pitch. Sometimes the catcher has to give a true answer to the manager's question, "Does he have it anymore?" The character in the lead role is always the pitcher. The lines and the moods change. On the summit you meet the diplomat, the comedian, the growler, the Shakespearean actor, the accused, or the accuser.[9]

Garagiola caught Murry Dickson when both played for the Cardinals and the Pirates. Dickson claimed he had six pitches (plenty), but Garagiola swore it was more. Later, at the end of his career, Garagiola, then with the New York Giants, faced Dickson, then with the Philadelphia Phillies. Garagiola struck out and when manager Leo Durocher asked him about the pitch, Garagiola called it "A roundhouse American Legion submarine curve ball." And he called Dickson "Thomas Edison Dickson" for inventing it.[10]

One thing about Garagiola was that he never tired of baseball or talking about it. He moved on to broadcasting for the Yankees, and that moved him into the orbit of the entertainment and electronic communications world. His horizons broadened from the broadcast booth to the TV studio, from baseball to game shows, to serving as company to millions of Americans just waking up.

Garagiola, who straddled the worlds of sports and non-sports, once had his hat grabbed off his head by an elderly woman at spring training in St. Petersburg, Florida. "Now I know who you are," the woman said. Garagiola fired back with, "You wouldn't do that to Johnny Carson, would you?" The woman replied, "I don't like Johnny Carson."[11]

Even nearly 20 years into his broadcast career, Garagiola was surprised to be recognized out of context, just walking down the street or the like, as compared to after a banquet speech. "It's a crazy world," Garagiola said. "I'm not an actor, I'm a bubble-gum card guy."[12]

Garagiola did appear on bubble-gum cards several times. With the passage of time, some cards that were once valued at one penny have matured into cards worth $25 to $70. Those with his autograph on them may be sold for hundreds of dollars. That well describes the arc of Garagiola's career.

Garagiola never drifted away from baseball even when he was becoming more popular hosting shows such as *Sale of the Century* and *To Tell the Truth*. He also subbed for Johnny Carson on *The Tonight Show* at times, as well as being one of those good-morning regulars on *Today*.

"There'll always be a tinge or a ton of baseball in my life," Garagiola said. "There's very little that I can't associate with in baseball. I wear two rings—my wedding ring and my World Series ring."[13]

Garagiola kept the laughs going whatever he did. He never pretended to be a better player than he was and could chuckle when someone made such a flattering comment about his hitting days that not even he could repeat it without blushing. "The longer I stay away from the game, the better I get," Garagiola said, thinking of banquet raves about him. "Just the other night at a dinner I was introduced as a baseball immortal."[14]

Promotion aside, Garagiola knew where he stood in the firmament. He once joked to All-Star shortstop Phil Rizzuto, who played only for the Yankees, "You never knew the thrill of walking into a clubhouse and wondering if your uniform would still be hanging there."[15]

Garagiola hung around long enough in the majors, though not as long as he might have preferred since he was retired before turning 30. The second and third careers as a public speaker and as an electronic speaker had much more longevity to them, and there was little doubt Garagiola had a blast.

One might say he practiced by telling stories about his youth and baseball to his three children when they were young. They asked for his "little boy" stories.[16] It was Roy Campanella who said that players had to have some little boy in them to succeed at baseball.

Being born in the 1920s, playing in the 1940s and 1950s, and sticking around the game for a lifetime, Garagiola also had perspective on changes. Ballparks morphed into relative palaces from the ones he played in. Domed stadiums popped up in locales around the country to prevent so many rainouts in cities susceptible to getting soaked all summer long.

It took time for some people to get used to indoor ball, and Garagiola liked to tell the story about a pitcher named DeWayne Buice when he first encountered the Kingdome in Seattle. "It's like playing inside the Goodyear Blimp," Buice said.[17]

But not to everyone. For Rocky Bridges, the one-time shortstop turned minor league manager, the newfangled buildings seemed like luxury hotels. He lived in the park when he managed Phoenix, then in AAA ball. "All I needed was a TV, a bathroom and a bed," Bridges said. "I got them and now I don't have to walk too far to the park."[18] He could fall out of bed and be at work.

Actually, Bridges did pretty well on the one-liners himself, though he did not utter as many of them. He understood that he was a journeyman in his 11-year Major League career and said, "I'm in the twilight of a mediocre career. I've had more numbers on my back than a bingo board."[19] Garagiola probably wished that he said that about his own career, but he could not obtain a monopoly on fresh comments.

Still, the success of Garagiola stemmed from being naturally witty and remembering the baseball stories he heard along the way.

Garagiola also transcended eras in Major League baseball from when salaries were around $7,000 a year to when they grew to be closer to $7 million a year. He heard old-timer Herman Franks, a San Francisco Giants manager, compare changes in the way players were treated. "It used to be that you could kick a player's butt," Franks said. "Now you have to kiss it."[20] Garagiola likely quoted that because he agreed with the sentiment.

Garagiola's books are like a rock group's greatest hits albums. He included all of the oldies-but-goodies the way he heard them or the way he told them over the years. And, as usual, Garagiola was his own foil in many of the tales.

The old catcher said he loved to examine new equipment whenever it came along. And that was well before the high-tech world we now live in. "You could go crazy in the on-deck circle alone," Garagiola said of modern-day stuff, from weighted rings for bats and other simulated heavy bats, to resin bags. When Garagiola played, the accepted norm for making your bat feel lighter was to swing two bats in the on-deck circle. That's what he did, though he did make a mistake once. "I took one last, good warm-up swing with the two bats, then flipped them aside and walked up to the plate. Problem was I just tossed away both bats and now I'm standing at home plate empty handed." At first he thought the Dodgers' catcher had stolen his bat. Then Garagiola realized his gaffe, walked back to the dugout and picked up a bat. He struck out on three pitches. "I never even swung the bat."[21]

When in doubt when reminiscing, Garagiola could always return to the bad old days with the Pirates. He did so partially because there was always something to say about manager Fred Haney, who had better luck later in his career, winning two National League pennants and one World Series with the Milwaukee Braves. "I guess it was either a case of having a good sense of humor or never checking into a hotel room on a high floor," Garagiola said of Haney's Pirates days. "I tried to cheer him up. I said, 'Don't worry, Fred. Things will get better. After all, you've been in last place before.' He just looked at me sand said, 'You ought to know. You helped put me there.'"[22]

During his long career as a ball player, but more so as a sports banquet speaker and a broadcaster, Joe Garagiola put people in seats, or kept them in their home seats listening to the story of a game. He barely slowed down as he aged, doing cable commentary for the California Angels for one year and then between 1998 and 2012 working as a color man for the Arizona

Diamondbacks, a team his son Joe Jr., served as general manager. In 2009, the Diamondbacks named the press box in his honor.

"The blessings I've had," Garagiola said on that occasion. "I've had a tremendous ride."[23]

On February 22, 2013, Garagiola announced his retirement from broadcasting, 57 years after he began that career and at age 87.

Garagiola lived in Arizona for years and so he was a natural fit for the Diamondbacks. He had only recently moved into a retirement community and so had his old buddy Yogi Berra, though in a different state. Berra would pass away in September of 2015.

Before that, during one of their chats, Garagiola asked Yogi how his new place was. Berra replied, "It's all right, but geez, they've got a lot of old people here."[24]

Garagiola, who passed away on March 23, 2016 at 90, may have aged, but he never grew old.

13. Lefty Gomez

"Your mom and dad are in the ballpark, aren't they? Well, they should be pretty impressed that the great Gomez is asking you for advice in this critical situation."—Said to Yankees shortstop Phil Rizzuto when he was a nervous rookie and Gomez summoned him to the mound for show[1]

VERNON "LEFTY" GOMEZ WAS A GOOD ENOUGH PITCHER to be selected for seven All-Star teams and to be voted into the Baseball Hall of Fame. But he also made sure he had fun during his 14 seasons in the majors.

He earned his nickname "Lefty" because he was a southpaw, and "El Goofo" and "Goofy" Gomez for his sense of humor, his occasional offbeat actions, and most definitely because of his story-telling ability on the banquet circuit. It was as difficult to keep up with Gomez's quips as it was his fastball.

Gomez won as many as 26 games in a season, 24 another time, and 21 two other times while finishing 87 games over .500. When asked to explain his success, other than pitching for the New York Yankees during one of their greatest eras in the 1930s, Gomez said, "Clean living and a fast outfield."[2]

One of Gomez's themes, as he attributed those winning ways to an outfield that included Joe DiMaggio and a bullpen that contained Johnny Murphy, was, "I'd rather be lucky than good." Most would say he was both.[3]

The one sadness of Gomez's playing days was that his left arm gave out too soon, costing him his bread-and-butter. When he went into the Army during World War II, he was given shots to prevent various illnesses. "That shot you just gave me won't do the slightest bit of good," Gomez told the medical man. "Confidentially, doc, that arm has been dead for two years." Similarly, when Gomez applied for a job at Wilson Sporting Goods after his playing days, the form asked the reason for leaving his last place of employment. "I couldn't get anyone out," he said.[4]

Gomez was a slick talker, never at a loss for a response to a question, never slow on the uptake before an audience. One of his close friends was DiMaggio, who was a shy rookie and young player, and then a standoffish veteran. In the beginning, when DiMaggio was gaining fame, he was in demand to speak at various sporting banquets. Gomez roomed with DiMaggio and DiMaggio always insisted he come along to the dinners. DiMaggio would stand up at the podium, greet the crowds with a few hello words, and then introduce Gomez. DiMaggio sat down and Gomez spoke. He was so entertaining that no one in the audience complained that he overshadowed the scheduled featured speaker. Gomez did joke that DiMaggio always kept the swag from these events, however.

Gomez was born in California of half–Spanish and half–Irish ancestry, but was sometimes referred to as "The Singular Senor." In the 1930s, with Gomez as the cornerstone of the pitching staff, the Yankees won five World Series. Of the seven Series games Gomez started, he won six of them; the other was a no-decision. Gomez never shied away from action on the big stage and certainly that contributed to his Hall of Fame credentials.

When he was a young man, both in the minors with the San Francisco Seals, and in his early years with the Yankees, Gomez was skinnier than a cigarette. He stood 6-foot-2, but weighed barely over 150 pounds. He gained velocity on his fastball when he gained heft on his body.

Gomez was also good friends with Babe Ruth, but "The Sultan of Swat" made fun of Gomez's famously poor hitting. For years Ruth bet Gomez $500 that he would not get ten hits in a season. The Babe usually lost those wagers, but it was close every season. A couple of times Gomez did not make it and other times he finished with 11 safeties. Since Gomez's lifetime batting average was .147, it was a risk worth taking for Ruth each year.

One time Gomez said he closed his eyes and went four-for-four on Opening Day, giving Ruth a start. But he followed that up with a 42-game hitless streak.

When the All-Star Game began in 1933, Gomez was the American League's starting pitcher. Ironically, he got the first RBI in the midsummer classic's history. He was also the winning hurler. Ruth, naturally enough, hit the first home run. As a young player Ruth took a shine to Gomez and gave him advice about the game that stuck with him. "Babe taught me the basics of baseball," Gomez said. "'Win the game for your teammates and know that without the fans you're nothing."[5]

That sounds almost too philosophically serious for Gomez, but he did not dwell on the side of seriousness very often. More Lefty–like was the comment he made when someone asked if he was planning to write an autobiography. "Why would I write a book about my life?" he responded. "I lived it."[6]

He lived it with relish. Gomez was just 15 when he met the great Satchel Paige for the first time in a semi-pro game. Paige was mowing down the hitters wherever he pitched for dollars, in exhibitions or in Negro Leagues games. For this one, Paige had pledged to strike out the first nine men he faced—and came through. "The hitters complained they couldn't see the fire, only the ashes left on the plate," said an impressed Gomez. "Satch could wipe you out on charisma alone."[7]

The same might have been said for Gomez when he got older. But he also came by the moniker "Goofy" honestly. One day while traveling by train to a game in Washington, D.C., members of the Yankees were reading a newspaper story about an Albert Einstein invention. Just making sure, a sportswriter asked Gomez if he knew who Einstein was. "Sure," Gomez replied. "He's an inventor … like me." The follow-up question naturally was what had Gomez invented. "A revolving fishbowl for tropical fish," Gomez said. "They stay in one spot as the bowl turns. The fish conserve energy and live ten years longer."[8]

It is not clear if that theory has ever been debunked.

Gomez learned how to fly planes. He played the saxophone. He married actress June O'Dea. And he hung out with DiMaggio when he was married to Marilyn Monroe. Gomez was a loyal pal and a man who enjoyed life away from the diamond, as well as on it.

His baseball stories are legendary. Gomez blessed Detroit Tigers future Hall of Famer Charlie Gehringer with his nickname "The Mechanical Man," because all you had to do was wind him up and he hit .300. Gomez, making remarks at his own expense, explained his special pitch, a go-fer ball. This was one that he threw and it went for two bases, three bases or a home run. Indeed, with slight modification, the words "gopher ball" became a synonym for a home run.

When he was just a Yankees rookie being sent down to the minors in St. Paul, Minnesota, Gomez still believed he could be a good hitter in the majors. He wangled a bat contract out of Hillerich & Bradsby, alias Louisville Slugger. Although the company did grant Gomez a deal, it was not a particularly munificent one. "I received $1, two bats and a set of golf clubs," Gomez said.[9] Even at that, once the bat-maker got a load of Gomez swinging in the American League, it probably felt it had given up too much in the arrangement.

Gomez poked fun at his own hitting. For a while Gomez was a teammate of Joe Sewell, a shortstop who made the Hall of Fame and who was stingy with his at-bats. Although Sewell was no power hitter, he practically never struck out. "A great hitter," Gomez said. "One year he struck out three times in over 600 at-bats. Well, I'll tell you what, I did better than that. I struck out five times in one game. Took him more than 600 swings and I did it in one day."[10] (Actually, he never struck out more than three times in a game.)

There were certain Hall of Fame hitters—the hitters who did well against any pitcher regardless of reputation—whom Gomez did not like to face. The Yankees faced the New York Giants in the 1936 World Series, and star outfielder Mel Ott came to the plate. While Ott waited for a pitch, Gomez looked skyward and followed the progress of a passing airplane. Gomez told catcher Bill Dickey if he held onto the ball long enough he hoped Ott would go away. He told reporters, "I didn't want to throw the ball. He couldn't hit it while I was still holding it."[11]

A similar story was told about Gomez doing the same on the mound when muscular Jimmie Foxx was at the plate. In any case, in 1969, when Americans put a man on the moon and Gomez was watching the event on television, it was noted that the astronauts were walking around picking up chunks of what NASA told the world was rocks. Gomez had a different take. "I said to my wife, 'I know what that is. It's a ball Jimmie Foxx off me.'"[12]

In another infamous incident, Gomez said before one game that he had been reading in the newspaper columns about how smart second baseman Tony Lazzeri was. Lazzeri would later make the Hall of Fame, too. "That's all we ever read about," Gomez said of Lazzeri's brain power. "One day I was pitching to Hank Greenberg. There was man on first and one out and the batter hit a perfect double-play ball back to me. Lazzeri is standing halfway between first and second. Instead of throwing the ball to [shortstop Frank] Crosetti, I threw it to Lazzeri.

"He comes up to me laughing and wants to know why I threw him the ball. I told him I'd been reading how smart he was and just wanted to see what he would do with it."[13]

The team fined Gomez $100 for the play.

Going back to the holding the ball trick. Gomez told the story so many times he may have altered the details over the years. This is how he spelled it out in 1941. "The bases were full and nobody was out," he said. "Also, there was a tough hitter at bat. So I just held the ball. 'Go ahead and pitch,' the umpire said. 'That would be a foolish thing to do,' I answered.

'As long as I hold this ball they can't hurt me. But who knows what will happen if I let it go.'" What finally happened? "I was right in the first place," Gomez said.[14]

During Gomez's years with the Yanks they won most of the time, including seven pennants. He set the record for going 6–0 in the Series, the most wins without a loss. But once in a while the Yankees lost in the World Series, as they did in five games to the St. Louis Cardinals in 1942.

When the defeat was in the books and the New York locker room was gloomy, Gomez, being Gomez, sought to break the tension. He climbed up on a trunk and said, "Attention, everybody! All be on hand for the Yankee victory party tonight—at the Automat at 50th and Broadway. Bring your own nickels!"[15] Well, this was one year without champagne, so Gomez must have figured they should eat apple pie instead of humble pie.

Gomez's marriage was about as adventurous as his story-telling. When he was courting O'Dea, who starred in "Of Thee I Sing" but who later gave up her career to be a housewife, she did not know much about baseball. She thought everyone played every day, including the pitcher. As Lefty's guest at Yankee Stadium for her first game, O'Dea tried to sooth her upset boyfriend when he lost to the Washington Senators 2–1. "Never mind, honey, you'll beat them tomorrow," she said. "Tomorrow!" Gomez shouted. "You must have me mixed up with Iron Man Joe McGinnity."[16]

It should be no surprise that a man of Gomez's wit and proclivity for banter made friends with the New York sportswriters. During Gomez's career, sportswriters did not always venture into the locker room for postgame quotes. They wrote their game stories, their play-by-play, fairly straight. Before television, the readers of their newspapers needed to know the facts about every play. They had some radio to rely on, but otherwise the writers were the source of what happened. Columnists were beginning to perform those pre-game and post-game visits, getting to know the ball players better than they had from a distance in the past.

Gomez left the Yankees after the 1942 season (he pitched one more big-league game for the Washington Senators in 1943) because his arm was worn out. When he departed from New York one columnist talked about what life with Lefty had been like.

> Gomez is by far the wittiest of ball players. The funniest guy maybe in modern baseball. There is nothing subtle about Lefty. He cracks wise and then helps you laugh. It is spontaneous fun, never raspy or vindictive. Most of his stories are at the expense of the pitcher, himself. Without animus, without malice, he is liked universally.[17]

While Gomez was loved in the dugout by teammates, he could get on his manager's nerves with his own energy, conversation and chatter on days he wasn't pitching. Once, Hall of Fame manager Joe McCarthy blew his cool after Gomez tried to burn up energy by chinning himself on a pipe in the dugout. "For God's sake, go down to the bullpen, or in the clubhouse," McCarthy ordered. "Go some place! You're driving me crazy."[18]

Once, after Gomez got picked off second base, his manager asked what had happened. Gomez, notorious as the non-hitter, said he didn't know because he had never been there before. There were several reasons why McCarthy was driven batty by Gomez's commentary, and some of those occurred when he spoke directly to the pitcher. After Gomez once threw to the wrong base, McCarthy asked him what he was thinking. "There's too many Italians out on this team," Gomez said, ostensibly being confused between Lazzeri and Crosetti. "I can't tell them apart." McCarthy jibed that there was another Italian in the outfield—DiMaggio. "Why didn't you throw the ball into centerfield then?" he asked. "There's an Italian out there."[19]

If Gomez had a follow-up answer to that it was not recorded, or he did keep his mouth shut.

Once, on a train transporting the Yankees through Windsor, Canada, into Detroit, there was a stop in that country, but the players did not get off. Still, Gomez yelled for the porter. "Send the customs men this way," Gomez said. "I have something to declare." The porter pointed out that he hadn't gotten off the train, so how could he have acquired anything? "I want to declare 180 pounds of dope," Gomez said. This came as a surprise to the porter, who asked where the dope was. "Right here," Gomez said, putting his hand on outfielder George Selkirk.[20]

Gomez was elected to the Baseball Hall of Fame in 1972, when he was still around (for another 17 years) to enjoy it. He was chosen by the Veterans Committee, along with Ross Youngs and Will Harridge, and joined the group elected by the BBWAA, who chose Sandy Koufax, Yogi Berra, and Early Wynn. That year the special committee formed to review the histories of Negro Leagues players who had been shut out of the majors added Josh Gibson and Buck Leonard. This was the year after Satchel Paige was the first of that group elected.

By the time he was elected, roughly 30 years had passed since his retirement, so Gomez did not believe he was ever going to be selected for the Hall of Fame. But there he was in 1972, delivering an acceptance speech. It was a rather surprisingly short one given Gomez's loquacious manner. In part he said, "This is indeed the greatest pleasure I've ever had in my life." He credited DiMaggio for chasing down his mistake pitches hit to the deepest reaches of Yankee Stadium's center field and reliever Johnny Murphy for saving games that Gomez left early.[21]

Many sportswriters wrote nice things about Gomez when he was elected to the Hall, and many of them had never seen him pitch, but enjoyed listening to his jokes.

Discussing Gomez's plaque, which includes lifetime highlights, one writer said, "They won't have room for the essential Lefty Gomez, all those warm, wonderful stories. If they did, Gomez's plaque would weigh 256 tons."[22]

In older age, Gomez had heart surgery and when he took ill for the final time he was hospitalized. He was with family when he passed away, and later his son Gery told people that Gomez's final words were about baseball.

"He was having trouble breathing Friday morning," the younger Gomez said of his father the day before he died. "The nurse was trying to assess how bad the pain was and how to deal with it. 'On a scale of one to 10 how hard are you pitching?' Lefty looked at the fellow—it was a male nurse—and he said, 'Who's hitting?' 'Jimmie Foxx,' said the nurse. And dad said, 'Then it would be a four.' Those were his last words. The last thing he uttered was a little joke about baseball."[23] Figures.

Gomez died only a few days shy of his 56th anniversary.

"We had such a good time, all that laughter," said his wife June, who probably heard more Lefty jokes than any other human being.[24]

At the memorial service for Gomez, a guitarist played "Take Me Out to the Ballgame." It was Gomez's own idea and request. The congregation that had gathered to pay him tribute fittingly sang along. It is not known if he envisioned that occurring, but it definitely seemed appropriate.

Surely, Gomez would have engaged in a hearty laugh.

14. Bill Veeck

"I never thought I'd live to see the day that I'd be a major leaguer. For a minute I felt like Babe Ruth."—*Eddie Gaedel, the midget sent up to the plate to hit for the St. Louis Browns in August of 1951 as a publicity stunt*[1]

EVERYONE LOVED BILL VEECK, owner of the Cleveland Indians, St. Louis Browns, and Chicago White Sox (twice). Players, fans, sportswriters, all of them. And ultimately the Baseball Hall of Fame, too. But not other owners. They despised him because they were stuffed shirts, as he put it, conservative men who sought to drain the fun from the game, who believed it should be taken so seriously they disliked creative promotions.

There is no doubt that Veeck, who spent his youth working for the Chicago Cubs while his father was president of that team, and later for the Wrigley family, was the fan-friendliest baseball executive of all time. He had a sense of humor and, as passionate as he was about winning, Veeck understood that there was only going to be one World Series champion per season. He wanted to make sure that supporters of other teams around baseball had just as good a time when they came to the ballpark, even if their team was not the champ.

It should be noted up front, however, that Veeck was the owner of the Cleveland Indians the last time that franchise did win a world title in 1948.

Some said that Veeck ran a circus, not a ball club. In reality, he ran a ball club that was always open to suggestions for ways to have fun in between getting the other guys out. Veeck's father, also named William, invented Ladies Day when he supervised the Cubs. The younger Bill turned the event into an art form, once importing orchids from Hawaii for every lady who entered the park on Ladies Day.

Veeck designed and dressed his White Sox in shorts one year. It didn't take. He put their last names on the backs of jerseys. That did take. He had future Hall of Famers Luis Aparicio and Nellie Fox, the keystone combination that reflected the shortest players on his Chicago club, kidnapped at ray-gun-point in the outfield by midget Martians.

Veeck held court in the "Bard's Room" at Comiskey Park, drinking after games with sportswriters. He sent Eddie Gaedel, a midget standing 3-foot-7, to the plate in a Browns game—with orders not to swing upon pain of death. Although tempted, Gaedel did not swing, and with his miniature strike zone did earn the base on balls that Veeck was angling for.

While he was always working telephones with hopes of making a trade that would improve his team (the White Sox won an American League pennant in 1959 under Veeck), the boss was never content to sit idle and wait for the world to come along with him. Veeck invented the exploding scoreboard at Comiskey, too, setting off fireworks when a home-team player smacked a home run. They still do that at U.S. Cellular Field (the new Comiskey).

The man they called "Sportshirt Bill" because he refused to wear a sport coat and tie under any circumstance pulled off his most famous stunt when he sent Gaedel to the plate for his single at-bat. Veeck knew that there was likely to be American League opposition to the move, so he signed Gaedel to a professional contract going into the weekend so it would not be received until the dawn of the new business week. By then, most of Gaedel's fame would have been recorded.

Veeck said he got the idea for sending the little man to the plate after reading a James Thurber story in the *Saturday Evening Post*. Veeck stashed the idea in his brain and pulled Thurber out a decade after the tale showed up in print. The protagonist in Thurber's story who came to bat measured in at 2-foot-9.

Three decades after Gaedel's solo appearance in a big league game occurred, Veeck reflected on the phenomenal attention the event sparked. "I can't talk to anybody from St. Louis without them telling me they were there," said Veeck, who was aware that attendance at Sportsman's Park was 18,369.[2]

Sure enough, Gaedel never got to take a second at-bat because American League President Will Harridge banned him from the sport before the laughter even died down around the country. Veeck immediately accused Harridge of discriminating against "little people. I'm puzzled, baffled and aggrieved by Mr. Harridge's ruling. We're paying a lot of guys good money to get on base and when they don't do it, nobody sympathizes with us. But when this little guy goes to the plate and draws a walk on his only time at-bat, they call it 'conduct detrimental to baseball.'"[3] It was not an argument Veeck was going to win with a hanging judge.

Veeck was born February 9, 1914. His dad, a former sportswriter, ran the Cubs from 1917 to 1933. It is said that the younger Veeck got the idea to plant the famous ivy on the outfield walls at Wrigley Field when he was 13. However, other stories indicate it was the idea of owner Philip Wrigley, who wanted something colorful planted on the walls, and Veeck came up with ivy in 1937 while the ball park was being renovated.

During World War II, Veeck served with the Marines in the South Pacific. Part of his right leg was crushed by his anti-artillery gun, and 36 surgeries over the years resulted in the amputation of his right leg somewhat piece by piece. Veeck used a wooden leg for decades, but as a constant smoker, he had an ashtray built into it.

Veeck could never find enough time in a day to do things so he pretended it offered more than 24 hours per calendar-page flip. He slept just four hours a night, drank coffee by the gallon, chain-smoked, never ate breakfast, did not eat a healthy lunch, and all of that taken together probably means he was lucky to live to 71.

An idea man who never stopped the wheels turning in his head, Veeck tried to make the most of those other 20 hours a day. Ignoring the likelihood that others might be asleep while he was keeping those elongated hours, Veeck telephoned people at any time. Sometimes it seemed a telephone was growing out of his ear. He would have loved cell phones.

Veeck never stood on formality. He said that cab drivers and bartenders were just about the smartest people around—that they knew everything. That's because their clients told them everything.

It may have been that Chattanooga owner Joe Engel was tabbed "The Barnum of the Bushes," but Veeck was regularly compared with P. T. Barnum from the Major League standpoint.

Aside from his humorous bent, Veeck was on the side of the angels when it came to human rights. In the 1940s, the Philadelphia Phillies, at the time an embarrassingly poor team, came up for sale. Veeck had been running the Milwaukee AAA franchise and his goal was to run a Major League club.

His plan was to buy the terrible Phillies but turn around the team's fortunes immediately by stocking the talent-weak team with stars from the Negro Leagues. Baseball's color line was still in effect, and there had not been an African American in the majors since Moses Fleetwood Walker in 1884. Veeck envisioned hiring stars such as Satchel Paige, Josh

Gibson, Cool Papa Bell, and Buck Leonard. Only he made the mistake of talking about this plan to the wrong people. His idea was leaked to rigid segregationist Kenesaw Mountain Landis, the commissioner, who made sure the Phillies found another buyer. Some people do not believe that Veeck story, but others do, and it seems consistent with his character.

It took until 1947, when the Brooklyn Dodgers employed Jackie Robinson, for the color barrier to be broken. A few months after Robinson made his debut, Veeck hired Larry Doby as an outfielder for the Indians, and Doby became the second African American big league player and the first in the American League.

In 1948, Veeck sought out Paige and made him a 42-year-old rookie. Paige still had enough stuff to star in relief for that Indians' championship club and later made All-Star teams. Paige and Veeck remained lifelong friends. Veeck used Abe Saperstein, owner of the all-black Harlem Globetrotters traveling basketball team, as a conduit. Paige also impressed a skeptical manager Lou Boudreau in a short tryout. *The Sporting News* embarrassed itself by criticizing Veeck as a travesty. When Paige began winning, Veeck sent a telegram to *Sporting News* kingpin J. G. Taylor Spink that in part read, "He definitely is in line For The Sporting News 'Rookie of the Year' Award."[4]

Veeck's brain moved faster than most comedians' mouths. He was constantly thinking of ways to spice up baseball. By dying in 1986, Veeck, who often complained to fellow owners that they were making the game boring, he missed out on how baseball decided to make itself more entertaining. He may not have agreed with the influx of mascots, the fan games, and junk put on videoboards, but he would have had to admit owners were trying harder than they had.

In Cleveland, his Indians set attendance records, shooting way over 2 million fans. Nowadays the best-drawing teams bring in well over 3 million. So from that standpoint, even though Veeck repeatedly said baseball officials were killing the game, it is more financially successful than ever.

Well before Major League Baseball made the change, Veeck suggested the traditional American and National Leagues be split into divisions. No one bought it at the time. Veeck was a hit in Cleveland, popular as all get-out in Chicago, but flopped in St. Louis. He realized the Browns were doomed, going up against the Cardinals, and wanted to move the team to Baltimore. But owners wanted to see him drummed out of the game and did not approve a move for the Browns to become the Baltimore Orioles until after Veeck sold the team.

"Big-league owners always breathed deep sighs of relief every time they rid themselves of Bill Veeck," one sportswriter noted, "an uncontrollable maverick whose imaginative ideas, promotional flair and pixie sense of humor outraged the establishment. By nature and habit they are stand-patters. Wild William is not."[5]

While it is a lesser-known chapter of Veeck's ownership and entrepreneurial career, the fun and games he presided over in Milwaukee with that old minor league club more than a decade before the big-league Braves staked the territory, was pretty much a dress rehearsal for Veeck's Major League tenures.

This is when his promotions first emerged. Veeck gave things away to fans. Unlike today, when the booty is some routine baseball-related item passed out to children as they pass through the gate, Veeck creatively selected random fans to receive prizes. He gave away a 200-pound block of ice and live lobsters. As he moved up the ranks, his promotions became complex. Periodically he would give away live livestock—and wonder why no one claimed it. Famed White Sox organist Nancy Faust once added an animal to her farm menagerie when that happened.

Whatever he did in Milwaukee worked. Attendance jumped from 75,000 to 250,000 between 1940 and 1942. Between 1947 and 1948, Cleveland Indians attendance jumped by 1.1 million fans to more than 2.6 million.

Once, in Cleveland, when it was announced there was going to be a special appreciation day for a ball player, a fan wrote in, seemingly tongue-in-cheek, saying the well-paid player didn't really need all of the gifts he was going to get. Instead, how about having a day for a fan? The author was named Joe Early, and ultimately there was a "Good Old Joe Early Day." Early was a World War II veteran from Lakewood, Ohio, who worked as a security guard at a Cleveland manufacturing plant. Veeck ran with the idea. Early was the star of the show, but Veeck made it an all-fan extravaganza, giving away live turkeys, rabbits and guinea pigs, bushels of apples, tomatoes and peaches.

Then came Early, who it was announced would be receiving a new house for him and his wife, which Veeck claimed was "early American architecture." A flat-bed truck appeared on the field, toting a shabby outhouse. Next came the presentation of a car. This was a Model T, about to fall apart. As a bonus, it was set up as a clown car, with only female models jumping out. After the gag gifts made everyone laugh, the real stuff was handed over, including a new car, luggage, clothes, and a dog. Plus Early was presented with a lifetime baseball pass to American League games.[6]

The people who best got Veeck, his motives and his charms, were the fans whom he entertained, and the newspaper guys who wrote the stories about how he entertained them. Headline writers described Veeck as a dying breed for years before he actually died. Veeck never was actually part of a breed. He was a one-of-a-kind owner.

One of Veeck's great friends in the game was Hall of Fame first baseman Hank Greenberg, who made his reputation on the diamond for the Detroit Tigers. He cut his teeth in the front office working for Veeck. For years, Greenberg told the world that Veeck belonged in the Hall of Fame. When the subject was broached to Veeck by a sportswriter, he recoiled. "I would have to refuse it if I were put in the Hall of Fame," was his first reaction. "If there is no room there for Luis Aparicio, for Phil Rizzuto, for Pee Wee Reese, for Nellie Fox, then there is surely no room for a scuffler who couldn't hit .001."[7]

Hall of Famer Bill Veeck was probably the most popular Major League owner of all time. He put fan enjoyment first and never saw a creative entertainment stunt he didn't like.

However, it must be observed that eventually all four of those middle infielders, little men all, by coincidence, were voted into the Hall of Fame. So was Veeck, though not until 1991, five years after he died. In the long run he surely would have been satisfied to be enshrined next to august company.

Veeck penned a few books, all autobiographical, but the best-known was "Veeck—As In Wreck," to clarify the pronunciation of his name. Contained in those pages was a chapter called "Every Day Was Mardi Gras," focusing on the grand season when the Indians won the pennant and the World Series and set a big-league attendance record.

Between doubleheaders we had shows featuring colorful and dramatic fireworks displays and circus acts. The philosophy behind this is simple. I have always loved fireworks and circus acts. My tastes, I have found, are so average that anything that appeals strongly to me is probably going to appeal to most of the customers. The first night game after we got our license, we had fireworks displays showing a flame-eating pelican, two planes in a dogfight, and finally, a plane sinking a battleship in a thrilling encounter at sea. At least the plane was supposed to sink the battleship. Something got fouled up in the inner working—and this is the truth— the battleship pulled a complete upset on us and knocked down the plane. Ah well, the fortunes of war.[8]

Veeck was a success in Milwaukee and a hero in Cleveland, but he couldn't do much to save the Browns in St. Louis. He had always wanted to run a team in Chicago. That went back to his boyhood with the Cubs. With two teams in the City of Big Shoulders, that gave him two shots. The Wrigley family was not about to part with the Cubs. Through some shrewd maneuvering, some helpful financial allies, and a lot of desire, Veeck acquired the White Sox. And it came just in time for the Sox to win their first pennant in 40 years, or since the Black Sox debacle of 1919.

He was described as an elf, not a clown, a mischievous planner, in Chicago. He espoused some of his promotional philosophy while assuming command. "This is an illusionary business," Veeck said. "The people who go to a ball game go away with nothing more to show for it than what's in their heads. You can't destroy the illusion. You have to give them more vivid pictures to carry away."[9]

Many people used the word "handicapped" around Veeck because of his continuously shrinking right leg. They didn't know Veeck. Once, Veeck received a letter from a religious official who asked if he wasn't embarrassed to be pictured playing tennis in shorts or with his artificial leg removed. Veeck's answer? "I wrote and asked him if people with artificial teeth stopped smiling," Veeck said.[10]

In 1981, Veeck was presented with a Lifetime Achievement Award from *Baseball Magazine*, and his pal Hank Greenberg did the honors at the ceremony. "In 1948, when he drew 2.6 million people fans into the Cleveland park it was like parting the Red Sea," Greenberg said.[11]

Veeck bought and sold the White Sox a couple of times, and when he got out he could read the handwriting of the sport's future. Baseball was no longer going to be available for individual owners like him. Major corporations, with endlessly deep pockets, were going to run the game. He said baseball wasn't as much fun as it had been before the 1980s.

He also joked about that leg, saying his most valuable players through the years were the surgeons that kept on operating on him, doctors who helped him survive. Instead of pitching and hitting he credited "the remarkable skills of modern medical science" for his longevity in the game.[12]

During the last few years of his life, after disposing of his final connections with the White Sox, Veeck didn't get along with the succeeding team ownership. But as someone who still lived in Chicago, he wasn't going to deprive himself of baseball. So he took to attending Cubs games, sitting in the bleachers, shirtless, soaking up the sun, much like many of the other denizens.

Bill Veeck had come full circle, rooting for the team he first worked for as a teenager so long before. Appropriately enough, he was merely hanging out with the fans sharing beers and baseball stories. At the end, he was just another fan. That's probably what Veeck's strongest allegiance to the game had been all along.

15. Jim Bouton

> "F-You, Shakespeare!"—*Cincinnati Reds star Pete Rose, reacting to pitcher Jim Bouton's inside-the-team book look at the 1969 Seattle Pilots season*[1]

WHEN JIM BOUTON KEPT A DIARY of the one-and-only season of the Seattle Pilots expansion team in 1969 (before they expanded right on to Milwaukee to become the Brewers), nobody thought that much about it.

The reaction was powerful in 1970 when *Ball Four* hit the bookshelves. The reason people like Pete Rose and Commissioner Bowie Kuhn were so exorcised at Bouton was their belief that he had violated the understood rule of the locker room: what happens inside the team's private domain stays there.

Ball Four became a smash hit, reprinted many times and selling more than two million copies. It is a baseball classic, rife with humor and penetrating observations, and transformed Bouton from a hanging-on, once-successful New York Yankees hurler into someone known for wielding a wickedly funny pen and who could hold his own in conversation with talk show hosts.

Bouton was at the tail end of a career that had reached World Series highs in New York marked by a 21-victory campaign. Arm woes had cut short his effectiveness and ultimately ended his Major League career. In desperation, trying to salvage the last moments of life at the highest level of the sport, Bouton resorted to throwing the knuckleball he had learned as a kid. While the knuckler did not perpetuate Bouton's Major League career for long, it did allow him to remain active in semi-pro leagues and the like for decades, pitching for a ridiculously long time, even past the advent of senior citizenhood.

It's probably too bad that Bouton did not rely on the knuckler a little bit sooner than he did. "It's a wonderful pitch," Bouton said. "It defies logic. It flutters up there at grandma speed and renders strong men helpless."[2]

That occurred when *Ball Four* was released as well. Strong men collapsed in laughter. The people who didn't laugh were the conservative administrators of baseball and selected players who hated simply that it was written more than what it said. Kuhn was so affronted by the idea that young men on the loose on road trips chased after women that he demanded Bouton issue a statement indicating the book was fiction.

That was not going to happen because the stories were true, true, true. Most people, even baseball fans, even residents of Seattle, don't remember the Pilots ever existed, but Bouton immortalized them. Never was so entertaining a volume written about such an inconsequential, losing team.

It should be noted that the book was not even Bouton's idea originally. Leonard Shecter, a prominent sportswriter for the *New York Post*, pitched the master plan of keeping a season-long diary. Shecter was credited as the editor.

Bouton documented his time with the Pilots from his arrival at spring training in Arizona, when baseball was busily seeking to avoid a long, debilitating strike as those uppity players finally got representation that could shake up the establishment. Union director Marvin Miller was trying to protect the players' pension plan. Bouton had publicly sided with the union.

When the Pilots' general manager, Marvin Milkes, greeted Bouton, Milkes told him nothing said about the strike would be held against him. Bouton cocked a suspicious eye at a baseball executive shaking hands and uttering comments about starting fresh. He wondered "where, on a scale of one to 10, a guy who talks too much falls between a former alcoholic and a moral degenerate."[3]

Bouton was not above semi-insulting banter with teammates either. Early, as catcher Greg Goossen darted from his crouch after a bunt yelling, "First base! First base!" to the pitcher, he watched in amazement as the hurler scooped it up and threw it to second, leaving everyone safe. "Goose, he had to consider the source," Bouton shouted to Goossen. Two years later, when they ran into one another, Goossen recited the line back at Bouton.[4] He apparently did not appreciate it.

Bouton's musings indicated that he did not particularly trust manager Joe Schultz or the coaching staff, and there were hints they didn't win his respect, either. Bouton also made fun of himself in the book, simultaneously revealing the type of superstitions or off-the-field things ballplayers sometimes think affect whether or not they make the team or get to play.

"My hair was quite long and the sideburns were thick and heavy," Bouton said of obtaining a haircut during an era when college students in particular had taken to wearing their hair long. "I didn't want to have a long-hair image, so I got a really short haircut and look like a storm trooper. It's terrible.... You never can tell how spring training is going to go. I could be one of those borderline cases and the difference between the club and not making it might be the length of my hair."[5]

Heavens, you mean baseball is not a meritocracy and your hair could get you cut? No one suggested Bouton didn't know what he was talking about. He knew that the baseball establishment was conservative.

Early on, Bouton didn't mind Schultz's approach. In spring training he stopped by often to say nice things of encouragement. Bouton considered this good strategy and good to hear since those vying for spots on an expansion team roster are almost all, by definition, bottom feeders in the league. "He may look like Nikita Khrushchev, but it means a lot anyway," Bouton said. "I'm sure most of us here feel like leftovers and outcasts and marginal players and it doesn't hurt when the manager massages your ego a little bit."[6]

Bouton sought to learn a pickoff move to second base from fellow pitcher Mike Marshall. Marshall was well known as a mathematical whiz and often explained things in formulas and theorems that other ball players couldn't understand. After Marshall told Bouton that his pickoff worked so well because he leaned back when he threw, Bouton asked why. "Newton's Third Law," Marshall said.[7]

The response baffled Bouton and he wrote, "Of course. Except the last time I tried his pick-off motion I heard grinding noises in my shoulder."[8]

Bowie Kuhn and Pete Rose aside, Bouton's revelatory book became wildly popular. It also led Bouton to write other light-hearted baseball books. He authored *I'm Glad You Didn't Take It Personally*; *I Managed Good, But Boy Did They Play Bad* and *Foul Ball*.

Joining the baseball establishment in damning Bouton were some older, more conservative sportswriters. Leader of the pack was Dick Young, columnist at the *New York Daily News*. His review of *Ball Four* was scathing. He did not seem likely to share schnapps with Bouton on Christmas. "I feel sorry for Jim Bouton," Young wrote. "He is a social leper. He didn't catch it. He developed it. People like this, embittered people, sit down in their time of deepest rejection and write. They write, oh hell, everybody stinks, everybody but me, and it makes them feel better."[9]

That was certainly one extreme take on *Ball Four*, which actually made a lot of people feel good. It was so off-the-wall a description that Bouton said he did not even know what Young meant. But the well-known sportswriter's attention on the book probably helped sales, Bouton thought.

Bouton's bestseller led him to a job as a TV sportscaster in New York. Bouton thought he was destined for radio. That was before he got exponentially more famous from *Ball Four* than he had at any time in his life apart from his 21- and 18-game winning seasons for the Yankees. But perhaps not. "Then, all of a sudden I got sexy," Bouton said.[10]

That is different from being qualified for a new field, but he didn't turn away opportunity, either, especially with the right arm that had carried him for decades turning to mush.

Bouton jumped right to the major leagues of a New York station's newscast without doing an apprenticeship in the minors and replaced a respected veteran in the lineup. Bouton stumbled a little bit, and those who disliked the displacement of Lou Broda, the old guy, were not complimentary. "Bouton, you better shape up. Your stuff is terrible. You're not doing the job and if don't get a helluva lot better real fast, you're gone." That was not a fan letter, but a talking-to delivered face-to-face in a bar by a news broadcaster. "I don't see why the hell ABC would ever replace Boda with you. Boda's a pro. He's knowledgeable about sports. He knows the broadcasting business."[11]

Apparently Bouton was not being touted for rookie-of-the-year. His approach was to read sports the way he wrote *Ball Four*, as if sports were not a life-and-death venture and he could talk up the games with a sense of humor.

When someone in the news center pulled a prank on Bouton, he retaliated with a note on the bulletin board designed to shake people up and perhaps make them think before picking on him again. He wrote, in part, that he was writing another book and it would include a chapter on the TV newsroom. He urged people to share anecdotes and stories about so-and-so's sex life or other wild stories and about degenerate film editors. "But if you don't send me any anecdotes I'm going to have to make them up myself and I'm sure you don't want that." He signed it, "Yours in sport, Jim Bouton."[12]

Bouton said that when he finished *Ball Four* he knew it was a good book, a funny book, and an honest book. Somebody later accused him of being only 97 percent honest. Hard to figure out what that meant. But he was aware that the baseball establishment was not used to such honesty, with the word as a synonym for being outspoken. "It didn't take any superbrain to know that baseball and baseball players weren't used to 97 percent honesty, maybe not even 50 percent," Bouton said.[13]

Bouton's diary-keeping in Seattle was actually cut short when he was shipped to the Houston Astros in August. He began the 1970 season with the Astros, but was 4–6 with a 5.40 earned run average when he was optioned to the minors.

That summer, Bouton began floating comments about what the book contained so he could get some attention flowing and people would be teased into buying it. "I was going to write a book when I got famous," he said. "But I couldn't wait any longer." Also, "If the book was a movie, it would be rated X."[14]

Ball Four made its debut in the dearly-departed *Look* magazine. Bouton was quite nervous by the time his words showed up in print, partially because he was not pitching well and was afraid his career was going to come to a screeching halt. He talked to some friends in the game and asked what they thought might happen. Essentially, he was told that it all depended on how he was pitching at the time. If he was throwing poorly, he was going to be in trouble. "If I was a winning pitcher I could be Jack The Ripper in my spare time and people would pat me on the head," Bouton said he realized.[15]

Only Bouton was pitching like Jack the Ripper.

For a while he was paranoid that he was demoted because of the furor surrounding *Ball Four* and then had to face the fact that his pitching was lousy enough on its own merit for him to be sent down. That's when Bouton went into TV. It was likely his Major League pitching career was kaput.

Strangely, and remarkably, Bouton did surface briefly with the Atlanta Braves in 1978, brandishing his knuckleball, but finished only 1–3. A big-league comeback after eight years was very unusual, but it didn't last. For that matter, the TV gig didn't last either, at least not as a long-term, full-time career. Bouton was still hot, though, because *Ball Four* was a smash. He lectured at colleges, which in the 1970s were where non-conformists hung out.

Bouton was brutally straightforward in *Ball Four*, writing down what he thought. When a player talks the way Bouton wrote during the course of a season, the sportswriters and sportscasters dissect every word, put a spin on it and pass judgment on it. Bouton was damning in many ways, but he didn't mention his thoughts aloud while the Pilots were playing out their only season. Everyone got to read about it, including Seattle management and his teammates, a year later.

For one thing, Bouton, who has spent most of his life in the northeastern part of the United States, said he could not stand listening to first baseman Don Mincher speak because he talked with a Southern accent. Mincher, who passed away in 2012, was from Huntsville, Alabama. "I keep hearing that big southern accent of his," Bouton said. "It's prejudice, I know, but every time I hear a southern accent, I think: Stupid. A picture of George Wallace pops into my mind. It's like Lenny Bruce [the comedian] saying he could never associate a nuclear scientist with a southern accent." While acknowledging that surely there were baseball players who disliked his northern accent, Bouton added, "I've often thought that the best way to get through professional baseball is never to let on you have an education."[16]

Bouton had crossed the age DMZ into his 30s, was fighting to keep his career alive, and despised rookies with potential on the Pilots. One of them, named Dick Baney, had a fastball that made Bouton jealous. He said he hated him. Baney told Bouton that he once wrote him a fan letter and Bouton didn't answer it. Bouton didn't remember it, but thought it could well have happened years earlier. "When did you write it?" Bouton said. "When I was about six," Baney said. "If there's one thing I hate, it's a smart-ass rookie," Bouton wrote.[17]

Bouton's second book was popular, too, though not on the 100-must-read baseball books of all time. His third effort was mostly writing the introduction to a book about managers, though he brought his own style to the effort and added personal comments about each. "I could never be a big-league manager," Bouton wrote. "One reason is that no one would let me have it. Another reason is that I wouldn't want the job. It seems to me that managers are lonely and that their lives aren't exciting enough."[18] Bouton said that he did not want to visit Cincinnati and Cleveland 25 times and thought it was more fun sitting in the back of the bus with teammates drinking beer than sitting up front with coaches.

Bouton said that the all-time best motivational speech he heard was delivered by a minor-league manager. Don Hoak, the one-time third baseman for the Pittsburgh Pirates and a member of that franchise's 1960 World Series club, was managing the AAA Columbus Jets in the International League. Hoak held up his thumb and forefinger and informed his charges that "I just want to remind each and every one of you that you are this far away from big-league pussy."[19]

Bouton felt there were two Leo Durochers, Leo the Good and Leo the Bad. One would have been great to play for and the other not so great. After *Ball Four* came out, Bouton heard that Durocher panned the book without reading it and added that Bouton would never play on one of his teams. Well, that ship had sailed anyway.

The author said that it changed his image of Durocher from a guy who would do anything to win. "I had always felt that Leo would play a convicted rapist if he could turn the double play," Bouton said.[20] Of course, that was in 1973 and Bouton couldn't get away with saying that nowadays, never mind Durocher actually using a player with that stain on his record.

In 2005, while living a completely different life in western Massachusetts, Bouton became involved in an effort to save an old, historic ballpark from destruction. The effort also ended up becoming a diary-type book.

Bouton, on the side of the little man, and on the opposite side from baseball magnates who come to the sport through massively rich corporations and then extort the populace of their team's home cities into shelling out for new stadiums, was motivated by that circumstance. "You are no doubt familiar with America's most costly hostage crisis," he wrote, "perpetrated by the owners of professional sports teams. 'Build us a new stadium,' they warn, 'or you'll never see your team again.'"[21]

Bouton and friends opposed a rich owner who wanted to replace a park where baseball had been played since 1892, under the threat of moving the minor league franchise elsewhere. A battle ensued, politics intervened, but the ball park is still standing and the community does have a team.

Still, Bouton's biggest and everlasting fame is tied to writing *Ball Four*. It remains fun and entertaining 45 years after it was released. Readers might not recall who the players or personalities were, or even who the Seattle Pilots were, but the way the season unfolds is exactly how many think life must be on any hopeless team.

The foibles of bad baseball teams are universal. Pitchers get knocked around. Hitters strike out. Fielders boot ground balls. One major failing of the Seattle Pilots, in pitcher Bouton's mind, was a failure to convert double-plays. At one point, Bouton asked the bullpen what he called a trivia question. "What's it called when you get two out with one ground ball?" Bouton said. Veteran catcher Jim Pagliaroni spoke up. "Wait," he said. "I remember from some of the other clubs I used to be with. I think they called it a double play."[22]

That's what life was like with the 1969 Seattle Pilots. Just ask Jim Bouton.

16. Bo Belinsky

"Chutzpah like that, I never heard of, and he's only half–Jewish."—Los Angeles Angels public relations man Irving Kaze on Bo Belinsky's brashness in holding out for more money as a rookie[1]

PITCHING A NO-HITTER FOR HIS FOURTH WIN in the majors did it. That transformed Bo Belinsky from a rookie only baseball aficionados had heard of into a baseball "star" everyone in Hollywood wanted to meet.

He was young, handsome and a playboy, and Belinsky was quickly linked to starlets as an out-and-about-town, youthful gadabout. He dated actress Mamie Van Doren and drove a Thunderbird convertible. Never shy, Belinsky cultivated fame, fortune and a good time, although not necessarily in that order.

It was 1962 and the world was a different place, awakening from the slumber of the 1950s with radical new ideas on the horizon. Belinsky was already 25 and wise in the ways of the world. He held fascination for beautiful women and it soon became apparent that he was more fascinated with them than he was with pitching.

Belinsky probably milked more fame from minimal diamond contributions than any other player who ever lived. Even in his attention-getting rookie season with the no-hitter, Belinsky finished just 10–11 for the Angels. In parts of eight seasons, the best mark Belinsky recorded was 9–8 in 1964. Lifetime his won-lost record was 28–51.

But boy did he entertain, with his mouth and his exploits. Somehow, for a few short years Belinsky was Hollywood royalty without truly being part of Hollywood at all. Belinsky excelled at the art of mingling and hanging out, of being seen with the right people, and being capable of charming them.

Actually, Belinsky came ready-made to the majors as a player old-timers relished calling "colorful." He just gained a wider audience and following in the big leagues than he had in the minors. Belinsky was fully formed as colorful in the minors, a strange creature recognized for his quirks the moment he opened his mouth.

Belinsky came from Trenton, New Jersey, where his pitching background was quite limited. Eventually, a Pittsburgh Pirates scout found him and signed him. Belinsky received no bonus and thought the deal was for $185 a week. When he read it again he realized it was for $185 a month. With no other career prospects, Belinsky gave pitching a try anyway. "I either go away to play ball or hang around Trenton robbing old ladies of their pocketbooks, or holding up drugstores," he said. "Not literally."[2]

When Belinsky was sent to his first posting in Brunswick, Georgia, he said he packed his pool stick. It is possible that Belinsky was a better pool player than baseball player. "I took my pool cue and that saved me," he said. "Without that I would have been on the corner eating cupcakes. At first I stayed in the Oglethorpe Hotel. It was a ridiculous hotel. I think Andrew Jackson stayed there. I don't challenge the ball players. I take on the town hustlers. I win quarters, halves, that was big money."[3]

Belinsky was better at pool than pitching in those days and was cut. After working in a pottery factory, he joined the independent Alabama-Florida League. The Baltimore Orioles bought his rights, but Belinsky went to the Angels in the expansion draft. Even then he didn't do well in spring training, but somehow made the cut for the new team and got his shot. Life changed completely for Belinsky when he threw his no-hitter.

On May 5, 1962, Belinsky no-hit the Orioles. He took a little bit of satisfaction from it coming against a team that hadn't thought much of him. By then Belinsky was 4–0 and was the toast of L.A.

Certainly, Belinsky made a good first impression. "He could be the best pitcher on our club," said Angels pitching coach Marv Grissom. "His improvement just between his first and second starts for us was amazing. It's up to him, how much he wants to be the best, how hard he works, how well he looks after himself. He has all the tools and he's young. He shouldn't miss if he means business and I think he does."[4]

Grissom's entire analysis was a cautionary tale. Soon enough it was apparent that Belinsky put more energy into hoping things worked out with beautiful babes than he did into working out. It came across that Belinsky's main business was partying after hours. Surely, that was how he was always portrayed in newspapers at the time. He had catapulted from obscurity and sought to take advantage of his instant popularity.

You couldn't really blame him. The southpaw who did not play high school ball and said he never received much instruction as a pro, either, made stops in Brunswick, Georgia, Knoxville, Tennessee, Aberdeen, South Dakota, Amarillo, Texas, Stockton, California, Pensacola, Florida, Vancouver, British Columbia, and Little Rock, Arkansas, before sniffing the majors. Belinsky did credit Grissom's assistance with the Angels.

At times Belinsky was wild on the mound with those clubs. And at times he was wild off the mound. In Vancouver he punched someone who stole his coat. His mistake was using his left, pitching hand. "Heck, you know southpaw pitchers aren't too bright," he said.[5]

Belinsky was 6-foot-2, weighed 187 pounds, and relied on a fastball, curve and screwball. Some people read extra meaning into that last-mentioned pitch. He also signed for $6,000 in 1962, under penalty of being sent back to Little Rock. The no-hitter only weeks later solidified his status. "It was just one of those nights when nothing could go wrong," Belinsky said. "The Orioles just happened to get in the way."[6]

After he pitched the no-hitter, Belinsky's profile expanded and he made a deal for a replacement vehicle, upgrading to a bright red Cadillac convertible that was often seen on Sunset Strip. The combination of Belinsky's big-league renown and the flashy automobile made him a chick magnet.

Even *The Sporting News*, once published a story about Belinsky that was accompanied by photographs of him with Mamie Van Doren, a lesser-known, bikini-clad woman on a beach, and *Playboy* "Playmate of the Year" for 1965 Jo Collins, who became his wife. At other times he was seen squiring around Ann-Margret, Tina Louise, and Connie Stevens.

"I'm socially sharp," Belinsky said once.[7] He might have been winking; he might not. "It was a totally different world. I think everyone in their lifetime should have the experience of being a star in Los Angeles for one year. It was quite a town and it was mine for one year. That is something money couldn't buy."[8]

It was ironic that Belinsky threw his no-hitter against the Orioles. Some members of the team were old friends, notably Steve Barber, who talked to Belinsky before the game when he was 3–0, but still somewhat mortal. "I thought the only thing you ever did in the minors was chase broads," Barber said. "When did you have time to learn how to pitch?" Belinsky responded, "I didn't. It's just that the hitters up here are all fishcakes."[9] Fishcakes? That probably sent numerous readers running to their dictionaries. Somehow it translated.

Dean Chance, who later won a Cy Young Award as the best pitcher in the American League, was Belinsky's best friend in the game, and that dated back to the minors. "He was the guy giving everybody the hotfoot," Chance said of Belinsky in spring training of 1959. "He never ate. He lived on coffee and cigarettes. I had to laugh when he was big in L.A." Chance recalled a sandwich place creating a "Bo Special" named after Belinsky with meats, cheeses, tomatoes "and the works. The last guy to ever eat one would be Bo."[10]

Chance said Belinsky's reputation as a ladies man was well-earned.

> Nobody made it with girls the way Bo did. I never learned his secret. I just enjoyed watching him operate. When I roomed with him it was like rooming with a suitcase. I'd never see Bo at night. Into a town and gone. Albie Pearson [the Angels outfielder] roomed with him and said he had two jobs, one playing baseball, the other as Bo Belinsky's answering service."[11]

Belinsky and Van Doren were quite the visible couple and they announced their engagement. They never did marry, though. Belinsky's top-notch pitching lasted for only half a season before he slumped into that record of one game under .500. In 1963, Angels management shipped Belinsky back to the minors for a time. "Don't put the blame on Mamie," Belinsky said. "It's my teammates who just don't get me no runs."[12]

On one occasion with the Angels, the club had a team charter to New York. Besides the players and manager Bill Rigney, other passengers included Gene Autry, the famous singing cowboy who was the team owner, and general manager Fred Haney. When the staircase was lowered, a limousine pulled up. Autry, Haney and Rigney approached the car and Haney commented, "Now that's what I call service!" But the driver said, "This car isn't for you." A window in the limo rolled down and a beautiful, wealthy European countess shouted to Belinsky and Chance. "Oh, Bo! Oh, Dean!" The players climbed into the limo and left dumbfounded management standing in place and steaming.[13]

Chance said he was more bystander than participant as Los Angeles went wild for Bo. He said his reputation had preceded him to Angels camp and he lived up to his image. "Bo always had broads around, always," Chance said. "But after the no-hitter they were just better looking and a little more famous."[14]

Walter Winchell, the Hollywood gossip columnist, jumped on the Belinsky train early, and his notes in columns about Belinsky made him a hot topic in the celluloid town. Chance said that Winchell and Belinsky became friends. While teammates might have become jealous by the attention Belinsky received and his swinging ways, Chance insisted they did not, but were merely amused by their fellow pitcher's lifestyle.

Once, the team returned from an east coast road trip in the middle

Bo Belinsky (right), pictured with his Angels manager, Bill Rigney, was a passing comet on the baseball scene. He pitched a no-hitter as a rookie, dated Hollywood starlets, and was a chatterbox with sportswriters.

of the night, and when the players disembarked from the plane Winchell was there waiting for Bo with a trio of beautiful women. Chance said Belinsky didn't even bother to pick up his luggage, asking someone on the team to do so, and then disappeared into the night (or morning).

"As they walked off, everybody cheered," Chance said.[15]

When it came to parties, whether it was a small, cozy one in a hotel room, or a much larger one in a hotel ballroom, Belinsky never minded celebrations. "I had always liked champagne parties," Belinsky said. "I can't remember where I had my first one. I know it wasn't in Trenton. No one ever heard of champagne back there."[16]

When Belinsky was in prime night-owl form he prompted a baseball insider to speculate on whether playing the sport would shorten his career. The Angels put together a network of informants to rat him out when he was in night clubs too late.

In those days players made so little money it wasn't easy for Belinsky to stay up with his spending habits. He went to Venezuela to pitch winter ball and collect a little bit more cash. "I only turn out to be the most fabulous, colorful, goddamn pitcher in history down there," Belinsky said. "And for the money they give me they could take a chance on an infant. They could take a chance on a one-armed pitcher. I went down for $525 and expenses, and I set an all-time strikeout record down there and the all-time woman record!"[17]

Belinsky did hang out with women he had just met more frequently than teammates he spent the summer with. But he could be gracious. When Leon "Daddy Wags" Wagner hit a home run in a game Belinsky was pitching, Wagner said Belinsky showed him props. "I hit a home run for Bo and he said, 'Thank you, dad. Tha'ss beautiful. When I get a raise I'll drop you a few bucks.'"[18]

More than once the Angels told Belinsky to tone down his lifestyle. At times Belinsky even acknowledged that might be a smart thing to do for the good of his baseball career. But he also wondered about what one writer termed "the ravages of rest."

> I was going against the law of nature there for a little while. That nightlife was like cocaine on the brain. I go that way I'll wind up with cancer and TB. You know, it's a funny thing. I've gone a few times with no sleep at all and I come out and get 17 strikeouts. This is the first time I caught some sleep, but I wake up this morning with a goddamn sore throat and a lousy cold.[19]

Incidents like the brass being shown up by the limo, and punching a sportswriter (not so funny), combined with declining pitching results, made it easy for the Angels to send Belinsky to the minors and eventually on to the Philadelphia Phillies. Philadelphia was near Trenton, Belinsky's home, but he did not seem terribly nostalgic after living with the bright lights of the L.A. celebrity scene. "Philadelphia? A few of my friends been knifed there," he said.[20]

The 1964 Phillies are remembered for suffering through one of the great pennant-race collapses of all time over the last two weeks of the season. In the off-season they acquired Belinsky as well as ex–Pittsburgh Pirates slugging first baseman Dick Stuart. Stuart, it so happened, drove a gold Cadillac, somewhat complementary to Belinsky's red Cadillac. "We're sort of compatible," Belinsky observed.[21]

Stuart made it seem so. Stuart was viewed as a powerful slugger, but a terrible fielder who acquired the nickname, "Dr. Strangeglove." "Too bad I wasn't with the club last year. They could have blamed the whole thing on me," said Stuart.[22]

Belinsky was such a committed bachelor in the majors and attracted so much attention from writers who built his image that many married teammates did not want to go out with him. They felt that their wives would hear about it and be disturbed, even if they did nothing but sit and drink a few beers with Bo.

Many years later the baseball-football star Bo Jackson had an advertising deal that as its theme promoted the notion of "Bo Knows." The theme of an advertising campaign with basketball star Michael Jordan was "Be Like Mike." What Stuart learned as Belinsky's teammate was that while the sport's administrators despised Belinsky's behavior, players wanted to "Be Like Bo." "Just going by clubhouse talk," Stuart said, "probably all ball players wish they could be in his shoes."[23]

The Phillies remained pennant-less after Belinsky and Stuart joined the team. They wanted to be the guys who brought a world championship to town. Belinsky envisioned it. "Why, we'll put a dome over the goddamn river," he said, "and we'll make man-made waves and nobody will ever be able to bum-rap Philly again."[24]

Belinsky realized life would be different in staid Philadelphia compared to the Left Coast. He had made some money in endorsements with the Angels when he was a hot commodity. In Philly, not so much. Switching planets was going to take some getting used to for him.

"No guy should be sent to L.A. without the proper orientation course," Belinsky said. "When I saw all these broads around here, I was like a kid in a toy shop." When asked what happened, he said, "What happened? I lost the war."[25] Belinsky went out on the town in L.A. with teammates. One night he and other Angels went to the show at the Cocoanut Grove and Belinsky was invited onstage to introduce the players. "Who got this idea, I don't know," Bo said. "Someone must have sized up me up as the Polish Ed Sullivan."[26]

Belinsky did not pitch well in Philadelphia. Nor did he make much of a mark in cameo appearances with the Houston Astros, Pittsburgh Pirates or Cincinnati Reds. By the dawn of the new decade, Belinsky was nearly finished with the majors. Fortunately for him he had had a stint in Hawaii, where he took up surfing and decided he liked the environs. That's where he later settled.

Belinsky married Collins, the *Playboy* model, a union that lasted about six years, until 1975. He previously had been engaged to Van Doren for about seven months. They remained friends. "Our life was a circus," Van Doren said. "We were engaged on April Fool's Day and we broke the engagement on Halloween. It was a wild ride, but it was fun."[27]

Van Doren visited Belinsky at spring training in Clearwater, Florida, when he hooked up with the Phillies. Up until then Belinsky said he had been in his room at 9 p.m. regularly. That's because he considered Clearwater to be a boring, senior-citizen town. "It's a restful place," he said. "It's a great place if you take Serutan [a fiber laxative product]."[28]

In 1969, Belinsky was on his fifth comeback try, this time with the Pirates, following a 12–5 run with their Hawaii AAA club. The baseball did not take, but his marriage to Collins did, for a while. "I'm an amateur when it comes to love," Belinsky said. "Frankly, it gives me a nervous stomach, but I like it."[29]

By the mid–1970s, however, Belinsky realized he had a problem with substance abuse, alcohol and drugs. His marriage ended, but in 1976 he went clean and sober and stayed that way.

Belinsky relocated to Las Vegas, and when he died of a heart attack at 64 in 2001, the former pitcher had been suffering with a variety of ailments.

Long into baseball retirement, Bo Belinsky understood that he became as famous as any pitcher could have whose lifetime stat line read 28–51. "I probably got more out of 28 victories than any major leaguer who played the game," Belinsky said. "Anybody can be a known star if he wins 300 games. Let him try to be a known star winning only 28 games. I did it."[30]

17. Tug McGraw

> "He had a special spirit. The way he pounded his glove, the way he pounded his heart. He was one of the most memorable personalities I've ever met. He loved Philadelphia and Philadelphia loved him."—*Philadelphia Phillies board chairman Bill Giles*[1]

TWICE AN ICON ON CHAMPIONSHIP TEAMS, the reliever with the endearing hand twitch signifying his swiftly beating heart, Tug McGraw played baseball like a kid, meaning he always had fun.

McGraw named the 1973 theme of the run to the National League pennant for the New York Mets, proclaiming, "You Gotta Believe." And in 1980, when he registered the last out versus the Kansas City Royals for the Philadelphia Phillies, McGraw leapt so high he almost touched the sky. He was also part of the Mets' 1969 title team.

One thing about the southpaw closer was that he always believed. He kept clubhouses loose with his attitude and he was one of the world's great positive thinkers, even after he was afflicted with the brain tumor that killed him in 2004.

Even under pressure, in the tensest of situations which those late-inning relievers tend to find themselves in all of the time, McGraw would joke on the mound with teammates who strolled over from their infield spots to calm him down. "Can this get any hairier?" McGraw said if the bases were jammed. "You think I tried to do this?" The man for whom the description "free-spirited" was invented added, "If you can't make fun of yourself, who can you make fun of?"[2]

McGraw, who was born in California in 1944, made his Major League debut with the Mets in 1965, but was up and down between the big club and the minors for several years. He did not do himself any favors with managers who did not think he took the game seriously enough. Mets administrators were not particularly fond of his dog Pucci, either.

The hurler literally did ask how much is that doggie in the window. "I was on my way to barber college when I saw her in a window," McGraw said. "I went in and asked how much and the man said $10, so I bought her."³ The pooch called Pucci ripped up the flower bed outside the window of general manager Johnny Murphy's office and went to the bathroom outside coach Joe Pignatano's apartment.

One major leaguer managed by Casey Stengel, who could at least identify with McGraw's approach to life, was Mets manager Gil Hodges, who became most concerned about McGraw's maturity. "It was common knowledge that the guy was happy-go-lucky," Hodges said, "a little flighty, up in the air, not concentrating enough."⁴

Hodges had an argument. After all, McGraw was caught in the act of dropping balloons filled with water out of his hotel window. McGraw wanted to set up his camper in the Mets' parking lot as his in-season home, but was informed that zoning laws forbade it.

Actually, acting out with his big jump on the mound after securing the final out in the World Series was nothing new for McGraw, since during his days in the minors he behaved in a similar manner. When excited by an on-field development, McGraw liked to jump up and down on the mound like a kid on a pogo stick.

Initially, McGraw was going to be a starter for the Mets, but that didn't take and they had others who controlled that role, from future Hall of Famers Tom Seaver and Nolan Ryan to Jerry Koosman. After a few years, McGraw gravitated to the bullpen, and that is where he turned in his best work. Three times McGraw posted earned run averages under 2.00. He won 96 games and saved 180.

The world at large started to get to know McGraw in 1973, when his Mets were playing shaky ball and he inspired their comeback roll into the playoffs and on to the World Series, where they lost in seven games to the Oakland Athletics. That is when he coined the "Ya Gotta Believe" phrase that lives on in New York baseball lore.

By 1972, it was obvious that if McGraw ever started a game again it would be by accident. His only job for the first six or so innings was to stay alert in the Mets' bullpen. However, he did not even do that, instead resting up for big finishes.

"In the early innings, I fall asleep down here a lot," he said of the pen. "The bathroom is a good place. Put a couple of towels on the floor and get a pillow. It's nice and cool in there. Or in the golf cart with the big Mets' cap for a roof. But by the sixth or seventh inning I'm always awake. I start sniffing out those saves."⁵

McGraw also revealed that he often brought a snack to sustain him during the early innings, frequently barbecued spare ribs.

New York being New York, it made perfect sense to non-residents that the team had to install a protective screen over where the catchers caught the relievers' warm-ups in the Shea Stadium bullpen, though McGraw offered a defense. "Fans were throwing beer cans, beer, peanuts," he said. "Somebody even threw a big hunk of cement. It couldn't have been our fans. Must've been somebody else's fans."[6]

The 6-foot, 170-pound McGraw was beloved in New York, so they couldn't have been aiming at him. McGraw got by on a fastball, a curve, and a screwball. After being sent to the minors to learn another pitch—the screwball—when McGraw was brought back to New York, at first the manager and coaches wouldn't let him throw it and catchers wouldn't call it. Eventually, the screwball came to define his persona as well as his repertoire.

As proof of that New York popularity, McGraw's well-appreciated sense of humor got him into the cartoon business. With a partner named Mike Witte and a couple of other writers, McGraw developed a syndicated comic strip called "Scroogie." The panels were about baseball and the main character was "Scroogie," an alter ego for McGraw.

In one strip, Scroogie responds to a fan letter by saying, "Well, fellas, they call me Scroogie because my best pitch is a screwball." As Scroogie heads to the mailbox he thinks out loud: "That and the fact I'm a little nuts."[7]

In another strip, Scroogie is on a plane flying to spring training. "Well, here's to the new season," he says. "And here's to nine noble men of different race, creed and color, who labor together for a common ideal—even when many among them don't speak the same language." Pause. "Sort of like the U.S. Supreme Court."[8]

Drifting to the fan world, one strip focuses on a ball park spectator's passion for hot dogs. "I love ball park hot dogs!" he says. "I love the way they wrap 'em! I love the way they sell 'em! I love the way they taste! I love the texture, the smell, the feel! In fact, as far as I'm concerned, there's only one teeny-weenie thing they could do to make 'em better…. Cook 'em."[9]

The comic strip was such a smash that it kept running after a first baseball season and a second book came out, adding to Scroogie's fame.

While with the Phillies, one of McGraw's teammates was catcher Tim McCarver, who later enjoyed a lengthy broadcasting career. McCarver casually remarked that Tug and Scroogie reminded him of each other. McGraw made the silly mistake of asking if that was because they were both cool under pressure. McCarver said, "No, because whenever I see either of you on the pitcher's mound, I have to laugh."[10]

McGraw was good at making people laugh. In a strip in the second book, a pitcher is throwing a no-hitter and thinking of the spoils he would receive upon completion. "Just three more outs, guys. Don't fail me now!" he shouts. "You know what this no-hitter means to me!" A voice out of the scene replies, "A plaque next to Koufax in Cooperstown?" The pitcher's turn: "A seat next to Johnny on the Carson Show."[11]

The name on McGraw's birth certificate was Frank Edwin McGraw. As a baby, while breast-feeding him, his mother called him a little bit of a tugger, and the shortened version of that stuck. Somehow, his older brother Hank, who also was a fine baseball player during 12 years in the minors, escaped that kind of odd nickname fate.

For the longest time, McGraw didn't know what being part of Organized Baseball was about since he was so disorganized. "I have been organized only to the extent that the catcher has put down one, two, or three fingers—and I have thrown what he asked for," McGraw said.[12] He admitted that being on time was not necessarily one of his strengths, and that included getting to the ballpark at a specific time.

As a kid, McGraw wanted to be a fireman when he grew up. Hence, the picturing of the baseball-playing McGraw in a red fireman's helmet after he became a relief pitcher, which at the time was routinely referred to as being a "fireman." The baseball version was an analogy for the pitchers who came in and shut down the hot team.

McGraw's ambition changed when he became a fan of Mickey Mantle and Willie Mays. "I just love being a Major League player," McGraw said. "It may be a right-handed world, but I happen to think that the southpaws have a place in it somewhere."[13]

After occasionally being told that he behaved too immaturely and that was holding back his pitching career, McGraw served some time in the U.S. Marine Corps. That stint made him realize that others were probably right and he needed to shift his mindset. "They've taught me concentration and self-control," McGraw said of his 1960s Marines stay. "I used to go out there and jump around on the mound and wave my arms. I was pretty Little League-ish. You've got to go out there with a big-league attitude."[14]

Well, he was not completely cured of impish actions, but he did reserve them for special occasions.

For as fun-loving a guy as McGraw was, he did not have a happy childhood in northern California. His parents bickered, broke up, and eventually his mother, who suffered from mental illness, left the family. "Sports saved me," McGraw said. "My dad always encouraged us to play sports." While a great athlete when they were young, Tug's older brother (by 18 months) did not make the majors. "Funnily, he says he couldn't have been the athlete he was if I hadn't been there to compete with him. I never believed that, but he says it. He also has long said that when he saw me on the mound during Major League games, he felt like he was there with me, as if we were one."[15]

Once he reached the majors, McGraw, who was likely to be looking for a good time wherever he was or wherever he worked, took advantage of the lifestyle of a big-league ball player. "When I was with the Mets and Phillies, off the field culture was about 75 percent booze and tomatoes [women] and 10 percent drugs and other recreational treats," McGraw said.[16] "Now I'm not trying to sound like Wilt Chamberlain, but I usually did all right in the tomato department. When it came to that type of produce, I was always able to pick one out of the bunch."[17]

This was in the 1960s and 1970s, during the heart of the sexual revolution and when no one had yet heard of AIDS.

Even earlier, when McGraw was playing minor league ball in Jacksonville, he had an affair with a woman he met in the laundry room in his apartment complex. When she became pregnant, she went home to Louisiana. She gave birth to a son named Tim, who until the age of 11 believed that his step-father was his biological father. Then Tim found his birth certificate.

Tim's mother brought him to meet Tug, but the pitcher refused to acknowledge he was the father. Seven years later, when he saw how much the 18-year-old Tim resembled him, he accepted paternity. Eventually, father and son did develop a solid relationship and became close. Coincidental with that, Tim McGraw became one of the most successful and popular country singers in the world.

During his stay with the New York Mets, Tug McGraw recalled being thoroughly battered by the Pirates in depressing fashion. He was headed back to his hotel, but because the next day was a day off he changed his mind and detoured to a bar where he got stinking drunk. "I got so smashed I walked voluntarily into the police department and asked them to lock me up," McGraw said.[18] At first the officer he encountered refused, but apparently he was drunk enough to make his case and they did put him in a cell for the night.

After the Phillies won the 1980 World Series and McGraw played a key role, he was invited to appear on David Letterman's talk show. The producers said Letterman wanted to talk about drugs in baseball. McGraw said he would not go on if that was the topic. He would talk baseball. They agreed. But when he actually took his turn on the air, Letterman asked several questions about drug use amongst baseball players. McGraw was angry because he felt the pre-show deal had been violated.

Finally, McGraw said that he could name a player who took a brown pill. It was George Brett of the American League champion Kansas City Royals. Once he whetted the appetite of the host and the audience, McGraw said it was a suppository for hemorrhoids. "They went to a commercial break and I walked off the set," McGraw said.[19]

As the Phillies stormed to their first National League pennant since 1950 and claimed their first world title, McGraw was a key player as the ace relief man. His two trademarks on the mound became recognized by all baseball fans. He slapped his glove against his thigh and tapped his chest over his heart when he escaped close calls.

After being a star in New York for the Mets, a team that advanced to the seventh game of the 1973 World Series, McGraw was surprised when he was traded to the Phillies in December of 1974. "I had been traded down the New Jersey Turnpike to Philadelphia," McGraw said of the six-player deal.[20]

In 1980, the Phillies had to get past the Houston Astros in the National League Championship Series to reach the World Series. There were some tense moments and close calls. "It was like riding through an art gallery on a motorcycle," McGraw said.[21]

As Game Six of the World Series came down to McGraw pitching to Kansas City's Willie Wilson, security at Veterans Stadium, in the form of police on horseback, began ringing the field in a show of strength. The idea was to intimidate the crowd of 66,000 to stay in their seats instead of running onto the field. McGraw looked to one sideline and noticed one police horse taking a crap. "All of a sudden this horse lifts its tail and drops a big mud pie," McGraw said. "Right there. A strange sight to see before pitching the final out of the World Series, you know. I saw that happen and I just thought, 'Hmm, if I don't get out of this inning that's what I'm going to be in this city. I'm going to be horse s—t.'"[22]

Of course, McGraw made the clutch pitches and helped win the World Series crown for Philadelphia. That made him more popular than ever. McGraw signed every autograph he could, sometimes organizing the lines himself. He admitted he was "a flake," a common description of guys who are slightly off-kilter, but he didn't consider it an insult. Once when McGraw read in a Florida newspaper during spring training that a writer

Although relief pitcher Tug McGraw (left) and fellow pitcher Jerry Koosman look pretty hungry, McGraw was not known for his eating habits. A star closer for the Mets and Phillies, McGraw created his own comic strip in the funny pages for two years.

called him "a fruitcake," as in nutty as a fruitcake, he did not become indignant. Rather, he said, "Geez, I wasn't sure if that was a compliment or not."[23]

McGraw had the ability to make people laugh along with him, and he could laugh at himself. The winter after he was clobbered by the Pirates he was invited to speak at a Pittsburgh sports banquet. The organizers had the two Pirates players who had bombed him pick him up at the airport, and on the banquet program he was listed as "Pittsburgh Pirates batting practice pitcher."[24] It was pretty funny and McGraw laughed.

When McGraw retired from baseball in 1985 after 17 Major League seasons and 824 regular season games, he stayed in Philadelphia. Among his later activities was working for a local television station and doing some acting. He once played himself in an episode of "Everybody Loves Raymond."

17. Tug McGraw

McGraw was working as a spring training instructor for the Phillies in March of 2003 when he was hospitalized with a brain tumor. When he was diagnosed, a doctor told him he had just three weeks to live. That was one of the few times in his adult life McGraw didn't feel like laughing.

"I love to laugh," McGraw said. "Almost as much as I like to make others laugh. I've often joked that I am left-handed in every way, including my screwy sense of humor. But one of the downsides of living life as an unpredictable jokester is that when something's wrong, even those closest to you aren't sure when to take it seriously."[25]

This was that time. McGraw underwent surgery and at first it was announced that the cancer had been removed and he should get back to normal. However, that prognosis was incorrect, and McGraw passed away less than a year later.

The stilling of such a joyful voice was a sad experience for anyone who had met Tug McGraw during his many years in baseball.

18. Harry Caray

> "We don't need a house dog as our announcer. I think Caray is too great an asset to leave the city, particularly since the White Sox need assets. He is not always kindly, but is never dull."—*Chicago White Sox owner Bill Veeck upon hiring Harry Caray as a broadcaster*[1]

HE HAD A BIG MOUTH AND HE WAS PROUD OF IT. Harry Caray also had big glasses that became one of his trademarks.

There probably has never been a baseball announcer who had as much fun broadcasting the game to his audience and somehow made it clear over the airwaves. Harry Caray has been gone for 19 years now, but his name lives on with tradition at Wrigley Field during every seventh-inning stretch when a daily guest sings "Take Me Out to the Ballgame," and with the Chicago restaurant that bears his name. Somehow the food and spirits that are served in his name have outlived his voice. Even though the food is of high quality, that is a shame because the Harry Caray gravelly call of a game was something to savor.

The greatest irony of Caray's career and legacy is that he did not really want to lead the crowd in singing that old musical staple of the game, but White Sox owner Bill Veeck practically held him up against the wall to make him do it. Sure enough, it became an enduring connection to Caray, one which he carried across town to the Chicago Cubs, and which endures in tribute to this day. Strange how things work out.

Caray, who was born Harry Christopher Carabina in 1914, and adopted the more convenient Caray in the broadcast world, was one of baseball's great radio personalities. He made his reputation with the St. Louis Cardinals, spent a year with the Oakland Athletics, then became a Chicago institution, first with the White Sox and then with the Cubs.

Growing up in a tough neighborhood in St. Louis, Caray knew he had a face for radio. Later, some critics said Caray did not even have a voice for radio. He served apprenticeships in small markets and although baseball was his forte, Caray also later broadcast University of Missouri football, St. Louis University basketball, and even the NBA St. Louis Hawks games.

Long before Howard Cosell adopted the phrase "telling it like it is," Caray was a blunt man on the air. He took over St. Louis Cardinals broadcasts in 1945 and also managed to handle the St. Louis Browns games in 1945 and 1946.

He was not a broadcaster who schmoozed with players and became their buddies. He was more likely to alienate the home squad with his directness. If players made errors or pitchers got shelled, he did not sugar-coat. Caray seemed to possess a brilliant talent for selling beer, however, and with a Cardinals' main sponsor/owner being Budweiser/Anheuser-Busch, that was an important knack.

Caray's No. 1 broadcast trademark, a phrase that let the listener know that something special was going on, was "Holy cow!" The story went that Caray could not stand working with A's owner Charlie Finley, renowned for meddling with employees' assignments, for more than one season. Supposedly, his tolerance level boiled over when Finley wanted him to change his catch-phrase to "Holy mule!" Finley owned a mule that sometimes roamed the premises. He called it his mascot and named it Charlie-O. Well, it turned out Caray was more stubborn than the boss. That's how he came to work in Chicago.

Caray did not soften his ways in discussing White Sox players—hence Veeck's reference to his announcer's occasional shortage of kindliness. He also blitzed through broadcast partners at an alarming rate.

In some derring-do uniqueness, Caray occasionally chose to broadcast White Sox games from the bleachers, going shirtless at the same time to work on his tan. In this button-downed era of political correctness, it is difficult to imagine an announcer acting in that manner. Of course, Caray worked for Veeck, the most colorful owner in history. If Caray made news and made fans chortle, it was okay with Veeck.

Caray's popularity also transcended the ballpark crowd. He was notorious for taking advantage of Chicago night life, a denizen of the Rush Street bars or anywhere else they were serving late. Caray was no anonymous guy behind the microphone. White Sox fans could recognize him a mile away. He may well have shared a beer with them. In those days they called Caray "The Mayor of Rush Street."

When Caray accepted the Cubs job, it easily tripled his renown. Only the Cubs and the Atlanta Braves were linked to a cable television station beaming games into homes all over the land. With the Cubs also playing all, then most, of their games during the day, they acquired a wide and peculiar constituency. Baseball fans in other time zones could conveniently watch the Cubs, and they all got to know Harry Caray and the seventh-inning stretch ritual.

"Take Me Out to the Ballgame" is one of the most frequently played and sung songs across America. But Caray's regular home-game perpetuation of the tradition helped spread its popularity anew. It was not that Caray was a great vocalist, but his enthusiasm and his band-leader-style swinging the microphone was a treat. Caray was as much leader as singer, opening the radio booth window and letting the crowd's energy take over. He kicked off each performance with "All right. Lemme hear ya! Ah-one, ah-two, ah-three." At the end of the song, Caray would cry out, "Let's get some runs!"

Caray was such an overwhelming personality, and a broadcaster who could easily run off the rails with personal stories about his life out and about in Chicago, or merely digressing about the weather, that he did not always mesh well with other top-notch broadcasters who had more success and comfort elsewhere. For a time he partnered with Jimmy Piersall, who could be as much of a loose cannon as Caray, but Caray's settle-him-down partner for a while at the end of his life was Steve Stone.

There is little accounting for chemistry in the broadcast booth, but usually the bosses and the fans know when things click. Some might complain that there are plenty of homogenized voices in pro sports broadcasting today, but Caray was never confused with anyone else wielding a mike. When he came on the air to start a game, his signature greeting was "Hal-low everybody." Millions of Cubs fans can still hear that phrase rolling around in their heads.

It never was made clear why the Cardinals dumped Caray after a quarter of a century. The spokesmen at the time shied away from any direct comment, calling his dismissal "a marketing decision."[2] Infuriated by his firing, Caray went out and bought a six-pack of Schlitz beer so that when reporters wielding cameras came around seeking comment, he would be seen drinking the competition's product. It was a tiny measure of revenge that was very transient.

Later, Caray and Anheuser-Busch had a rapprochement and he sold the beer by the millions of kegs in Chicago. He even admitted that the brewery made him a rich man through his stock ownership. And, despite that one-time Schlitz aberration, Caray also conceded that when he drank beer it was Bud, and that's what he kept at home. "Hell, I'm a millionaire just on Anheuser-Busch stock," he said.[3]

For many years, the St. Louis Cardinals were the westernmost and southernmost Major League club. Even after baseball moved to the West Coast, Cardinals games were beamed all across the South, holding a sound monopoly before the Milwaukee Braves moved to Atlanta in 1966, and maintained a strong foothold in the mid-southern states for some time.

Caray said that once he was in a hotel room and received a call from a Memphis supporter who said he grew up listening to his Cardinals calls. He said he was Elvis Presley. "Harry Caray, I'm a great fan of yours," the voice on the phone told Caray.[4] He initially did not believe it, but came around when the man said to meet him in the lobby in ten minutes. It was indeed Elvis. Caray invited Presley to a game, but the singer declined, saying the fans would go wild. After the game, Caray went to Presley's house and they sat around drinking beer and eating ribs until 5:30 a.m. Elvis even sang a couple of songs. They later did that kind of thing all over again in Las Vegas. President Bill Clinton, who is from Arkansas, was another Caray fan growing up.

Caray hit 50 years in the broadcast booth in 1994 and said at the time, "I hope to do 50 more."[5] Not quite, but he did top out at an impressive 54 years.

For some it seemed somewhat miraculous that Caray, with his carousing habits ingrained and unlikely to be found in bed before 4 a.m., thrived in the industry as long as he did. "I like to go to a bar," said Caray, who was married three times. "I like to talk with the bartender. I like to make friends with the people at the bar. I've learned more from my business by listening to guys in bars who are the guys who listen [to his broadcasts]. I love it."[6]

It may not have been smooth as silk, and indeed Caray called his own voice "a whiskey baritone," but he bonded with the fans and they loved what he said.[7]

A *Boston Globe* writer undertook the scientific challenge of trying to describe Caray's voice.

> Anatomically, it begins somewhere in the bowels, where it's been soaking in plenty of that cold Budweiser. It climbs to his chest, looking like Indiana Jones scaling the cliff at the end of "The Temple of Doom." Then it coughs up the lozenge-lined throat, swirls in the mouth, meets in the center, and zap!—like the Death Star Weapon in "Star Wars"—through the microphone. Past the teeth, over the gums, look out Cubbies, here it comes.[8]

Well, that was certainly a game try. Whew. Caray amplified.

"You can call it a whiskey baritone at times," Caray said of his voice. "I remember the man I first auditioned with some 40 years ago describing it as having 'an exciting timbre to it.'"[9] Others took a crack at it. One anonymous broadcaster said of Caray's voice, "It sounds like a guy who got hit in the throat with a shovel and never recovered."[10]

Caray was liable to say anything about anybody in a uniform, depending on what happened on the field. Cubs catcher Jody Davis once prompted Caray to make an analogy between him and Davy Crockett, particularly the song that accompanied the old television show about the 19th-century pioneer. "Jo-dy, Jody Davis, catcher that knows no fear," Caray sang. Keeping with the theme, when Davis hit a foul ball back to the broadcast booth, Caray added, "Jo-dy, Jody Davis, his foul balls land in Harry's beer."[11]

Sometimes in the middle of a game Caray would simply drop the play-by-play doings and tell radio listeners about someone at the game from out of town. He once had President Ronald Reagan in the booth with him during the action.

Caray was so popular in Chicago that fans followed his movements as if he was Miss America on a visit. They monitored him when he went on a diet that included giving up booze for a while. Instead of drinking his usual beers or martini in 1982, he guzzled ice tea. One sportswriter noted that Caray mentioned his liquid refreshment switch seven times during an interview. During that same interview, which took place in Arizona as spring training was getting underway, Caray commented that he did not believe Tony LaRussa was qualified to be a big-league manager. LaRussa was at the beginning of his managing career, but long after Caray's death he was enshrined in the Baseball Hall of Fame in Cooperstown. Oops.

At the time, long after his role was cemented in Chicago, Caray said of his bitter parting from the Cardinals, "I always tell the story that I was expecting the gold watch and instead they gave me the pink slip."[12]

When he was at the top of his game, Caray earned about $275,000 in broadcast salary and much more from investments. He was a big enough name (thanks also to doing games on NBC) that he was a roast subject in Las Vegas, an event that raised $200,000 for the charity of his choice in 1988, the Maryville Academy in Des Plaines, Illinois, a suburb of Chicago. "This is going to be tougher than my second divorce," Caray said before the roast began with 2,300 people in attendance in Bally's Casino.[13]

Typical of roasts, invitees to the podium got off some good cracks. One came from Jack Buck, who once partnered with Caray in the booth and, it was rumored, did not get along well with him. Commenting on how three chartered planes of attendees showed up from Chicago to pay $100 apiece for this event, Buck said, "We could have held this in Peoria and it would have been a lot cheaper for all of us."[14]

Cubs pitcher Rick Sutcliffe was afraid to let loose, well aware of Caray's acid tongue and his wide audience on WGN Cubs games across the nation. "Do you think I'm going to get up here in front of 3,000 people and roast him when he can roast me next summer in front of 8 million," Sutcliffe said. "Well, if you think the odds are bad in the casino...."[15]

At one point Caray told the organizers to hurry things up so he could go gamble in the casino. On road trips with Chicago teams, Caray often played gin rummy with renowned baseball writer Jerome Holtzman. "What I remember most about these games, which usually lasted until 3 or 4 a.m.," Holtzman said, "is that every time he was about to win a hand he would shout, 'What do you make a martini with?' Pause. 'Gin!'"[16]

Caray was an A-list celebrity in Chicago. He cultivated the attention, true, but even when he was seeking a break from the limelight eating dinner, he was often surrounded by autograph seekers. That was the case when he left the ball yard after a game or when he was merely ready for an off-night main course. Holtzman wrote of being out with his wife and Caray on a Rush Street prowl and "he couldn't take two steps without being stopped. People also shouted greetings from across the street and from second-story windows."[17]

Caray had his troubles. He was hit by a car in St. Louis and said that was the only way he could get his name in the papers there. In Chicago, as Caray aged he had a stroke and everyone hung on the due date of his return.

Receiving the Ford Frick Award at the Baseball Hall of Fame in Cooperstown, New York, in 1989, Carey was a bit surprised. He was honored and even somewhat humbled. "I'm an opinionated guy," he said, "a free speech believer. I stepped on a lot of toes through the years. But I don't care. I'm merely a fan who happens to have a microphone and can express the game. I'm an agent of the fans ... my main source of pride is in pleasing the fans."[18]

Caray said his drinking declined to just a couple of pops a day after his stroke, "instead of 50 or 60 a day."[19] Probably an exaggeration, but there was no question that during Caray's just-shy-of 84 years of life he was a party boy.

When Caray passed away in 1998, his death produced many people recalling memories. More than a half-century in baseball meant that he had crossed paths with many of the best players in the world for decades, and innumerable fans.

Long-time Chicago baseball writer Paul Sullivan reminisced about the first time he met Caray, when he was pretty much just a copy boy and saw him in a bar. Then he reported probably the last in-depth interview Caray gave at the annual Cubs Convention only a couple of weeks before his death.

Caray recounted how his "Take Me Out to the Ballgame" singing was really an effort jump-started by Veeck. When the routine became popular, Veeck told Caray, "Harry, I've been waiting 45 years for the right guy to sing that song during the seventh inning. I've finally found the guy and that's you. Know why? Once a guy hears you, he knows he can sing better than you. So when you sing, he joins in. If you had a good singing voice, they'd be intimidated."[20]

So it was all a plot to get the fans to sing, which they continue to do until this day. How did Caray take the news? "And he was right," Caray said.[21]

Harry Caray lived long enough to see his son Skip and his grandson Chip follow him into baseball broadcasting booths, events that he termed a thrill. For one game in May of 1991, all three of the Carays shared the broadcast booth at a Cubs–Atlanta Braves game.

Caray's funeral at Chicago's Holy Name Cathedral was geared to the man, if only because the words "Holy Cow" were part of the mass. Those who spoke about Caray did not dwell on the somber, and when his casket was carried out of the church the organ played, "Take Me Out to the Ballgame." What else could have been more appropriate?

Pete Vonachen, owner of the Peoria Chiefs minor-league team and a friend of Caray's for nearly a half-century, said, "If I gave everyone in here one of the drinks we left behind, not one of you could pass a Breathalyzer."[22] The biggest surprise in that statement was that Caray ever left a drink behind. He had to be referring to the post-stroke Harry. Vonachen did report that Caray's doctor allowed some leeway in his non-drinking sentence, telling the broadcaster, "You can have two martinis if the Cubs make it to the World Series." Vonachen added, "The doctor sure went out on the limb on that one."[23]

In August of 1999, Cubs officials dedicated a statue of Caray outside of Wrigley Field. The bronze shows Caray as if rising on the shoulders of Cubs fans, grinning wildly, and holding out a microphone for those patrons to sing "Take Me Out to the Ballgame."

During his declining years Caray told a friend, Grant DePorter, who operated his restaurant, that he guessed he drank 73,000 glasses or bottles of Budweiser beer during the course of his life. On the second anniversary of Caray's death in 2000, DePorter organized a toast to Caray that he hoped would result in some 73,000 people lifting a glass in his memory around the world.[24]

It was a gesture Harry Caray most certainly have appreciated—especially if they all followed by singing "Take Me Out to the Ballgame" in unison. You would hear him from somewhere above exclaiming, "Let's get some runs!"

19. Ron Luciano

"Well, you idiot, you just blew your perfect game. You blew that one, you clown."—*New York Yankees catcher Thurman Munson on the first ball called by home plate umpire Ron Luciano*[1]

NOT MANY UMPIRES ARE POPULAR WITH FANS. Mostly, fans subscribe to the theory that the umpire is out to get their favorite team with obviously bad calls. Rarely do fans get to know much about an individual umpire. For the most part, they don't even know what they look like, sound like, or act like away from the diamond. Very few umpires cross the line from anonymous man in blue to a public personality who provides entertainment.

Ron Luciano was as different as it could get and provided more fun and laughs than all other umpires in baseball history combined, even good-natured arbiters like Eric Gregg. Luciano was the Good Humor umpire, a naturally gregarious guy who admitted that he loved to talk and definitely had show-biz blood coursing through his veins.

If baseball umpires are viewed as starched-shirt Major League employees (just the way the administrators of the game like them), Luciano was a Hawaiian shirt of bright hues. For Luciano, working the bases was performance art. A batter thrown out at first was not merely a recipient of the traditional thumb in the air. Luciano shot him dead, pointing his forefinger as if he was a lawbreaker being sent to Boot Hill.

Luciano could act a good game, talk a good game, and, as it turned out, write a good game. He co-authored five light-hearted books about baseball, the first one a smash hit called *The Umpire Strikes Back*. In the 1980s, the title was an obvious play on the name of one of the *Star Wars* movies, *The Empire Strikes Back*.

If Luciano hadn't been a Major League umpire between 1969 and 1979, basically because of his love of baseball, he might have made a living as a touring stand-up comic in nightclubs.

Ron Luciano was born in Endicott, New York, in 1937 and was a first-rate, two-way tackle for the Syracuse University football team. At 6-foot-4 and 260 pounds, he was big enough and talented enough to be drafted by the Detroit Lions. Injuries slowed and ruined his pro football career after just two games with the Buffalo Bills. By 1964, Luciano was in the umpiring profession, starting in Class A minor league ball. He reached the majors five years later. The American League did not realize what it was getting.

Luciano was loud, funny, flamboyant and unabashed. He talked to catchers in their squat and batters when they stepped into the box to hit. He made energetic calls, often pointing his finger repeatedly, kicking one foot in the air, or putting his entire arm into an emphatic decision. He could banter with the best of them and uttered one-liners to reporters. He was also a marvelous raconteur, repeating with great description some of the more off-beat anecdotes that occurred on the field that fans might otherwise not hear. Luciano had a great ear for picking up dialogue and reveled in relaying stories.

Hall of Fame manager Earl Weaver and Luciano famously feuded over calls. Luciano said Weaver's problem was that he always held a grudge long after a play was decided. With other managers, the next game was a new day, he said. Of course, there were managers like Billy Martin who straddled a fine line. "I've already forgotten how you screwed me yesterday with the worst call I've ever seen," Martin told Luciano before another game in a series. "Today's a brand new day."[2]

It was for Hippolito Pena, too, a pitcher trying to make the Yankees' roster. Only he didn't seem to have his usual stuff when he went to the mound. Pena had hidden the fact from the team that he had an accident in the off-season. He actually was trying to make the cut with a broken wrist, shoulder bone and ribs. "Now, if Pena could hide those injuries, he shouldn't be pitching for the Yankees, he should be working for the CIA," Luciano said.[3]

Luciano worked the 1973 All-Star Game, the 1974 World Series, and three League Championship Series. One year players gave one of only two "excellent" ratings to Luciano for his season's umpiring work.

Some players begged Luciano not to shoot them when he called them out, but Luciano gave no mercy on that quarter. He admitted that occasionally he got carried away being playful with his actions. During his career there were 52 Major League umps, and the other 51 acted in the same manner, which is to say comparatively subdued. Luciano stood out. He didn't mind and he was having fun.

> Bill Haller [another umpire] told me once, "You set a new record tonight. You called a guy out 17 times—on the same play." If I call something wrong I do it 17 times. Most of the other umpires don't like it. I come across as a clown and they're all conservative. John Birch is to the left of them. They say I make a travesty out of the game. But I'll take some of the flak off them. It's gotten so the players tolerate me. The nice ones don't mind.[4]

Luciano joked that he had become a factor in some managers' strategy. "Gene Mauch has more signals than anybody," Luciano said. "If somebody blows his nose, three guys steal. Mauch has a $100 or $150 fine if someone misses a sign. And it's double if they miss it because they're talking to Luciano."[5]

Organized baseball is at its happiest when umpires are seen (behaving sedately) and not heard, but Luciano was not a good fit with that expectation. He never pretended he was perfect, that alone probably being a violation of the umpire code, but he thought he was a good umpire, if more colorful than all the others. "We're only supposed to have done a good job if we're able to walk off the field without anyone realizing we had been there," Luciano said. "Bull. We're part of it, too."[6]

Luciano, who was a bird watcher, carried binoculars with him on road trips and once got into trouble because someone thought he was looking into hotel windows as a voyeur. He became such a well-known personality that he was able to break into the book market, and that led him to a two-year national baseball color man broadcast gig when he retired from umpiring.

"I'm not as egotistical as I make out," Luciano said while he was still active. "But I miss a lot of plays. Nestor Chylak is so much better than I am it's ridiculous. So is Bill Haller. I don't understand rain. As a football player, you play through it. If I see two drops, that's it. I stop the game. I cannot handle rain. I am completely befuddled by it."[7]

As might be expected, Luciano said working the plate is much more challenging than being an umpire on the base paths. He once said a perfect day in the field would be the third-base ump who made no calls all day long. That doesn't happen at home plate calling balls and strikes. "By far it's the toughest," Luciano said. "There are, on average, some 260 pitches per game. So maybe batters swing at 70 or 80. That's 190 split-second decisions. Even God can't make it out on 190 split-second decisions."[8]

It was not very surprising, either, that Luciano might have a bit of affection in his heart for players who also seemed to act out of the mainstream. Reliever John Wetteland entertained Luciano. The ump became intrigued when he learned that Wetteland worked on his poetry and played poetry-related games while in the bullpen. He also admired a Wetteland comment: "In my spare time I enjoy serving doughnuts on another planet."[9] Seemed like a neat part-time job.

Luciano and Weaver were like finalists for a Golden Gloves championship. Luciano kept getting assigned to Weaver's games and Weaver, who was known as an All-Star ump baiter, made sure to get on his nerves. Once, Weaver was suspended for three games for questioning "the integrity" of an umpire (Luciano, naturally). Another time Luciano had to apologize to Weaver for comments he made in an interview that amounted to saying that he hoped any team in the American League won the pennant except Weaver's Baltimore Orioles and he hoped Weaver never won another game. That was deemed by Major League Baseball as prejudicial against the Orioles when Luciano was supposed to be impartial. "To start with, I've got a big mouth and I said a lot of dumb things," Luciano said. "Everybody makes mistakes and I guess I'm at the top of the ladder when it comes to saying dumb things."[10]

Luciano's first book was "The Umpire Strikes Back," released in 1982, and it became a big bestseller. The back of the book promoted it as "Here is Ron Luciano, the funniest ump ever to call balls and strikes, a huge and awesome legend who leaps and spins and shoots players with an index finger while screaming OUTOUTOUT!!!"[11]

There were no breaks in a Luciano monologue when he was on the field (and he did periodically miss a play when otherwise distracted by his own conversation), but he said he was startled when he went into television. The producer gave him three major topics to discuss, and when he asked how long he had, he was told 30 seconds. "Thirty seconds!" Luciano wrote. "I can barely say my name in 30 seconds, even without including a middle initial. I started sweating, causing my make-up to run. I realized I was about to embarrass myself on national television."[12] Imagine, big, burly football player Ron Luciano wearing make-up.

Luciano said he never aspired to be a television commentator. "My voice is perfect for mime and my face is made for radio," he said.[13]

Of course, Luciano had never planned to become an umpire, either. His intention was to become a pro football player, which he achieved for about ten minutes. Umpiring was a replacement gig for football.

Very much a raw arbiter when he began in Rookie Leagues in the 1960s in Florida, Luciano said he was surprised that managers at home plate looked at him as if he had just landed from Mars when he wished them luck. He also didn't know he had it within his power to have the park's lights turned on when the sky was dimming. Once he learned that he did, he relished the vision-improving lights for calling balls and strikes. "Well, once I found out, I got real good at it," Luciano said. "Two o'clock in the afternoon, let's have the lights. Power companies all over the league got to love me."[14]

Luciano said he learned the hard way about becoming an umpire, including coming to terms with a decent strike zone. However, along the way he ejected a manager or two from a game. Once, early on, he was in a lousy mood because he knew he was calling a bad game. It did not help his perspective to have one of the managers screaming and swearing at him constantly. They say there are magic words in the umpire world that will get a manager tossed, and to Luciano this fellow crossed the line. The umpire took charge and threw the manager out of the game. "Just that simply, the problem was solved," Luciano said. "He continued screaming at me for a few more minutes, but suddenly he was gone and it was quiet and peaceful and beautiful on the field once again. I immediately realized I was on to something good."[15]

Luciano said being behind the plate was a job with great responsibility, fast-paced and packed with action. Life was busy as the home-plate umpire. During one of those brief pre-game discussions at the plate between the umps and the managers that fans do not hear as they anxiously await the first pitch, the protagonists might discuss the ground rules. For the most part Luciano thought that was a waste of time because nothing had changed since the last time the teams had played in that park. He believed most managers agreed that was just a time-killer.

> Fences don't move. Trees don't grow in the outfield. After you've worked in a ball park dozens of times you know all its peculiarities. Once, in Anaheim, I asked the managers if they wanted to go over the ground rules. The Angels' manager, Jim Fregosi, looked at me and laughed. "What's the use?" Fregosi said. "You're just gonna make 'em up as you go along anyway."[16]

In almost every way, you could say that Luciano was a non-conformist in baseball. He brought his own style to the sport and that could offend the serious-minded purist with no sense of humor. Most of those types could be found in upper management or the league office.

Luciano said what he thought when posed with a question, but what he thought, and what came out of his mouth was not always politic. The issue was that as an umpire he had to remain 100 percent neutral. So he had to be careful in his insults of Earl Weaver. He happened to mention once that he did not like the city of Baltimore either, not just the Baltimore Orioles. That did not make him any friends in Baltimore. But beyond that it meant to so many that Luciano could not call a fair and honest game if it involved the Orioles. That's when baseball administrative management stepped in and swatted Luciano with fines.

Weaver accused Luciano of being biased against the Orioles, said that in a close call Luciano might lean in favor of the other team, and demanded that Luciano be banned from calling Baltimore games. For his part, Luciano accused Weaver of being ... short. At 5-foot-7, compared to Luciano's 6–4, that was true. The way Luciano put it was less than complimentary. "He's about three-foot-one," Luciano said. "I tell him to get his nose off my kneecap."[17]

Luciano did not have much of a governor on his thoughts, and that could do him harm occasionally. Luciano read Shakespeare and held a master's degree in mathematics. He did not seem to spend any time studying for a degree in diplomacy. When a sportswriter asked Luciano if he ever socialized with ballplayers after games, he essentially termed the suggestion ridiculous. "I'd never want to," Luciano said. "Most of them are too stupid. Let me tell you the level of intelligence of the average baseball player is very low. They're nowhere as smart as football players."[18]

That statement probably precluded earning Luciano post-game invitations. However, he did receive one from Detroit Tigers manager Ralph Houk to go out for a beer after pretty much losing the game for the Tigers with a call.

Luciano was a Major League umpire for 11 seasons, but got tired of the travel and seized the TV opening. "I've left laundry in almost every city in the country," he said of his umpiring tour.[19]

Luciano felt his umpiring career bridged changing times in the majors, from the pre-mascot to the San Diego Chicken Era, from pre-designated hitter in the American League, to the DH being established.

> When I started [baseball] was played by nine tough competitors on grass, in graceful ball parks. But while I was trying to answer the daily "Quiz O'Gram" on the exploding scoreboard a revolution was taking place around me. By the time I was finished there were 10 men on each side, the game was played indoors, on plastic, and I had to spend half my time watching out for a man dressed in a chicken suit who kept trying to kiss me.[20]

When Luciano was on—and that meant on-stage as well as on his game—he was a hoot to watch work as a sidebar to the game action. Anyone with half a sense of humor appreciated his efforts. One Chicago sportswriter waxed rhapsodic about what Luciano added to an otherwise routine Chicago White Sox–Cleveland Indians encounter. He called him the most interesting performer on the field. Luciano signaled strikes with his own style of enthusiasm, nothing short of glorious. The index finger goes straight out and then, as the arm comes back, Ron pivots spectacularly and jams his fist in the general direction of the batter's dugout. This umpire wants everyone to know. It's even more fun to watch the huge fellow work at first base. This is a tribute to Luciano's exuberance. At most games watching the first-base umpire is about as exciting as waiting for a traffic signal to change color.[21]

Despite once being a muscular football player, Luciano had two physical problems as he aged as an umpire. His weight was 260 in his prime, but baseball officials wanted him to trim down. He got down to 240, bounced back up, dieted again, but after he gave up smoking his new nervous habit was eating, and he challenged the scale at 300 pounds. Also, his eyesight began to fail. Umpires are supposed to be able to match eagles for sharp vision. Although Luciano had prescription glasses, he couldn't wear them doing his job (since everyone teases umpires about what they can't see anyway), or even in public, lest word get out.

So when he moved from umpiring to the TV booth, Luciano said the change was a relief. "It's a great weight off my shoulders," Luciano said. "I can wear glasses from now on in restaurants and read the menu and I don't have to lie about my weight."[22]

Luciano's broadcast career lasted only a few years. Somewhat surprisingly to many, his book writing career lasted much longer as he and co-author David Fisher produced five lively baseball books.

Whether he was an umpire on the field, doing his thing in front of thousands of appreciative baseball fans (and some skeptical baseball players and managers), or writing up wonderful memories and telling stories that made readers chuckle, Luciano came across as an affable, happy-go-lucky man.

The reality, it turned out, was far different. On January 18, 1995, Ron Luciano was found dead in his own garage in Endicott, New York, the community where he was raised. The cause of death was carbon monoxide poisoning, and suicide was the cause. The majority of the world did not know it, but Luciano had been troubled by depression for a long time. He was 57 when he died.

Old friends said Luciano loved making others laugh, something he accomplished with regularity. They said they thought there was a better chance after completing college that he would become an actor rather than an umpire.

"He was a classic," said Ken Kaiser, a veteran umpire. "There was only one Luciano."[23]

20. Jay Johnstone

"Introducing my roomie, the Moon Man."—*Jimmy Piersall*[1]

JIMMY PIERSALL? PIERSALL WAS A BASEBALL personality many believed came from another planet, so that would have made two players sharing a room who were in orbit.

Jay Johnstone was a good enough outfielder to stick around the majors for 20 seasons from 1966 to 1985. He batted .267 with 102 home runs and 10,000 laughs. Perhaps that's why eight teams provided employment, including the Los Angeles Dodgers twice and both teams in Chicago.

Johnstone, born in Manchester, Connecticut, in 1945, was both witty and a prankster, making him a dangerous practitioner of humor. He could utter the outrageous and perform it, too. He was uninhibited and unabashed.

A hint of personality might be gleaned from the titles of the books Johnstone co-authored with sportswriter Rick Talley. He wrote *Temporary Insanity*, *Over the Edge*, and *Some of My Best Friends Are Crazy*. You might not be able to tell a book by its cover, but you should have been able to tell these books by their titles.

"I can't think of anybody I'd rather have in a clubhouse than Jay Johnstone," said long-time Dodgers manager Tom Lasorda. "But he wrote a book? What, with a fire extinguisher? Shaving cream?"[2] While admiring Johnstone's hard-working nature on the field, Lasorda also credited him for keeping the clubhouse loosey-goosey, even if the boss had to fine him sometimes just to make a point that he had stepped over the line. "Some people are naturally funny, you know?" Lasorda said. "But Jay is more than funny. He's crazy. There are a lot of people in asylums who are saner than Jay Johnstone. He's also devious. He must sit up nights thinking of things to do to me."[3]

Johnstone did not shrink from such descriptions or deny them. He embraced his image, believing his hijinks came naturally.

> I've been called everything from "Moon Man" and "Crazy Jay" to "My Favorite Martian" and "The Disappearing Man." I've been described as flaky, spacey and a clown. But I prefer to think of myself as a throwback to another era—one of a vanishing breed of ball players who find health, happiness, and a certain degree of satisfaction in throwing creamed pies, and putting hot stuff in somebody's undershorts.[4]

Johnstone blew plausible deniability with that introspective statement, but he pretty much revealed he had trained for his bizarre actions with a time machine.

Just about anything was fair game for Johnstone's sense of humor, even if he was catching teammates on a bad day and there was a 50–50 chance the object of his prank was going to smash his head into a locker. One such occasion arose when relief pitcher Steve Howe was shelled. Relievers, it is said, are supposed to put out the blaze, not turn it into a conflagration. That's why they sometimes call relievers firemen. "However, there are times when even I wonder why I do the things I do," Johnstone said. "Now, I could have left it alone. Instead, I slipped down to the groundskeepers' room and appropriated this giant, red, five-gallon gasoline can, which I hung up in Howe's locker with his name written on the can."[5]

This was one of those times when Howe was not in a mood to chuckle at himself. Johnstone said the pitcher promptly blamed someone else for making fun of him. "This was perfect, as far as I was concerned," said Johnstone, who stood around with a who-me look on his face. "It's always more satisfying when somebody else gets blamed for your stuff."[6] Howe, who blamed fellow pitcher Jerry Reuss, took revenge on him the next day by doing something unmentionable to Reuss' shoes in the bathroom.

Not only is it satisfying to get away with the crime, it is best when the protagonist is an eyewitness to his misdemeanor. Sometimes, though, a delayed fuse means the prankster cannot see his handiwork. That happened once when Johnstone put the substance Capsolin in pitcher Dave Goltz's underwear before he dressed to drive home from a game with his wife and baby. Johnstone disguised the ointment and was left to imagine its impact as Goltz left the park. "It is the hottest stuff ever to come out of a tube," Johnstone said.[7] He later learned that Goltz moved at supersonic speed on the freeway and immediately jumped into the shower when he got to his house.

While Johnstone might well have fit in with a full-time role on *Laugh-In*, he was serious about baseball. He was just wedded to the notion that he should enjoy himself while playing the game.

In the mid–1970s, when he got into 120-plus games a few years in a row (something that did not often occur since Johnstone was often relegated to back-up outfielder and pinch-hitter), he hit .329 and .318 in consecutive years. The second season, in late August, he was leading the National League in batting at .345. Johnstone felt that several teams had overlooked his potential and failed to help him improve. He also admitted that he did not work out as hard as he might have during the off-season for years. At age 29 and 30 he classified as a late bloomer during those two glory years.

"It didn't help that I made the mistake of going home each winter and putting my bat and glove in a closet," Johnstone said. "There's no way you can do that and expect to hold a job. I've since learned that you can't lay off and you've got to put in time every day. I should have gone to winter leagues long before I did."[8] Forty years ago, players didn't work out nearly as regularly over the winter. They sometimes worked second jobs or just loafed if they were in the smaller percentage of players who made enough money to do so. They worked their way back into top shape in spring training.

Of course, when it came to gags, Johnstone was always in mid-season form. Johnstone had standards in his humor, implementing an idea no one else would have thought of or dared try. Once, at Vero Beach, in a move sure to endear himself to Lasorda, Johnstone was at the root of a plot that locked the manager in his motel room. Rope was placed around the door handle and tied to a tree at 4 a.m. When Lasorda picked up his phone to call the front desk for help, he discovered the telephone line was dead because its inner pieces had been dismantled.

Larsorda missed breakfast and had difficulty making the team bus that day after a laundryman responded to his shouts for help. "Oh, he was mad," Johnstone said. "Not just because he was tied in his room, but he missed breakfast. Tommy's a guy who never met a meal he didn't like."[9]

Once, also with the Dodgers, for whom Johnstone played four seasons, he and Reuss disguised themselves as the groundskeepers and took over the role of dragging the infield in the fifth inning. "Sometimes you've got to do something to relieve the pressure," was Johnstone's explanation for the move.[10]

Johnstone's personality and bat milked two decades out of the big leagues, but nobody expected him to turn into a bestselling author who produced sequels. Turns out Johnstone writing about the silly stuff, sight gags included, could be about as funny as the genuine article.

A somewhat amazed Johnstone took a somewhat perverse pleasure in having his debut volume, *Temporary Insanity*, banned at Dodger Stadium,

20. JAY JOHNSTONE

which sold other Dodgers-related books. "Was it because I wasn't hitting?" said Johnstone, who was still employed by the team at the time. "Was I having an affair with the groundskeeper's wife or the publicity director's secretary? Or was I finally being nailed for using the manager's telephone?"[11] Dodgers management ruled that the book contained "objectionable" language in a couple of places. Johnstone merely quoted a player's rant. But that was apparently a sin.

In later books, Johnstone was quite happy to include offbeat events that occurred to other players, including those indulging in baseball in Latin America over the winter. Lasorda, he noted, once spent a night in jail for partially disrobing on a field in the Dominican Republic after being tossed from a game.

Johnstone's span in the majors included the time period when baseball players were awarded single hotel rooms and no longer shared lodging with a roommate on the road. Johnstone, however, missed having a late-night pal around to talk with, cover for him when violating curfew, or share watching pro wrestling on the tube. "I was the Mr. Clean of roommates," Johnstone said. "Felix Unger in spikes. I even vacuumed. U.S. Marine J. Johnstone, ready for inspection, sir! I even won a game for the Phillies once because I was neat."[12] Johnstone claimed he was hit in the foot with a pitch. The ump refused to award him first base until he saw the ball scuffed with the red shoe polish from Johnstone's footwear.

To the amazement of many, Johnstone actually served two years in the Marines, an unlikely candidate for the type of discipline usually expected of those men in uniform. "The Marines say they build a few good men," he said. "Well, if you can't baffle 'em with brains, baffle 'em with bull."[13]

Johnstone was surrounded by characters during his seasons with the Dodgers, but they all didn't have the same broad reputation that he did. Dodgers second baseman Steve Sax smacked a deep double, sped past first base, rounded second base and fell down, obviously injured. Lasorda and the trainer rushed out to help him. "Where did you get hurt?" Lasorda asked, concerned over his player's body parts. "Over there," Sax said, pointing to the first-base line.[14]

The time that Johnstone took the field as a pseudo-groundskeeper, Lasorda fined him $200 for being out of uniform. He was lucky he was not fined another time for being in uniform. Johnstone was spotted in full Dodgers regalia waiting in line at a ballpark concession stand—during a game. It was non-stop between Johnstone and Lasorda. That time Johnstone tied the motel room door closed? Lasorda made sure Johnstone's clothes were missing after the exhibition game, and he had to ride the bus home in his underwear.

Lasorda was known for holding court in his Dodger Stadium office with Hollywood celebrities, and the walls were decorated with his favorite autographed pictures of stars. One time Lasorda returned to the office and discovered that all his souvenir pictures had been taken down and replaced with autographed pictures of Johnstone, Reuss and another pitcher, Don Stanhouse. Lasorda began screaming about the disruption of his prized possessions, but Johnstone responded, "How many games did those guys [Frank] Sinatra and [Don] Rickles ever win for you?"[15]

Johnstone may have had goofy tendencies, but sometimes his lighthearted approach to the game was tinged with alternative explanations. Like the time with the Phillies when the club held Photo Day and Johnstone took the field wearing a colorful umbrella hat.

> That wasn't a gag. It was just plain, good sense. You guys don't know it, but it must have been 130 degrees on that Astro Turf. The sun was brutal out there. You could have broiled a steak out there. Our caps are red, and red, like black, absorbs sunlight. My umbrella hat is multi-colored and it reflects light. Those other guys were gasping for breath and I stayed cool … and they call me a kook.[16]

End of science lesson for the day. And no, Paris fashion experts did not call.

Johnstone was also very fond of firecrackers, and not only on the Fourth of July. Sometimes he set them off in the clubhouse, which made it seem as if war had broken out. Other times he maneuvered to set off the firecrackers near another player's feet. One time he sneaked up on broadcaster Joe Garagiola, who was interviewing Dick Allen, then with the Phillies, when Johnstone "bombed" them. "Garagiola nearly swallowed his microphone," Johnstone said. "Allen, he didn't know what to do. He was feeling around his body, looking for bullet holes, I think. He figured he'd been shot."[17] This was a long-distance attack, and Johnstone was in the dugout with teammates while this was going on.

Johnstone had a similar relationship with Phillies manager Danny Ozark to what he had with Lasorda, although perhaps not as extreme. He tested Ozark's patience often, taking infield practice when he was told to take outfield practice and the like. But Ozark seemed to enjoy his presence. "He's kind of a goofball," Ozark said. "One day, like those old Dodgers, he'll end up at third base with two other guys. Sometimes I'm afraid to use him as a pinch runner. I got the feeling he doesn't have the faintest idea where second base is. Jay Johnstone is all right. Everybody else is just nuts."[18]

During Johnstone's tenure in Philadelphia from 1974 to 1978, whenever he hit a home run, the team flashed the message "Crazy Jay" and a cartoon character on its videoboard. No one could say that Johnstone did not bring that on himself.

Johnstone did take risks with teammates. He always hoped he was keeping them loose, but that wasn't always going to be a slam-dunk either. Once, after Dodgers second baseman Davey Lopes dropped a pop-up, he returned to the locker room and found one of his spare uniforms displayed with a watermelon on top of it serving as a head, sporting dark glasses and holding a cane. Another time when shortstop Bill Russell made an error, he found one of his gloves swathed in bandages.

Johnstone was regularly on the lookout for kindred spirits in the majors, those guys on other teams whose approach to the game was a little offbeat, too. Once, he made a list of such players that he called "Crazies Of The Nineties." They included pitcher Roger McDowell for keeping a snake named Larry above his locker and holding a service for the reptile when it died.

Also, he took note of pitcher Steve Bedrosian drenching his manager, Nick Leyva, when he gained his first big-league victory by dumping a bucket of water on him, the equivalent of a Gatorade shower. "At least they could have heated up the water," Leyva said.[19]

Johnstone cited the story of former power hitter Darrell Evans and his wife, who said they saw a UFO. "I am envious because I have never seen a flying saucer," Johnstone wrote, "although I did hang around one spring with Bo Belinsky."[20] That's probably equal on the life-experience chart.

California Angels manager Bill Rigney did admit that he roomed Johnstone with Piersall by design, his main goal being not to let the flakes infect any other impressionable player on the team. Insisting that he had been a quiet kid in high school, not the class clown, Johnstone said Piersall was an influence on him. "I only learned those crazy jokes when I went to the Angels and met Jimmy Piersall," Johnstone said.[21]

Piersall was an outstanding center fielder and said that when he met young Johnstone, the knowledge he sought to pass on was not how to give a hot foot, but how to play the outfield. "I tried to pass off a few things I had learned through the years," Piersall said. "I tried to teach Jay how to practice against the walls in the outfield, how to know the opposing hitters."[22]

Johnstone was always a far better hitter than fielder, so there was not much evidence those lessons took. As far as absorbing a humorous approach to the game, that seemed to sink in. If an introduction to life in the big leagues and southern California was enforced by Piersall, Johnstone was also influenced by Bo Belinsky and his running mate, Dean Chance. Never did that group pass up the opportunity to have a good time. "They were three very interesting people to be around, to say the least," Johnstone said.[23]

It was not terribly surprising that with his gift for humor, Johnstone was given a shot in the broadcast booth after he retired. He was a radio commentator for the New York Yankees in 1989–1990 and a broadcaster for the Phillies in 1992–1993. He also broadcast college baseball on the West Coast and had a company called Sporthings, which aided charitable organizations by gathering sports items for auctions. He also did some corporate speaking.

The designated hitter came along while Johnstone was playing, but he spent most of his time in the National League. He got a laugh out of hearing about pitchers who spent their long careers in the American League and hardly ever came to the plate. Reliever Dan Quisenberry got to bat for just the third time in his 616th game, and Johnstone was tickled that he employed a Mel Ott hitting style, raising one leg before swinging. It didn't help. Quisenberry grounded out. "I wasn't sure if I was lifting the right leg," Quisenberry reported. "Besides, I thought they were in a zone defense and they were playing man-to-man."[24]

Johnstone seemed to relish his image. He never backed off from the crazy description and used it about himself when it was convenient, such as at the end of his first book. "Maybe some day a rookie will hear my name mentioned and say, 'Jay Johnstone? He was so crazy that when he came into the hotel room, his pillow jumped out the window.' And that kid might have a chance in this game."[25]

Johnstone never seemed to change, whether as a young player or an older broadcaster. When he was with the Yankees, he wrote, "If you see me on a New York bus or subway, make sure you come up to say hello. We'll talk baseball. You tell me what's wrong with the Yankees and I'll give you George Steinbrenner's phone number."[26]

21. Bill Lee

"He's getting the ball over. He looks like a legitimate hurler out there."—Brockton Rox team official Hoffman Wolff on Bill Lee pitching a game at 63[1]

THE TITLE OF SATCHEL PAIGE'S AUTOBIOGRAPHY is *Maybe I'll Pitch Forever*. Well, Bill Lee is trying to do it.

As Lee marched past 70 he was still periodically showing up on a pitching mound to teach whippersnappers a half-century younger a little lesson about how location and control can outperform sheer speed on a fastball.

During his prime, the southpaw hurling for the Boston Red Sox and Montreal Expos was known as "Spaceman." The nickname was bestowed because of Lee's unconventional ways. He said anything he felt like, teased his managers and other players, hinted that he smoked marijuana regularly, and might well have been blackballed from the majors when he could still win after a career spanning 1969–1982.

Born in Burbank, California, Lee has been living in Vermont in recent years. His lifetime Major League record was 119–90 with a 3.62 earned run average and a million laughs. He was viewed as the king of the counterculture in the big leagues during his era and always spoke his mind.

Famously, Lee referred to Red Sox manager Don Zimmer as "a gerbil" and said Zimmer did not understand pitching. "Gerbils have big, puffy cheeks, store food, waddle a lot, and kids love 'em," Lee said. "Zim and I have a lot in common, but he tries to win at all costs and I try to enjoy at all costs."[2]

Many a time, listeners did not understand what Lee was talking about. He was putting them on when they were looking for deeper meaning, but he also had genuine emotions. He was so ticked off at the Red Sox when they traded away outfielder Bernie Carbo, his friend, that he jumped the team for a day as a protest. When asked why he did it, Lee was virtually incredulous. It seemed obvious to him. "Get some degrees in sociology, economics, and psychology and then I'll tell you," he said. "Friendship is first with me, then competition."[3]

There was never any indication that Lee minded being called Spaceman. Jokes were made about him periodically returning to planet Earth and the like. Lee was more logical than many people who thought they were wiser, and smarter than most ball players who couldn't understand him. He was just out on the edge in a conservative sport, but not in a way that the conservatives could identify with. Lee reveled in writing an autobiographical book called *The Wrong Stuff*. He was pictured on the cover wearing a Red Sox cap with a propeller on top and a space jet-pack on his back.

Lee said he did not get into much trouble as a kid, but perhaps this was true confessions time. He said he once cut off his younger brother's curly hair because he was better looking. "Transformed him into a normal mortal and robbed him of his strange powers," Lee said.[4]

There were some other outward signs of rebellion in daily life for Lee, too, one example coming when he was seven years old. Growing up in a Catholic household, he became weary of practicing First Holy Communion, and his refusal to go to church any longer for that would have been headlines in a local paper if commonly known.

"It really made me nuts," he said. "It was so boring! We would do it every day for hours. I just couldn't take it. It had become the Catholic version of Chinese water torture." So one day he pulled out his toy Roy Rogers handcuffs, hid the key, and locked himself to his bedpost. "It took my mother hours to get me unshackled."[5]

One of Lee's major influences in sports while he was growing up was his aunt, Annabelle Lee, who may have had a faster fastball than he did, at least until Bill finished high school. "(She) could really bring it," Lee said. "My aunt pitched the first perfect game in the history of the Women's Semi-Pro Hardball League in Chicago and had a lifetime ERA of 1.17. That was her idea of the Equal Rights Amendment."[6]

Lee was a good observer and developed a sardonic wit to accompany his thoughts about things he had seen. A southpaw who stood 6-foot-3 and weighed 205 pounds, Lee pitched collegiately for the University of Southern California, where one of his teammates was future 300-game-winner and Hall of Famer Tom Seaver. During his heyday with the New York Mets and later the Cincinnati Reds and Chicago White Sox, Seaver was almost stocky and was a powerful thrower. But when he first became a Trojan, he was not quite as sturdy. Lee thought of him as a small guy. "Seaver pitched only one year for us—1965—but an extraordinary thing happened to him in that short time," Lee said. "He must have gotten exposed to some gamma rays because he just suddenly filled out and got those big legs that resulted in that patented Tom Seaver delivery and turned him into a human dynamo."[7]

Actually, many around baseball thought that Lee might have experienced prolonged exposure to gamma rays. It would have fit with his Spaceman persona, anyway. Before he was Spaceman, Lee was a more or less normal college player who was working to get better and become a more attractive prospect for Major League scouts. During the summers of 1966 and 1967, Lee played in the Alaska Baseball League, always one of the top destinations for college players trying to hone their skills. He suited up for the Alaska Goldpanners, and while he was in Fairbanks he met his future wife, Mary Lou, who was a former Miss Alaska. This was not the only time Alaska would play a role in Lee's life.

Lee had to earn the Spaceman nickname, and while he gave credit to the late *Boston Herald* sportswriter George Kimball for calling him "Space Cowboy," that version did not stick. *Boston Globe* sportswriter Peter Gammons called Lee "The Ace From Space." Close. Lee believes that infielder John Kennedy awarded him the Spaceman title.

> A reporter had mentioned something to him about one of the lunar launches. Kennedy pointed to me and said, "We don't need to watch that. We have our own spaceman right over there." I was never offended by the appellation. I just thought it was off the mark. I would have preferred to be known as Earth Man.[8]

Lee said there was a behind-the-scenes method to his madness image with reporters. He felt he had been taken advantage of as a young player and misunderstood. So he retaliated on purpose by mangling his answers to questions. "So I started to lead them down a verbal primrose path," he said. "They would ask why I did a certain pitch and I would do five minutes on Einstein's theory of curved space."[9]

Lee won 17 games three years in a row, 1973–1975, for the Red Sox. He was a very reliable member of Boston's starting rotation. He made his only All-Star team in 1973. A serious injury suffered during a brawl with the hated New York Yankees in 1976 halted that streak, and Lee's differences with manager Zimmer did not help his status with Boston. He and a few other players—Ferguson Jenkins, Rick Wise, Jim Willoughby, and Bernie Carbo—were known as a clubhouse clique called "The Buffalo Heads." The group's sole goal seemed to be making sure they had some fun while they were in the majors. But they were in the boss' doghouse and soon enough became ex–Red Sox.

When historians think of fun-loving baseball players, Lee's name always surfaces, in one way or another. Lee called himself a "Roman Catholic Zen Buddhist," evidence he never did really get past that First Holy Communion role. He was once fined $250 by Major League Baseball for saying he sprinkled marijuana on buckwheat pancakes. Not that anyone saw this; he only said it.

This incident began with Lee being cornered in the Red Sox locker room by reporters who quizzed him on whether or not the team had a drug problem. He said it sure did. "I think the entire team abused nicotine, caffeine and alcohol far too much," Lee said.[10]

When the writers persisted on the topic of marijuana as a possible problem, again Lee said no. Smoking marijuana was no problem at all, as he had showed by using it for years. Headlines blared that Lee admitted smoking dope.

Naturally, that led to big-league administrators fining him. Commissioner Bowie Kuhn demanded that a check be made out to Major League Baseball and said it would be donated to charity. Lee said he didn't trust that procedure, figuring the cash would end up in a "Let's Bring Back Richard Nixon" fund. Instead, Lee chose his own charitable cause, a religious mission in rural Alaska named St. Mary's, and that's how he paid off the fine.[11]

It might be said that Lee was ahead of his time on the marijuana issue. In 2016, Lee gave an interview to ESPN's Dan LeBatard when he claimed to have smoked marijuana in 1972 with George W. Bush, the future president, at the Boston Museum of Science. Bush never commented on the assertion.

Lee looked positively on the changes in American society legalizing marijuana in selected states such as Colorado and Alaska and said he would like to grow it, but is waiting for it to be legalized in his home state of Vermont. "It's amazing they haven't legalized it," Lee told *Men's Journal* when he was running for governor in 2016.

When the Red Sox shipped Lee out, he landed in Montreal with the Expos. He had one additional fine season with the Expos, winning 16 games in 1979. Lee's tenure ended in Montreal when he again protested a management decision to trade a friend, Rodney Scott. This time when he walked out on the team, he never returned and no other club picked up his contract.

That put Lee into exile from the majors at age 35. It may be said, however, that Lee never truly retired. Although he never threw another pitch in the majors after 1982, Lee played for numerous semi-pro teams, formed touring teams, and began making solo pitching guest appearances for teams in independent leagues. He was a broadcaster in Canada and somehow stayed in baseball doing odds and ends—so far, forever.

In 2008, when Lee was 61, he returned to the Alaska Goldpanners in Fairbanks to pitch as a visiting celebrity, and got the win in the game.

Appropriately, when Lee wrote another book he titled it *Have Glove, Will Travel*, and that was no accidental naming. For three decades after leaving the majors, Lee was on a roll. Somehow his arm, which was never a repository of Bob Gibson speed, held together. "Location, location, location" did not only apply to real estate purchases, but also was critical to Lee continuing his wild tour. He got batters out by fooling them, not overpowering them. Many times, depending on the competition, Lee played first base when he wasn't pitching. He could never get enough baseball.

Bill Lee's nickname with the Boston Red Sox and Montreal Expos was "Spaceman," which was pretty much all you had to know about him. Lee was a solid left-hander, but an A-plus wit.

In fact, in his 60s, Lee was making bats, some for Major Leaguers like Red Sox slugger David Ortiz. When he won a game at 63 for the Brockton, Massachusetts, suburban Boston team (a charity appearance at the request of a friend), some wondered how he did it. "I lift wood and make bats for a living," Lee said in 2010. "This is fun for me. It doesn't take anything out of you to pitch."[12]

More than 6,000 fans turned out for the game, and Lee gave them a treat, starting with the "eephus" pitch, a blooper-type throw he had developed since his big-league days. The pitch yielded a single, but Lee turned to other weapons to escape the inning. For one so determined to have fun in baseball, Lee was careful not to over-emphasize the significance of the sport in daily life.

When he was pitching, to help calm his nerves, he adopted a motto that kept things in perspective. "I think about the cosmic snowball theory," said Lee, citing a theory that was probably not one of Einstein's. "A few million years from now the sun will burn out and lose its gravitational pull. The earth will turn into a giant snowball and be hurled through space. When that happens it won't matter if I get this guy out."[13]

Lee did not want to retire from Major League Baseball when the Expos released him and no one picked him up. He got angry, but he made a commitment to himself.

> Now I could travel the world searching for the game in its purest form. I made up my mind to play wherever I could find a diamond for any team that needed my talents. Hardball, softball, stick ball, Wiffle ball, cricket, pay me in cash, pay me in pelts, pay me not at all—it did not matter. If you owned a club of Nerf-ball playing kangaroos with a home park situated just beyond the dark side of the moon, and you needed someone to fill that last spot on your roster, I would catch the next space shuttle.[14]

That's how it came to pass that Lee continued playing baseball in so many different venues, for whoever asked. It kept him young, at least. Of course, he kept writing about it all as well, and wherever Lee traveled adventures of one sort or another were sure to follow.

During his four years with the Expos, Lee did develop a fan base in Canada. So he stuck around Quebec and played semi-pro ball. For a former big-leaguer, especially one who only very recently had been facing top-notch hitters, the competition was not significant. That's one reason Lee said he got high smoking marijuana during games.

Lee's team, Verdun, made the playoffs and faced Longueuil. The way Lee described the makeup of the squads, he portrayed the other guys as upscale suburbanites and his teammates as inner city toughs.

> Longueuil players visited bistros. Verdun players hung out in bars. Longueuil players dressed in Ralph Lauren. Verdun players dressed in Ralph Kramden. Longueuil players ate pate, escargots and croissants. Verdun players? They ate players from Longueuil. Their team bested us in three straight to send us home for the winter.[15]

Once, while killing time wandering around Moncton, New Brunswick, better known for its hockey players than its baseball players, Lee walked into a cemetery. "There I found the headstone of Ronald McDonald," Lee said. "'Oh, how sad,' I thought. 'No one told me he had died. It occurred to me that I had stumbled upon the lost Cemetery of Clowns. I spent the next three days searching for Bozo and Emmett Kelley. Never did find them.'"[16]

Lee did need a passport for some of his travels, like the 1998 trip to Russia as part of a baseball squad. Russia is known for many things, including vodka, caviar, peculiar figure-skating judging, and Lenin's tomb, but baseball is not high on the list. A professor friend of Lee's, whom he once played against in college, pulled together a team for the journey. Some of them had even played organized ball, but no one else had reached Lee's exalted Major League status. Off to Moscow they went on a friendship mission of sorts. Moscow was still rebounding from the long rule of Communism and had not quite morphed into the free-wheeling, much more modernistic city it became. The players did not stay in luxurious hotels. Likewise, their hosts had not advanced to an international level of sophistication either.

> Our guides resembled Soviet espionage agents straight out of central casting. Blond flat-tops, opaque gray eyes, broad features, broad shoulders, broad everything. Neither of them subscribed to GQ. They dressed in ill-fitting black suits, too tight in the chest and too tight in the waist. Fresh white shirts, but no ties. The cuffs of their pants stopped an inch shy of their ankles. They wore heavy white athletic socks with sandals. I had seen this look before, on undercover cops working the streets of South Boston in the seventies.[17]

One of Lee's most bizarre roles on the mound occurred when he was invited for a weekend appearance in Pennsylvania. Lee was paid $2,500, which he thought was okay. Then he realized he was expected to pitch complete games for both teams both days to earn his check. He ended up throwing 64 innings without a rest. The irony did not escape Lee, who had long opposed the use of the designated hitter as an example of too much specialization in the world. "Yet here I was, the designated pitcher," Lee said, "doomed to stay on the mound till the final inning, never allowed to take my turn at the plate. The ultimate one-dimensional chucker."[18]

During those touring days, Lee maintained his ties to Montreal and Canada and was appalled when the Expos went into league receivership and seemed bound for Washington, D.C. He was one of the last holdouts of believers who felt the team should and would stick to Quebec.

> Listen, 90 percent of all Canadian fans are massing at the border. If you think you're going to take this ballclub and move it down to Washington, I don't think so. It can't be north of town because the Baltimore organization would have something to say about that. It can't be downtown because no one goes downtown after July 1 in Washington. At least that's what I remember.[19]

The Spaceman was wrong about that one.

As someone who retained allegiance to the Canadian club that cut him, Lee said he would not transfer his feelings to Washington. "The only way I'm coming to Washington is if I'm elected," he said, "and if I do I will paint the White House pink and turn it into a Mexican restaurant."[20]

Actually Lee did announce a candidacy for the presidency in the 1980s, running on the Rhinoceros Party ticket, a campaign which did not take the country by storm, at least partially because he was living in Canada at the time. One writer noted that Lee was not the first spaceman to campaign for the office, citing U.S. Senator and former astronaut John Glenn. "I was way ahead of Glenn," Lee said. "I knew there was no point going up there. I didn't have to go into space to be in orbit."[21] Funny, many of Lee's baseball teammates had said that all along. "I live in Canada because I've got a lot of plaid shirts. I'd live anywhere they'd let me play baseball."[22]

Lee figured he was as qualified as anyone else who had not been embroiled in a sex scandal thrusting him onto the cover of *People* magazine. He said he would not accept major campaign donations, limiting them to 25 cents because he was running "a two-bit campaign." Lee's first act as a president, he said, would be to "Get ride of the designated hitter. The DH rule is what's evil in America."[23]

Having traveled to all 50 states and played ball in many, Lee thought he could relate to people everywhere, even on a basic level. "I'm one of the few people who've been to every state and know every state capital," Lee said. "Not only that, but I've been to a Stuckey's in almost every state, or driven by one."[24]

Lee committed to Carl Sagan being in his cabinet and basketball star Larry Bird as minister of sport. He wanted Hunter S. Thompson, the radical writer, as his vice president. Comedian and social activist Dick Gregory would be minister of health. Alas, Lee never got to make those kinds of appointments.

There was also a foreign policy platform that included channeling military budgets into sports budgets, with the Russians determined to best the U.S. at its own national pastime of baseball. "God knows we can't have a third World War," Lee said. "It'd be like Jim Kaat pitching for the Russians and me pitching for the U.S. An hour, 43-minute ball game. We'll all be good and crispy, but we'll still be No. 1."[25]

Lee never mellowed out (at least not more than he had when he was in his 20s and throwing for the Sox). He never sold his soul for corporate work. He stayed true to his self and pretty much played the part of Bill Lee wherever he traveled, for whomever he spoke, and to whomever he gave baseball advice.

A few years ago, Lee addressed a group of Cape Cod League summer college players, a league comparable to the Alaska Baseball League where he had twice played. Purist that he always was, Lee decried the use of aluminum bats in college in favor of the wood bats featured in the Cape league.

He also said that players on steroids would not ruin baseball—at the time Barry Bonds was a hot topic after setting the all-time home-run record with 762.

> People say he's on the juice. But just look at the ingredients of the milk we're all drinking; it's got hormones, chemicals. So we're all on the juice. No, I don't think it's bad for the game because I think the game will survive. It's a strong game, stronger than ever. You can't kill it. You won't ever kill it. People have tried and failed.[26]

More than most, Bill Lee spent his energy over the years very much trying to keep baseball alive in several corners of the planet, and even in outer space.

22. Steve Lyons

> "He seemed to be an island of hard-working, blue collar sanity at a time when many of the higher-paid Red Sox players were lazy and complaining, the baseball equivalents of gasbag floats in the Macy's Turkey Day Parade."—*Horror writer/Red Sox fan Stephen King on why he liked Steve Lyons' playing style*[1]

EVEN UTILITYMAN STEVE LYONS ACKNOWLEDGED he was just an average baseball player, but by being adaptable, holding down spots in the outfield and infield, wherever he was asked to play, whenever he was asked to play, he spent nine years in the majors.

A lifetime .252 hitter, Lyons, who was born in 1960 in Tacoma, Washington, came up through the Red Sox chain as a top prospect, but never turned into a star. Although he kept coming and going from Boston, Lyons actually played more games with the Chicago White Sox. The most he hit in a single season was .280 with Chicago. Like Jay Johnstone, Lyons was known for practical jokes and keeping teammates on their toes in the clubhouse. It was one way to keep busy when he was hardly playing.

For starters, one of Lyons' books, *PsychoAnalysis*, was printed as if he were writing in Hebrew, where the reader reads from the back and reads to the front. Lyons offers some true confessions about his boyish habits of committing pranks. "I always got a kick out of putting shaving cream on the phone receiver and telling someone they had a phone call," he said. "Or giving hot foots, putting atomic balm in a guy's jock."[2]

The most games Lyons played in one season for the Red Sox was 133 in his rookie season of 1985. Rarely did he approach 100 appearances. He played six positions that year, and that was typical of Lyons' career. "I've always been a utility player," Lyons said in 1991, "so I'll probably always be known as one. I'd like to be known as one of the more valuable players and I feel I have to."[3]

22. STEVE LYONS

Lyons had his memorable nickname of "Psycho" attached to him while he was still in the minors. But he did not change his ways when he was promoted to the majors. He was still psycho.

One of Lyons' better jokes was initiating on-field games of tic-tac-toe with opposing first basemen at game's start by drawing a board in the dirt next to the bag with his spikes and playing an X in a square. Each half-inning a player would draw in an X or an O. "You had to finish the game before they dragged the infield in the fifth inning," Lyons said.[4] He said only two first basemen around the American League ignored him, refusing to play.

That was a little bit offbeat, but the one thing that more baseball fans remember about Lyons (to them, proving he was psycho) was an incident when cameras caught him standing on first base while playing for the White Sox. That was the day in 1990 when Lyons dropped his pants during a stoppage in play, with the aim of cleaning dirt out of them.

Seeking a base hit against the Detroit Tigers, Lyons dropped a bunt. Speeding down the first-base line, Lyons saw that the play on him would be close, so he dove into first base, looking for that extra edge. Pitcher Dan Petry fielded the ball and sprinted for the base to head off Lyons. Pitcher and runner arrived close together, but umpire Jim Evans called Lyons safe. Petry did not see it that way and got mixed up in an argument. Time was out and Lyons waited safely on first base. But he did not stand still. The slide had sent a bunch of small pebbles down the front of Lyons' pants. When he stood up, they trickled down his legs to the tight bottoms of the pants, where they got stuck just above his socks.

> With Petry and Evans still creating a commotion right there in front me, I literally forgot I was standing in front of 15,000 fans and did what anybody would do—I started shaking the dirt out of my pants. I undid the belt, unsnapped the snaps of my pants, and even unzipped the zipper. With the first tug, my pants fell to around my knees. With another tug my pants crumpled down around my ankles. Then it hit me. Bent over and nearly naked from the waist down, the only thing between me and an X rating was my sliding shorts! In a flash I had those pants back up around my waist where they belonged.[5]

First baseman Cecil Fielder started laughing. Petry and Evans stopped arguing. Lyons blushed fire-engine red. When play resumed, Lyons was out at second base on a force play. As he trotted back to the dugout, women began waving $1 bills at him and yelling, "Take it off!" Teammate Jack McDowell suggested that Lyons obtain a part-time job as a stripper.[6]

Playgirl magazine, which featured nude men in its centerfolds the way *Playboy* featured nude women, contacted Lyons for a guest shot. He turned down that opportunity, however. It was the incident that never went away, the single best-recalled moment of Lyons' Major League career. It was not a premeditated move, but Lyons heard about it for years. The story drifted into baseball lore and people began labeling Lyons as the guy who dropped his pants during a game.

That was partially because Lyons was only a part-time player most of his career. He was not a big-time power hitter, nor did he hit clutch home runs to win a World Series. As he once told a reporter, he had to think carefully about his approach, knowing he was looked at solely as a bench guy.

Lyons said no matter what he did he always thought he was normal, perhaps because he was living in a baseball environment. People believed he dreamed up stunts when he was bench-ridden for lack of anything better to do like pay attention to the game, yet he insisted everything he got involved in was spontaneous.

But Lyons was also a menace away from the field, overcome by the camaraderie of being on a ballclub. Even when he was still playing at AAA Pawtucket in the Red Sox chain, he could be counted on to be at the center of the action.

"We had guys sneak into other players' rooms, short sheet their beds, steal all the light bulbs, turn up the heat, and fill up a wastepaper basket with water and lean it against the door," Lyons said.[7]

Lyons went into each season aware that he had little chance to play in every game. That meant he had to find other ways to shove himself into the spotlight. The crazy stuff did the job. As a back-up, Lyons had to seize the moment when he got a chance. He also had to modify his goals as each season began. "I can't set career goals like other players," Lyons said. "I can't say, 'I'd like to get 150 hits this year' because I don't play often enough. So my biggest goals this year are to appear on 'Late Night With David Letterman' and be on the cover of *GQ*."[8]

Everyone who becomes a professional ball player dreams of making it to the majors. They think their stay in the minors will be transitory. They are sure that even if they start out in the lowest rung in the majors, they will work their way up and become big leaguers. For some the dream dies quickly. They either recognize their abilities that once carried them to stardom in high school or even college don't translate to a more competitive level, or someone in authority tells them that's it.

Lyons was sort of halfway in-between in this environment. He learned quickly that advancement would not be easy, but he also did not give up and he was not sent into exile. Still, after only nine days of professional ball he realized he was going to be in for a battle.

22. Steve Lyons

> We lost nine straight games, our bus caught fire, our driver died, and I'd seen people act towards each other in ways I'd never seen before. We almost dropped our shortstop out the back window, and I was hitting about .220. I was cold, tired and hungry, and I began to realize just how long the road to the big leagues was going to be.[9]

Lyons made it sound as if having a sense of humor was a pretty good attribute upon learning the distance between the low minors and the majors in everything from transportation to level of play. The difference between Class A and the majors was class, no class and all class.

Similar things happened when Lyons went off to play winter ball in Puerto Rico. Having advanced to AAA ball, he thought that if he showed well in the off-season someone would believe he could become a big-leaguer. The money, some $4,500 a month, was more than he made in the United States, but he discovered he had to pay for his own housing, food and rental car. It did not help his state of mind that he played poorly, which matched the 6–16 start of his team. "I was hitting about .230 and made seven errors at third base," Lyons said. "That's not as bad as it sounds, considering our infield looked as if the grass was cut by cattle grazing after games."[10]

Lyons was still playing in the AA minors in New Britain, Connecticut in the Red Sox chain, when he gained his nickname of "Psycho." It was not a nickname that he relished, nor one that he expected. It was hung on him by catcher Marc Sullivan one day after Lyons had a terrible day at the plate. After striking out for the third time, Lyons went berserk. He threw down his bat, kicked his batting helmet and then sat in the dugout swearing at himself. Sullivan said he was acting like a psycho, and that was it.

Sometimes Lyons portrayed himself as an innocent bystander. He bonded with fans in some ballparks. At one time he was sent down to AAA by the White Sox, but ended up back in the majors with the Red Sox. Some of his old friends in the center field bleachers welcomed him back by acting out the famous shower scene from the Alfred Hitchcock movie *Psycho*. As Lyons put it, "complete with back lighting, a shower curtain and 15 extras wielding fake knives. Dee, a shapely blonde, was the unanimous selection to be the shower victim."[11]

Chris Berman, the ESPN announcer who was exceptionally clever at coining nicknames for players that were more than one-word jobs, also labeled Lyons later. On the occasion when Lyons made a highlight-reel fielding play in the majors and the catch was shown on screen, Berman said, "And here's Steve Lyons, and tigers, and bears, oh my!"[12]

Lyons had plenty of ups and downs in his career, one stretch up with a Major League team and another down with a minor-league club.

In 1992, he was back with Pawtucket and injured a hamstring. Rather than stew about the problem during one game he decided to alleviate boredom by selling popcorn. He slipped away to a concession stand, cajoled the workers into lending him the proper attire and set off for the box seats wearing an apron. As he adopted the typical selling slogan of "Popcorn, here!" fans recognized him and asked for autographs. He bartered his signature for popcorn sales.

Although he became renowned for practical jokes, Lyons later backed off from that reputation. Or at least, according to the first book he wrote, he did so, saying that yeah, he was often involved, but he was not always the instigator.

Lyons was playing for the Montreal Expos in 1992 when manager Tom Runnells was fired. Lyons had only been with the club for ten days, so it wasn't his fault. Runnells showed class by leaving individual notes in players' lockers, thanking them for their efforts. The note Lyons found in his locker had a slightly different tone. It read, "I didn't really want you here anyway. It was a front office decision. Thanks for going two-for-10 in the at-bats I gave you. It helped me get fired. Tom Runnells."[13]

Of course, Runnells did not write that. Nor did he write the other notes that appeared in the lockers. They were substitutes penned by catcher Rick Cerone and his evil sense of humor. Lyons said it took some time for the veterans on the team to convince the young players that Runnells really hadn't authored them.

Lyons knew that he did not have the natural talent to succeed like the top players, so he put his heart into the game and made sure he hustled like a Pete Rose. He knew that was the best approach for him, and he knew that was the kind of thing that might get him noticed by the brass more than playing jokes would. Organizations don't think players who are at the bottom of the pecking order are funny enough to keep around if they can't hit or provide other value. "Even when I played the outfield I always threw the ball hard back to the infield after catching a fly," Lyons said. "I wanted to get the ball to the pitcher as quickly as possible so the game can get started again."[14]

Lyons said he may have come across as hypocritical to fans at one time because he was running out walks a la Rose, but didn't always run out pop-ups or grounders when he knew the defense had him dead to rights. "People started thinking it was all a big act, so this year [1984] I've hustled on everything. And playing the infield is more suited to my personality anyway. There's too much standing around in the outfield."[15]

Lyons did not actually make it to the big club in Boston until 1985, but he played in 133 games that season. He was the regular center fielder. That did not last, though. One thing Lyons did make his mark with was his personality. He was the same old Steve, the Psycho, but on a bigger stage. That meant more people noticed if he did anything goofy. Lyons was primarily a third baseman, but the Red Sox had future Hall of Famer Wade Boggs in front of him. He actually got a chance to play more often than pinch-hitting and pinch-running because of injuries, and found himself in center field.

That season it seemed fans were more focused on making Lyons laugh than he was on making them laugh. Lyons was hitting well and the fans were appreciative. Fans yelled from the stands to him to throw them a ball one day. They said they would autograph it and throw it back with signatures wishing him a happy June 3, 25th birthday. Sure enough, that's exactly what happened. "When the game ended they threw it back and there were about 20 signatures on it," Lyons said.[16]

Somehow it is difficult envisioning a group of fans doing that for Albert Belle or Carl Everett, given their frequent surliness to reporters and in public.

Although Lyons made a good impression with his hustle and by starting out strongly at the plate before declining to a .264 final average, he was his own comedy miscue film in one game against the Texas Rangers in May of the next season. If the Sox hadn't pulled out the game, 5–4, Lyons may have been optioned to Mars, never mind AAA, and he knew it.

> I had made an error that cost a run, overthrew a cut-off man, messed up a sacrifice bunt and got picked off. When Marty [Barrett] hit the ball, I was determined to make up for it by scoring the tying run. As I got to third, I took a look back and thought the ball had been caught. If I was thrown out in this situation, I'd never see the field again this season, so I put my head down and ran back to second.
> As I slid in, I heard Barrett saying, "What are you doing here?" I knew we both couldn't stay on the same base, so I took off back to third and dived in, trying to beat the throw. I never saw the ball go into the dugout. My face was buried in the dirt.[17]

With the ball out of play, Lyons was given a free base, which was the tying run. It was no wonder manager John McNamara's analysis sounded a bit dizzy after watching that. "I don't believe I've ever seen anything quite like it," McNamara said. "But I'll take it."[18] It was a surreal happy ending.

In 1986, a suburban Boston radio station in Marlboro, Massachusetts, hired Lyons to file short reports from spring training and during the season. Another reporter raised the question of how Lyons would handle things if he was the star of a game. It was not a situation he anticipated occurring too often since as always he was a utility player without a regular job in the field. But Lyons took the question seriously, if that is the proper word, saying he might have to include himself in a radio snippet if he did something special. Then he made up a scenario. "Hi, everyone," Lyons said. "This is Steve Lyons at Fenway Park with the hero of the Red Sox' 5–3 win over the Yankees—myself. Do you think this clutch home run will persuade manager John McNamara to put you in the starting lineup more often? What kind of stupid question is that? You trying to get me into trouble or something?"[19]

One irony of Lyons working for a Marlboro radio station was that his father, Dick, had been a star high school athlete in nearby Hudson, though Steve never spent any time there. His grandmother still lived in the area, and he and his mother and grandmother all went to dinner at the Marlboro Country Club. When Lyons' AA team won its league title he gave the championship ring to his dad. "I never get tired of hearing my father's name being thrown around," Lyons said. "It's a big thrill for me to hear he was such a fine athlete. People are always coming up to me and telling me they knew him or played against him."[20]

After his Major League playing days ended, Lyons became a baseball broadcaster. He was a regular for Fox Sports, but was fired in the middle of the American League playoffs in 2006 for making a racially insensitive remark about Hispanics that related to Lou Piniella. Piniella said he did not think Lyons was prejudiced and was only joking.

Lyons had been hired with the goal of being edgy and outrageous, but he often ran the risk between being blunt and too blunt. Still, Lyons has also worked as a baseball broadcaster for the Los Angeles Dodgers, Arizona Diamondbacks, and, starting in 2014, the Red Sox.

One thing Lyons had at his fingertips was a storehouse of offbeat, funny baseball stories, sometimes those he was directly involved in and sometimes just things he witnessed or heard about while in big-league dugouts or clubhouses. Lyons always said he was not a traditional baseball trivia expert. "That kind of stuff rarely sticks in my brain," Lyons said. "So if you've got a trivia question for me I probably don't have the answer."[21]

But he did have a favorite story about an unusual minor league, extended spring training triple play that Buck Showalter, now the manager of the Baltimore Orioles, told him. "The opposing team [not Showalter's] turned an unassisted triple play without touching the ball," Lyons said.[22]

There were runners on first and second. The batter faced a 3–2 count. Showalter ordered a double steal. The hitter swung and popped the ball up. The umpires invoked the infield fly rule. So that was one out. The runner on first base was running, but did not tag up after the ball was caught. The runner on second base did return to the bag. And that's where he was standing when the first-base runner, oblivious to the circumstances, passed him. So that was two outs. But the runner on second, who was not much more aware, was actually hit by the pop-up when it came down for out No. 3.

It was an almost unimaginable scenario, virtually impossible to duplicate. But it was a triple play. Showalter, as minor league managers are typically required to do, filed his game report with the big club's front office, and was immediately telephoned to explain what happened.

And if anyone thinks that was wacky, remember that when Steve Lyons wrote one of his books it appeared in print upside-down and backwards.

Maybe that was another way Lyons earned the nickname "Psycho."

23. Ozzie Guillen

"He has more fun than anyone else who plays the game. For a lot of players, it's a job. Ozzie Guillen doesn't fall into that category. I'm not saying other guys don't enjoy it. But if they do, they don't show it."—*Then–Yankees coach Don Zimmer*[1]

WHEN OZZIE GUILLEN SPOKE TO A WRITER for *Sports Illustrated* in 2006, he uttered a memorable comment. "I will tell the truth, whether you like it or not," Guillen said.[2]

That turned out to be fascinatingly accurate self-description for the years of Guillen's tenure as manager of the Chicago White Sox, the franchise he represented for most of his career on the diamond as a shortstop.

Guillen, a native of Venezuela who became a United States citizen around that time, was the man at the helm when the White Sox ended an 88-year drought and won baseball's World Series in 2005. His theme song might as well have been Frank Sinatra's "My Way."

A creative speaker with a devil-may-care attitude about what he said (although he was wise enough to go off the record after his daily press briefing for other comments in the Sox's dugout), Guillen was a monstrous breath of fresh air as a big-league skipper. He occasionally came up short by failing to have a governor on his speech, and it cost him periodically. But anyone who spent much time around Guillen had to be delighted with such a frank, outspoken man answering questions and dispensing monologues. If not for those darned politically correct comments in an ever-critical world, Guillen might still be running a big-league team, and he probably should be again someday soon.

Candor is Guillen's middle name. As a player, Guillen, who was born in 1964, broke into the majors with the White Sox in 1985 and played for 16 seasons, most of them with Chicago. He averaged .264, but his strength was fielding. He was the American League "Rookie of the Year," a three-time All-Star and a Gold Glove winner. He considered himself a disciple of and follower in the line of famed Venezuelan shortstops Chico Carrasquel, Luis Aparicio and Davey Concepción.

Guillen made a good impression in Chicago, especially with owner Jerry Reinsdorf, who considered him to be family. When the White Sox contacted him about their open managerial slot, Guillen was just coming off a World Series victory with the Florida Marlins. Guillen was the third-base coach for that team.

As most baseball figures would, Guillen attended the championship victory party. He was scheduled to meet with Sox general manager Kenny Williams, whom he knew as a former teammate. After he was hired, Guillen granted an interview with HBO Sports in which he admitted an out-of-the-ordinary preparation for the meeting with the brass for his dream job. When asked if he had read up on the team or rehearsed for the appearance, Guillen said he did not do those things. "I was hung over," he said. "Just because we just win the World Series. I was at Pudge Rodríguez's house and we had a party all night to celebrate the World Series."[3]

Guillen is quite fluent in English and always makes himself understood, but he does speak with an accent. He could be sensitive and liked to believe he fought for his players, his team, himself, and his organization. Feisty was another word that described Guillen, particularly if he believed those allegiances were under attack. "I like trouble," Guillen said. "Why not? A lot of people have their way to say stuff. I got my way. You know, all those little things about the game. People don't face it. Attack. Attack. I never take the first punch, never. Believe me, you throw me rocks, I'm gonna F-16 and just try to kill you. That's my style."[4] Guillen perceived that he did take the first punch most of the time, but he did not sit idle and let things roll off his shoulders.

Guillen was pretty much the same guy all along, but he had a broader forum to speak from when he became a manager and a larger stage still after he became a World Series–champion manager. He was more in demand, sometimes so much in demand for sound bites that it surprised him.

Always a hardcore player, giving 100 percent and making creative plays at short, sometimes Guillen's bat let him down. He had his moments hitting well, but he also had his slumps. One time in spring training fans yelled to Guillen and asked for a free bat. "Why would you want a .220 hitter's bat," he yelled to them. "To put in the fireplace?"[5]

Guillen was always competitive, an astute baseball man who knew his stuff. That's some of what the Sox hierarchy recalled about him when they were searching for a new manager in 2003. Those things, and perhaps also things he said in the past that revealed his attitude. "To me, second place is the first loser," he said. "That's all it is."[6]

Guillen's Q rating shot up when he took over as field boss of the White Sox. It's not easy to land a big-league managing job, and most baseball fans know the manager of each team. Guillen made himself higher profile yet as time passed. He had always wanted to become a big-league manager and he always believed he would. As a player, he told Sox teammates that one day he would hold down one of the coveted slots. He told sportswriters that as well.

Although Reinsdorf loved Guillen, former teammate Williams had his doubts if he was the right fit for the club. "We knew he had the knowledge and gamesmanship, but there was a goofball side of him and we thought that no one would take him seriously," Williams said of Guillen when he was hired in November of 2003. "Half the time we didn't."[7]

Familiarity might have hurt Guillen early in the process, but he sold himself in a four-hour-plus session with Williams. Guillen was the last of six candidates to be interviewed. "When I talked to Kenny I said, 'I'm going to be me,'" Guillen said. "'If you like it, you hire me. If you don't like it, make sure you pay for another first-class ticket to get me back home.'"[8]

Williams cited Guillen's passion and energy, among other things, as to why he chose him for the position, and Guillen did take the White Sox on a merry ride. Guillen said he was honored to get the job and hoped it would be the last Major League uniform he ever wore.

Guillen had never managed a minute in his life, but did bring three years of coaching experience to Chicago. Two months into the 2004 season as a rookie manager, Guillen had the White Sox in first place in their division. He said he was learning every day on the job, but when asked what grade he would give himself to date he was direct. "I think 'A' because I'm in first place," Guillen said. "If I was not in first place, it would be different. I'm in first place. If I was in last place, it might be a 'Z.'"[9]

Guillen imbued his team with a sense of enthusiasm, and he had good players to work with. What a journey it was in 2005 when the White Sox rolled to the American League pennant and won the World Series from the Houston Astros. The club had not won a Series since 1917, two years before the Black Sox nearly ruined the team and set it back for decades.

The Boston Red Sox drought that ran from 1918 to 2004 had been characterized as "The Curse of the Bambino" because the franchise had been silly enough to trade Babe Ruth to the New York Yankees. The Black

Sox scandal probably crippled the White Sox more than the exile of Ruth damaged the Red Sox long-term. At the least it was a close call, though few fans linked the two events as year after year passed without a White Sox championship trophy.

Guillen set the tone for the 2005 team, and when it was over he could celebrate by smoking a cigar and by bringing the World Series trophy to Venezuela to show off. That was a moment of great pride to him. The United States got to know Guillen that year in a more intimate way. Sometimes he made people laugh and sometimes he outraged them, but he became known as a sports figure with a frank tongue.

He was direct when he thought a player made a bonehead play and didn't shy away from saying it. If he was challenged, Guillen lashed back at a player. He issued a profanity-filled diatribe at Magglio Ordonez, who gave up the White Sox for the Detroit Tigers as a free agent.

Sometimes Guillen would get worked up about topics that came from left field, such as his monologue on heaven and hell. "Are you going to heaven?" he said. "Are you going to hell? We don't know. All I know is they put you in the ground and cover your ass with dirt. I ask my kids, 'Who came up with heaven and hell?' Somebody just made that up. You look it up in the dictionary? What do they say?"[10]

Huh?

During an in-game dispute with Texas Rangers manager Buck Showalter, regarded as a sharp cookie on the rules, some questioned if Guillen knew what he was talking about. When a ruling was made, Guillen was proven right and he gloated. "I never say anything about other managers," Guillen said, proceeding to do just that. "If I have any bad comments to make I'll keep them to myself. But Mr. Baseball [Showalter], who didn't even have a hit in Triple A, says things like that. He might be jealous. I might have more money, more houses and more cars. And I'm better looking."[11]

Guillen was an expert at holding court in the dugout before games. He answered questions, dealt with issues, and then went off the record and delivered some of his funniest remarks. Those could not be reported. Unfortunately for him, sometimes Guillen's comments were tinged by politically incorrect language. He was sent to the corner for some of them and ordered to undergo sensitivity training. His problem was not necessarily malice in his heart, but carelessness in his vocabulary in front of the wrong people.

Periodically, Guillen spoke of his kinship with past top-notch Venezuelan shortstops. Both Carrasquel and Aparicio starred for the White Sox, so he was merely continuing the linear connection. Even though Guillen did become an American citizen during his tenure as White Sox manager, he retained a strong connection to the South American country of his birth.

Despite being considered thin-skinned by some, Guillen was not above making fun of himself at certain times, either. "The Venezuelan people who know me don't feel proud because we're winning," he said. "They're proud because they go, 'How can this crazy man be the leader of a team?'"[12]

Guillen may have come off as a crazy man from a distance, but his players knew that he had their backs and he knew he was wiser about baseball than some believed. Guillen knew what he was good at—managing players—and what he shouldn't do. "I don't get involved in pitch selection," Guillen said. "First of all, I am not that smart. Second, I'm not that good. I trust my catchers."[13]

It didn't last long enough to be truly bothersome, but the White Sox did hit a speed bump late in the season that made some fans worry about them faltering and losing the division. There were a few uneasy moments. "I told my guys that we can't lose the division because I have 30,000 managers in the stands with me," Guillen said.[14]

During that slump Guillen remained pretty much an open book. E-mails poured into him criticizing the team's play and his managerial choices. He read them all. Some of them provoked steam coming out of his ears, but he still kept reading. "I'm getting hundreds every day," he said. "Sure, I read them. I only like reading the nasty ones. It hurts me very much to read some of the comments, but I think there's something to learn from even the ugly criticism. More so than reading the ones patting me on the (back). Of course, right now there aren't many nice ones to weed out."[15]

For Guillen to read these stabs in the back instead of the pats was difficult to stomach. But he has always dished it out. He told it like he saw it. That is his nature. He can't hold back if he thinks of something that must be said. He does not tap-dance around issues. He lets it fly. Guillen is also aware of how sometimes he ignites a firestorm. "People say, 'Ozzie Guillen is a bigmouth,'" Guillen said. "'He's so controversial.' No. People don't like it when you tell the truth."[16] Guillen doesn't subscribe to the white lie policy to spare someone's feelings. He is as subtle as a shotgun blast.

The White Sox rolled in 2005. It was a rollicking good time on the South Side. Chicago won 99 games, finishing six games ahead of the Cleveland Indians in the American League Central Division. The White Sox beat the defending champion Red Sox three straight games in the AL Division Series and then topped the Los Angeles Angels, 4–1, in the AL Championship Series before sweeping the Astros in four straight.

Tremendous starting pitching throughout the playoffs, coupled with clutch hitting, carried the White Sox. The victory made Guillen the first Latin American manager to win a World Series. He figured if he went back to Venezuela he might be able to make a living in a different field. "If I ran for president, I'd have a shot because I'm in the news every day," Guillen said. "I'm popular."[17]

To another scribe Guillen said he could probably be elected mayor of Chicago. Of course that didn't take into account all of the Cubs voters who might jam the ballot. Still, when the city threw the White Sox a celebratory parade, it was estimated that two million fans turned out to watch in Chicago's streets. Some of them might have been just baseball fans.

One always had to scrutinize Guillen's words to see if he meant what he said or he was just putting people on. Also, if the words attached to his name really signified the meaning or he was just coming close because his English was not always nuanced. Even if the words were read out loud, part of the job required reading Guillen's mind.

Guillen went on the record saying that it was okay to cheat in baseball, and that raised some eyebrows. He was not referring to the use of steroids or other performance-enhancing drugs. That was not okay. He was talking about fudging the rules in the old-style, traditional sense. To Guillen, that might mean throwing an occasional spitball or using a corked bat. In his mind, using those weapons meant looking for an edge, trying to squeeze every possible advantage out of a situation.

> If you're doing what you're not supposed to do and you don't get caught, keep doing it. Everybody cheats. If you don't get caught, you're a smart player. If you get caught, you cheated. To me, that's been part of the game for a long time. Corked bats have been forever. We don't know if Babe Ruth used a corked bat or [Joe] DiMaggio. Nobody checked those bats then. We don't know.[18]

Most White Sox players enjoyed playing for Guillen. He was unpredictable verbally, and he did criticize them by name in the media, but he appreciated hard work and dedication and he did make the boys chuckle. "He's a mess, but we love him," said infielder Gordon Beckham. "He's a fun mess."[19] That sounded like a compliment.

Guillen abhorred players not hustling. Once, when shortstop Alexei Ramirez jogged to first base instead of running all-out on a fly ball out in right field, Guillen let him have it. "The next time you do that," Guillen said, "you'll be running to Guatemala."[20]

As more time passed, Guillen grew savvier in dealings with the media. He knew what set off an attention frenzy, and some of his players were convinced the manager lit the fuse intentionally at times. If they were playing poorly, Guillen would feed the writers, TV guys and talk radio guys something to write that was off-topic. "There's a method to his madness," said pitcher John Danks. "Whenever we need the attention taken off us, or if he needs to do something to loosen us up, I think Ozzie knows what he is doing. Ozzie's a character, no doubt, but there have been times when he's said things or done things where it's almost planned."[21]

There was likely truth in Danks' observation. If someone asked Guillen directly, he might admit it, or just let the twinkle in his eye speak for him. Guillen's formal schooling may have ended when he was 16, but no one ever underestimated his intelligence.

Once with the White Sox, they fell into a 4–16 slump and it was time for more than handwringing. Assuming that Guillen was so depressed he could not function without professional assistance, a sportswriter seemingly innocently wondered if perhaps Guillen should take a time-out with the team psychologist. "That guy, if he took me on, he will retire," Guillen said of such a potential one-on-one session. "I guarantee you, he will quit. To me, mental? This is my 25th year in the big leagues. Before, we used to solve a mental problem with a vodka and a lot of Budweiser."[22]

The statute of limitations, or the patience of upper management, did eventually run out on Guillen's tenure in Chicago after he managed the White Sox for eight years. He moved on to the Marlins in Miami, where he had a home and where he had been part of a World Series success. But things went sour quickly in South Florida when the Marlins finished 69–93 in Guillen's only season at the helm, and where he ticked off the fan base with some ill-advised remarks about Fidel Castro. Somehow, it would not likely have been a firing offense if the Marlins had gone 93–69.

That was in 2012, and Guillen has not been prominent on the big-league scene since. Guillen was still only 53 in early 2017, however, quite young enough to manage again if someone called. As he said while still with the White Sox,

> I like the smell of the ballpark. I like the sound of the bat. That's the way I grew up since I was a baby. How many people have the opportunity to do what I do? I'm going to die doing this. I'm going to die on the field. I hope the day I die, I just like, go to the field and am gone. Game's over. Tomorrow's the funeral.[23]

24. Bob Uecker

"Bob Uecker is Brewers baseball."—Milwaukee Brewers owner Mark Attanasio and Major League Baseball Commissioner Bud Selig[1]

HE WAS GOOD ENOUGH TO PLAY Major League baseball for six seasons, but Bob Uecker was not good enough at the game to hang around the big leagues longer, or good enough to be a star. If you listen to Uecker, who was born in Milwaukee in 1935, he had to have a sense of humor because his lifetime average was .200.

But Uecker's sense of humor transcended many forums and locations, not merely big-league dugouts. The star of his own TV Show, "Mr. Belvedere," Uecker became known as "Mr. Baseball," nicknamed by talk show host Johnny Carson. Uecker spent a lot of time on Carson's couch making the nation laugh at his baseball stories and his self-deprecating shots at his own career. He also appeared in commercials and had a featured role as a broadcaster in the movie *Major League*.

Surrounded by wackos on the movie set, Uecker pretty much played it straight, with some bonus inflections applied to memorable lines. When "Wild Thing," the relief pitcher played by Charlie Sheen, uncorked a swift fastball and conked the mascot, Uecker said, "Juuuust a bit outside."

He broadcast games nationally, but has remained attached at the hip to the Milwaukee Brewers' booth for 40 years and counting. It is possible that of all the baseball funny men, Uecker is the heavyweight champ as the funniest of them all.

Never much of a power hitter, with 14 Major League home runs, or a hitter of any type, Uecker was an excellent defensive catcher. Hall of Famer Phil Niekro credited Uecker with giving him the confidence to stick with his knuckleball.

True to his own form, when Uecker was presented with the Ford Frick

Award in Cooperstown, his acceptance speech critiqued his limited career batting successes and tied them to other Hall of Fame pitchers.

> I wanted today to apologize to Ferguson Jenkins, Gaylord Perry, and Sandy Koufax for hitting home runs off them. I always thought it would keep them out of the Hall of Fame. Gaylord Perry, to this day, says that it's the worst moment in his whole life—not in his baseball career, but his life. The other day I said to him, "I don't remember hitting a home run against you," and he said, "5-5-63." He's got the date![2]

Uecker said he might have become a football player rather than a baseball player. "The first thing my dad ever bought me was a football," Uecker said. "He didn't know a lot about it. He came from the old country. We tried to pass it and throw it and kick it and we couldn't do it. It was very discouraging for him and for me. Finally, we had a nice enough neighbor who came over and put some air in it."[3]

Uecker was a National League player for the Braves, Phillies and St. Louis Cardinals. He was part of the St. Louis 1964 World Series champions. "I remember Gene Mauch in Philadelphia," Uecker said. "I'd be sitting there and he'd say, 'Grab a bat and stop this rally.'"[4]

Uecker said his sons played the game much the same way, citing strikeouts and a game-costing error. "I couldn't have been more proud," Uecker said. "I remember the people in the parking lot throwing eggs and rotten stuff at our car. What a beautiful day."[5]

Actually, despite hits coming sparingly to him, Uecker did have some regular success against Koufax in the mid–1960s when nobody else was hitting him. At one point Uecker's average against the southpaw was .400. "I can't him 'em all, so I just hit the best," Uecker said. "I've hit some real shots off Koufax. I mean real boomers. Why, some of 'em went 90 or 100 feet. But they wind up base hits and don't think Koufax doesn't remember it." When he heard that Koufax was adding a new pitch to his arsenal, Uecker said he didn't need it. "It's like giving Agent 007 another gun."[6]

Like any other sport, baseball teams have their stars, their regulars, and their back-ups. Uecker was a back-up catcher just about everywhere he went, and that meant he did more sitting in the dugout than standing in the batter's box. When he did not hit well, and he rarely did with his .200 average, Uecker seemed like just one of many other players who felt he would do better if he played more. Then he got some steady work with the Atlanta Braves in 1967.

"They're trying to ruin me," Uecker said of manager Billy Hitchcock playing him more regularly. "With those others teams I could always say I didn't get a chance. But now it's different. They're playing me too much and now I don't have any kind of excuse."[7]

"Uke," as Uecker is usually called, got so much action because the Braves traded away Gene Oliver and then incumbent Joe Torre got hurt. Uecker started playing behind the plate every day, on 90-degree days. Uecker was listed as 6-foot-1 and 190 pounds during his playing days, but said he lost 15 pounds in the heat of the summer while filling in for Torre. "It's a good thing Joe got back," Uecker said. "I was beginning to fade away."[8]

With every topic being fair game, Uecker was the biggest jokester in the clubhouse, teasing guys and flinging out one-liners. Teammates said he was a great guy to have around for laughs. "Yeah," Uecker said. "They all laugh like hell when they see me grab a bat."[9]

One spontaneous routine that perpetuated Uecker's reputation as a funny man was a pre-game act he pulled off before a Cardinals game. A band was preparing to play at the game, but took a break and left instruments around. Uecker picked up a tuba and began patrolling the outfield, trying to catch fly balls in it. When he ceased, Uecker played a few notes for the sportswriters. "I don't know how to play the thing," he said afterwards. "I did take clarinet lessons when I was in grade school, but I couldn't do anything with it so my parents took it away. They came to a recital and I couldn't play."[10]

Uecker's popular book, *Catcher in the Wry*, came out in 1982. The teaser line on the cover included this: "The man who made mediocrity famous!"[11] Uecker's introduction was brief, but to the point in a volume that was chockful of laughs.

> Most of what I have written here is true, especially those descriptions and examples of how I struggled to become a lifetime .200 hitter in the major leagues. Some of what I have written might have happened, but didn't, and some could have happened in the dark corners of my own imagination. I have not used any arrows, cartoon balloons, or parenthetical asides to tell you which is which.[12]

He thereby left us all on our own to laugh in the privacy of our own homes.

Uecker played before the big money spread to players throughout baseball. He was ahead of his time, a useful back-up catcher because of his fielding, but not quite as useful as a pinch-hitter since he couldn't really hit. But the way the game evolved into players earning *Monopoly* money, Uecker figured that if he was just a little big younger his phone would have been ringing off the hook for teams to give him $150,000 a year to play 60 games or maybe $200,000 a year to play 30 games.

Surviving six years on big-league rosters was an achievement Uecker always relished—and always joked about. "Anybody with ability can play in the big leagues," Uecker said. "To last as long as I did with the skills I had, with the numbers I produced, was a triumph of the human spirit."[13]

Although others throughout baseball history tried, no one was more successful at making fun of his own career than Uecker. If he had played any longer he probably would have been doing open microphone routines in Hollywood. But he got the most bang from his time in the bigs in humor, if not in big dollars. The man possessed the ability to adapt the language to his own needs. Uecker could likely talk his way out of any corner more readily than he could have hit his way out of a 0–2 count.

As most every player does, Uecker wished he could have played longer in the majors. He stuck around as long as he could, or as long as he could get a deal with a team. Then came the day when there was no deal to be had and retirement sneaked up on him, whether he wanted to take that drastic step or not.

The keen observation about retirement made by one-time boxing star Willie Pep resonated with Uecker. "First your legs go. Then your reflexes go. Then your friends go." Uecker's experience differed slightly. "My friends went first," Uecker said.

> In baseball the clues were more subtle. In my case I began to get the hint when my bubblegum card came out and there was a blank space on it where the picture was supposed to be. Sporting goods companies offered to pay me not to endorse their products. I got to the park for what the manager had announced would be a night game and found out they'd started at 1 p.m. I came to bat in the bottom of the ninth, two out, the bases loaded, my team trailing by a run and looked over at the other dugout and saw them already in their street clothes.[14]

The reader got the hint and so did Uecker, which is why he ended up looking for a new career at age 32. Fortunately for baseball and the listening public, Uecker did not become a full-time used-car salesman for the rest of his working life. By 1971, he was handling Milwaukee Brewers radio broadcasts, and he has never relinquished the role.

Radio led to more opportunities, including several spots in the series of Miller Lite beer commercials that used former professional athletes. In a memorable ad, Uecker brags about having terrific seats for a game. He sits in a crowded section, then is told he is in the wrong place and says, "I must be in the front row." The camera pans his section from a distance, and Uecker is sitting alone in what appear to be distant right-field seats. The ad became so famous that the Brewers created a statue of Uecker sitting in the way back of beyond in Miller Park.

Uecker was 14 years into his baseball broadcasting career and had made a splash with that advertising when he was cast in an ABC sitcom called "Mr. Belvedere." Uecker played a butler, a character inspired by Clifton Webb, a popular thespian from silent films.

Mr. Belvedere had references from Winston Churchill and famous

French chefs to obtain his job. "He's pretty much what I could be like," Uecker said of his TV alter ego. "A lot of his character was picked up from my own."[15] However, Mr. Belvedere was not a weak-hitting, second-string catcher in his role in the household he inhabited.

Uecker did experience a bit of an epiphany when he realized calling games from the broadcast booth gave him the same view of the diamond as he had when he was playing—from behind the plate, just a little higher up. "It's a lot safer up there and I don't get booed as much as I did when I was catching," Uecker said."[16]

Uecker also turned in memorable turns in front of the camera in the baseball movies *Major League* and *Major League II*. His role as Harry Doyle parodied all baseball announcers. Sometimes he spouted clichés. Sometimes he drank in the booth. Sometime he issued commentary that the viewer could see was false, just to be saying something positive about the team. A master of wry understatement was Harry Doyle. When a ball was hit deep, earmarked for home-run territory, Doyle said, "If that's not Shaquille O'Neal in left, it's out of here."[17]

During the 1989 off-season, Uecker suffered a mild heart attack, but he was back in the saddle for spring training only a month later. The initial news was alarming to fans, but Uecker seemed to recover quickly. It was no wonder that Uecker suffered the affliction when he did. He couldn't possibly have had much sleep during the week leading up to the attack since he was shooting *Mr. Belvedere*, worked on a batch of ten Miller Lite commercials, and did an appearance with Johnny Carson on *The Tonight Show*.

In his return to baseball, Uecker was his old self, joking around, making light of his health situation. "I tell ya, if I'm going to blow out someday, I want it to be at the ball park," Uecker said. "Really, it'd be great. I'd blow out, they'd cart me around the field a couple times, the fans would cheer, and poof, out the main gate. Gone."[18]

Since he wasn't ready to go, Uecker decided he had to listen to doctors' orders about diet and exercise, even if he wasn't sure that was the regimen he wanted to follow.

> The doctors have got me on this high-fiber diet. But I'm a little nervous about the effects. Dogs are starting to sniff my legs. My feeling had always been, "Hey, I've got a car. Why do I need to run?" But I've changed my approach. I couldn't believe how many flowers there were [from well-wishers]. I woke up one morning shortly after it happened and I was in kind of a fog. I saw all these flowers, but I couldn't hear any music. I thought my wife had bought me a real cheap funeral.[19]

Fortunately for Uecker, the heart attack represented a short intermission in his career, more like a long commercial than any significant break.

However, that was not the end of Uecker's health problems while he was in his 50s. Two years later, this time during the big-league season, Uecker had to call time out for surgery for an aneurysm of the abdominal aorta. Uecker had complained of lower back pains before he was diagnosed, and his operation took three hours.

Again in 2010, Uecker was sidelined for a while because of heart surgery during the season. This was a six-hour operation at age 75. He was out from April to July and actually returned to the broadcast booth ahead of doctors' plans, declaring himself fit enough with the statement, "I'm ready to rock and roll."[20]

In all cases, the repair jobs took and did not impair Uecker's gift of gab. When he came back, ten pounds underweight, partially due to a complicating staph infection, Uecker said he had to pay off his doctors with a bribe to release him, even though they did not want it. "I said, 'You guys wanna throw out a couple of first pitches?'" Uecker said. "'Then let me come back to work.'"[21]

Along the way during his decades broadcasting Brewers games, Uecker did have the opportunity to make appearances in places besides hospitals. In 1987 and 1988, he performed commentary on *Wrestlemania* with André the Giant. "That choking thing with Andre [who stood 7-foot-4 and weighed 520 pounds] wasn't in the script," Uecker said.[22]

However, those two fun jobs led to Uecker being selected for the celebrity wing of the World Wrestling Entertainment Hall of Fame in 2010. "I get to wear tights!" Uecker proclaimed.[23] Wearing tights in a big-league game is one thing Uecker never got to do. Maybe that was surprising given the nature of baseball humor in The World According to Uke. "At its liveliest, it is crude and shameless and irreverent," Uecker said. "It is army humor with more sweat."[24]

For a guy who seemed prepared to be shameless in pursuit of a laugh, Uecker had occasions when he worked to preserve his dignity while playing. One of those times occurred with the Cardinals while catching future Hall of Famer Bob Gibson, whose fastball could be mistaken for a bolt of lightning. The game was played in Milwaukee, and since that's where Uecker grew up he wanted to show well. It was pride by association that the pitcher was the great Bob Gibson.

> With two out in one of the late innings, and two strikes on the hitter, he let loose with a pitch that moved so sharply I didn't have time to raise my glove, and it smacked against my bare hand. It felt as if I had put my palm flat against a hot stove. I picked up the ball with my mitt, tagged the runner, walked away from the plate, walked into the dugout and up the runway toward the clubhouse, and then cut loose with a scream that would have made Johnny Weissmuller sound like a sissy.[25]

At the least it was probably a yell that Tarzan would have appreciated.

Uecker may have adopted a slower-paced schedule, but as he went on as Brewers broadcaster long past the standard retirement age, he stayed in baseball. The guy made up for a limited-length playing career with a super-length broadcast career.

In 2005, marking Uecker's 50th year in baseball and his 35th behind the mike with Milwaukee, the Brewers honored Uke. In 2009, the Brewers found another reason to honor him. Citing Uecker's connection to the old Milwaukee Braves (before they fled to Atlanta), they celebrated him as Milwaukee's first home-grown player, dating to his 1956 signing with the Braves. "I was also the first home-grown player sent out," Uecker said about being sent to the minors.[26]

Uecker, who never played for the Brewers because they weren't around when he was active, now has a number retired for him on the wall at Miller Park. The team chose 50 for Uecker's 50 years in baseball when they put it up in 2005.

"I'd like to do this again 50 years from now when I get to 100," Uecker said.[27]

Uecker is still going strong, still broadcasting those Brewers games. Less than 40 years to go.

Epilogue

"Anything that goes that far ought to have a stewardess on it."—Pitcher Paul Splittorff on a 420-foot George Brett home run[1]

THERE HAVE BEEN MANY OTHER FUNNY MEN in baseball history, for a moment in time, a season in time, or an entire career. Some of them meant to be funny and others acted that way by accident.

Mark Fidrych not only made people laugh, he made them feel good with his ingenuousness and innocence. The right-handed pitcher delighted fans during a brilliant 1976 season, coming out of nowhere to make the roster of the Detroit Tigers and emerging as the ace of the staff.

Fidrych was known for talking to the baseball, and something must have clicked because the ball seemed to obey him that unexpected year when he finished 19–9, led the American League in earned run average at 2.34, made the All-Star team and was chosen "Rookie of the Year." He sometimes got down on his knees and patted the ground on the mound to make it as smooth as he preferred.

The native of central Massachusetts was 21 when he hit the big-time and delighted fans from coast to coast. Some people referred to him as a mix of Dizzy Dean and Harpo Marx, partially because of his frizzy hair. Others say the somewhat loose-limbed hurler bore a resemblance to the *Sesame Street* character Big Bird, and that is how he gained his nickname "The Bird."

Fidrych was a phenomenon, a one-year wonder, because knee and arm injuries limited him to a lifetime 29–19 career mark. But for one brief, shining season he was Camelot.

When Fidrych was selected to start the All-Star Game for the AL, he said, "I guess this is my biggest thrill since I got a mini-bike when I was 14." When sportswriters asked if he thought he should be making more than the $16,000 he was getting, Fidrych said, "I never made this much money before and it's still pretty good for a guy who used to work in a gas station for about $2 an hour."[2]

Fidrych revealed that he started talking to the baseball even before he pitched in high school. "It's just my way of getting into a game, my way of concentrating," he said.[3] Apparently, no one had thought of that angle before.

Leading up to the All-Star Game, the writers were playful with Fidrych, asking if he talked to car engines when he worked at the gas station. He said he did (with a wink). Another question came from left field. Fidrych was asked when he noticed that his friends didn't act like him. "But they do," Fidrych said, breaking up the crowd.[4]

Fidrych was so popular that summer that it was figured he pitched in front of 900,000 people in his starts. At home the Tigers averaged fewer than 10,000 fans a game when he wasn't pitching, and when it was Fidrych's turn in the rotation 40,000 showed up.

The tragedy of Mark Fidrych, however, was twofold. For one season he could do no wrong. Then he suffered serious injuries and poof, it was all gone. He retreated to Massachusetts, bought a farm and raised a family. However, in 2009, an accident on that farm killed him at a young 54, way too soon.

First, Fidrych entertained the world with his presence and then he saddened it with his departure.

> "He's the only player in baseball who consistently hits my grease. He sees the ball so well, I guess he can pick out the dry side."—*Hall of Fame pitcher Gaylord Perry, admitting he threw a spitter, when talking about fellow Hall of Fame hitter Rod Carew*[5]

Moe Drabowsky enjoyed a peripatetic pitching career, suiting up for eight big-league teams, and "enjoyed" is probably the right word. Underrated as a pitcher (when he was on) and underrated as a comic when he was in the bullpen or dugout, Drabowsky was born in Poland in 1935 and died in Little Rock, Arkansas, in 2006. In between he pitched in 589 Major League games with an 88–105 record. Drabowsky suffered through numerous losing seasons, but mixed in excellent relief years of 6–0 and 6–1, mostly as a middle man after he turned 30.

Always on the lookout for an opportunity to play a prank, Drabowsky once gave the hot-foot—setting shoes on fire—to Commissioner Bowie Kuhn. He dreamed up creative ways to use the bullpen phone, doing impersonations on it or ordering pizzas. Whatever came to mind, Drabowsky tried it. "You never saw a shoe come off so fast in your life," Drabowsky said of the Kuhn incident.⁶ Drabowsky said he lay down a trail of lighter fluid from the trainer's room to the clubhouse to get Kuhn.

Pitching highlights were harder to come by than laughs, but in 1966, pitching for the Baltimore Orioles, Drabowsky struck out 11 men in 6⅔ innings against the Los Angeles Dodgers in a World Series game.

Once, Drabowsky, who had pitched for the Kansas City Athletics, was sitting in the Orioles' bullpen at Municipal Stadium. The A's hurler, Jim Nash, was pitching great against Drabowsky's club, but Drabowsky called one bullpen from the other and ordered them to get a reliever warmed up, imitating manager Alvin Dark's voice as he did so. No one expected Nash to need relief help, but the opponents scrambled to follow the order.

That was not Drabowsky's only bullpen call of note. Around the same time, he got Lew Krausse to begin warming up by using Dark's name, he made another call pretending to be A's owner Charlie Finley. Teammates listening in on those calls got the full flavor and Drabowsky left them in stitches.

After word got out about his telephone itch, Drabowsky received an abundance of fan mail. One note came from a youngster in South Dakota, whose comment arrived via telegram. It read: "Baseball needs more nuts like you."⁷

Another time Drabowsky approached Orioles teammate Paul Blair while wearing a snake around his neck. Blair thought it was a rubber snake, but it was the real thing and he was freaked out when the boa constrictor stuck out its tongue at him. Drabowsky also once put a snake in shortstop Luis Aparicio's underpants. And these were teammates!

Other Drabowsky greatest hits involved putting goldfish in the visiting team's water supply and borrowing a security guard's shotgun to shoot a voodoo doll hanging in a teammate's locker room, with the aim of changing his team's karma.

Just in case you thought this kind of stuff only happened in the movies, Drabowsky once put sneezing powder in the air conditioning system that was blowing air into a foe's locker room.

Drabowsky did find himself on the right mound at the wrong time on a couple of occasions. He threw the pitch that St. Louis Cardinals great Stan Musial connected with for his career 3,000th hit. Drabowsky soon volunteered his services to be the pitcher when Musial bashed his 4,000th hit. Musial retired before that opportunity arose. Also, Drabowsky was the losing pitcher when Early Wynn won his 300th game.

After retiring as a player in 1972 as a two-time World Series champion, Drabowsky served as a coach in the Baltimore minor-league system for 13 years. He battled multiple myeloma for years longer than doctors originally gave him to live with their diagnosis.

Drabowsky said his sense of humor kept him going on bad days. "It's been a major, major factor," Drabowsky said. "I don't get down very easily. I've always been positive. It doesn't matter what kind of condition you're in, you have to find some humor somewhere."[8]

> "I've seen him order everything on the menu except 'Thank you for dining with us.'"—*Braves teammate Jerry Royster on how much Dale Murphy could eat*[9]

In one of the strangest episodes in baseball history, one day out of the blue during the 1911 season, a man named Charlie Faust appeared in St. Louis, where the New York Giants were playing, and asked to meet with manager John McGraw. Faust told McGraw that a fortune teller back home in Kansas had told Faust that he would pitch the Giants to the championship.

The Giants were in a pennant race, so McGraw gave Faust a tryout. It was soon apparent that his arm did not have big-league stuff. But Faust knew his baseball, conveyed predictions and thoughts, and they turned out to be correct. In short order, Faust became a team mascot. Whenever he was around, the Giants won the game. Faust, who gained notoriety, went into vaudeville for $200 a week to tell stories about players and imitate them. However, as soon as Faust left for this new career, the Giants went on a losing streak. Faust rejoined the club, performed antics on the field, and the Giants cruised to the pennant. Faust gained a nickname—"Victory."

Faust's goal had been to pitch for the Giants, but his presence seemed to help them in a supernatural way. After New York clinched the pennant, twice McGraw inserted Faust into games as a hurler. In both instances, they were losing and Faust pitched the ninth inning.

Whatever magic Faust possessed ran out during the World Series. His Giants fell to the Philadelphia Athletics during Connie Mack's first A's dynasty. As for Faust, he ended up being institutionalized with mental problems and died in 1915.

> "I should have eat it. That would show them."—*While playing in the Dominican Winter League, Cincinnati Reds pitcher Pedro Borbon reacted to a black cat being thrown at him by fans and threw the cat to his catcher*[10]

"The best thing that ever happened to me was going nuts," Jimmy Piersall said of the nervous breakdown he had in the 1950s.[11]

It was a pretty strange thing to say. Piersall was a very funny man whose antics often entertained fans and whose commentary often entertained sportswriters. But some of his edginess and itchiness was genuine mental illness. He conquered that to experience a very solid Major League career and an excellent broadcasting career later, especially the time spent as a partner to Harry Caray.

Piersall had a 17-year Major League career from 1950 to 1967. He was an exceptional fielding center fielder and batted .272 lifetime. He made two All-Star teams and won two Gold Glove Awards. Piersall, who was born in Waterbury, Connecticut, in 1929, clouted 104 home runs in his career and famously back-pedaled around the bases to celebrate his 100th home run.

As a fielder, Piersall played very shallow because he was quick enough to catch up to balls hit deep toward the Fenway Park wall. When things were going badly at the park and fans booed, Piersall put his fingers in his ears to show he couldn't hear them. He also stuck out his tongue at the fans when they rubbed him wrong. During one very peculiar game in Cleveland, Piersall, who broke in with the Boston Red Sox but also was a regular with the Cleveland Indians and Los Angeles Angels, kicked a fan in the rear end that had burst onto the field.

Throughout the 1950s and into the 1960s, Piersall was regarded as a baseball character liable to do unpredictable things. He spit on a lineup card, led the right-field fans in Cleveland in a musical performance, and also had a genuine mental hospital stay in 1952.

The incidents, including the breakdown, made people wonder if Piersall was trying to be funny or was acting out because he was ill. At one point he said that he never planned any of his actions in advance. They were impromptu. Piersall wrote a book about his illness called *Fear Strikes Out*, and the volume was made into a movie as well.

He could very engaging, fun to be around, but a stigma was attached to someone who was mentally ill at that time in American history, and Piersall admitted that after he returned to the bigs (his talent was never in question), some players called him names like "nutty."

Being from New England, Piersall grew up a Red Sox fan, and it was a thrill for him to be signed by the team in 1947. Aside from any problems he had, Piersall had a sharp wit and wasn't scared to use it. "I hated the Yankees from the day I came out of my mother's womb," Piersall said.[12]

Piersall pulled a couple of memorable stunts against the Yankees.

Once, in Yankee Stadium while playing center, he ducked behind the Babe Ruth monument and hid there. Another time he sat down on second base and challenged notoriously poor-hitting Yankees relief pitcher Ryne Duren to hit the ball over his head.

The reason why Piersall hunkered down at the Ruth monument, he said, was the bad day his team was having. The Red Sox were getting shelled and there was a parade of relief pitchers going by. He said the umpire came out and told him he couldn't sit on the monument. "I'm talking to the Babe," Piersall said.[13]

Piersall was an excellent all-around athlete. He was a high school basketball star and the Boston Celtics drafted him. He got a hit in his first Major League at-bat. He began in the majors as a shortstop, partially because Dom DiMaggio still held down center field. He said that Hall of Fame shortstop Phil Rizzuto told him if he spent a year in the minors honing his skills, he would be a terrific big-league shortstop. Piersall's answer? "I hate playing shortstop."[14]

Near the end of Piersall's playing career, he ended up with the young New York Mets, playing for Casey Stengel. "Do you think New York is ready for me and Stengel together?" Piersall asked upon arrival.[15]

Piersall had worn No. 37 during his career, but remarkably, that was Stengel's number with the Mets. He suggested they wear 37A and 37B, but that did not come to pass.

Stengel said he thought Piersall would be good for the Mets and the Mets would be good for Piersall, and Piersall said he thought the expansion Mets were good for baseball. "I think the Mets and their fans are helping to save baseball," Piersall said, "and they are keeping the writers in business and it is better than being in Russia."[16]

During the last years of his career in California, Piersall appeared in an Elvis Presley movie and a TV episode of *The Lucy Show*, with Lucille Ball. Piersall spent years in the broadcast booth and then became a coach for the Chicago Cubs. He was the centerpiece of a Chicago sports talk show. So brutally honest that he once authored a book called *The Truth Hurts*, that was Piersall on the air and telling minor leaguers they couldn't cut it and they should go get another job.

Piersall had some legendary feuds with umpires, and he once got the heave-ho from an umpire whose last name was McKinley when he said, "They shot the wrong McKinley."[17]

In his 70s, Piersall was still touring the country doing baseball card shows and was a popular addition to any event. "I never hit like [Ted] Williams or Ruth," Piersall said, "but I've got as much publicity as any of them."[18]

"This wouldn't be a bad place to play if it wasn't for that wind. I guess that's like saying that hell wouldn't be such a bad place if it wasn't so hot."—*Jerry Reuss on pitching at Candlestick Park*[19]

Although many players of the past believe that there are fewer "characters," fewer "colorful" guys in baseball today, and that the modern player is too straight-laced and conservative, there will always be men who play Major League baseball that are funny to be around.

The law of averages dictates that.

Chapter Notes

Introduction

1. Eric Zweig, *Home Plate Don't Move* (Richmond Hill, ON: Firefly Books, 2006), 17.
2. *Ibid.*, 95.
3. *Ibid.*, 41.
4. Peter Handrinos, *The Funniest Baseball Book Ever* (Kansas City: Andrews McNeel, 2006), 51.
5. *Ibid.*, 51.
6. *Ibid.*, 127.
7. *Ibid.*, 127.

Chapter 1

1. Al Schacht, with Murray Goodman, *Clowning Through Baseball* (New York: Bantam Books, 1949), 72.
2. Lonnie Wheeler, "A Most Peculiar and Distinctive Career," *The Ohioans*, August 1987.
3. *Ibid.*
4. *Ibid.*
5. Gene Kessler, "Nick Altrock, The Ed Wynn of Game, Just Wiggles Ears and Goes Ahead Drawing Big Pay for His Clowning," *Chicago Journal*, October 5, 1933.
6. *Ibid.*
7. James M. Kahn, "Baseball's Court Jester Has No Secret Griefs," *New York Graphic*, October 10, 1925.
8. *Ibid.*
9. Joe Williams, "Humor Rare in Baseball, But Dodgers Boast Casey; Altrock Capitalized It," *New York World-Telegram*, March 9, 1938.
10. "Birthday Greeting from Ike Biggest Thrill for Altrock" (Baseball Hall of Fame Library Archives, unidentified), September 26, 1956.
11. "Altrock, 88, Dies; Baseball Comic," *Associated Press*, January 21, 1965.
12. "Schacht Leads Tributes to Altrock," *United Press International*, January 21, 1965.

Chapter 2

1. Baseball-reference.com biography page, Al Schacht.
2. Al Schacht and Murray Goodman, *Clowning Through Baseball* (New York: Bantam Books, 1949), 1.
3. *Ibid.*, 34.
4. *Ibid.*, 35.
5. *Ibid.*, 37.
6. *Ibid.*, 50.
7. Al Schacht and Murray Goodman, *G I Had Fun* (New York: G.P. Putnam's Sons, 1945), 31.
8. *Ibid.*, 36–37.
9. *Ibid.*, 37.
10. *Ibid.*, 38.
11. *Ibid.*, 73.
12. *Ibid.*, 73.
13. *Ibid.*, 85.
14. Al Schacht and Murray Goodman, *Clowning Through Baseball*, 53.
15. *Ibid.*, 96–97.
16. *Ibid.*, 100.

Chapter 3

1. Bob Broeg, "Colorful Hoyt Remembered as 'Merry Mortician,'" *St. Louis Post-Dispatch*, August 1984.
2. *Ibid.*

3. Bob Broeg, "Waite Hoyt: Articulate Winner," *The Sporting News*, November 27, 1976.
4. Furman Bisher, "Hoyt Paved Way for Jocks on Air," *The Sporting News*, June 21, 1980.
5. Curt Smith, *The Storytellers* (New York: Macmillan, New York, 1995), 58.
6. Bisher, "Hoyt Paved Way for Jocks on Air."
7. *Ibid.*
8. Broeg, "Colorful Hoyt Remembered as 'Merry Mortician.'"
9. *Ibid.*
10. Dick Reynolds, "Hoyt Says Babe Ruth Wasn't Fat or Drunk," *Richmond (IN) Paladium-Item*, September 5, 1982.
11. "Waite Hoyt, Pitcher, Sings at the Palace," *New York Times*, January 20, 1930.
12. Marshall Hunt, "Star Pitcher, Undertaker, Actor, That's Waite Hoyt of the Yankees," *New York Daily News*, January 7, 1929.
13. James Enright, "Roaring '20s—Golden Era for Waite," *The Sporting News*, August 7, 1965.
14. J. G. Taylor Spink, "Three and One," *The Sporting News*, April 2, 1942.
15. Russ Hodges, "Sounding Off," *The Sporting News*, August 25, 1954.
16. Tommy Holmes, "Hoyt to Plead Insanity after Boston Business," *Brooklyn Eagle*, July 2, 1937.
17. Joe Vila, "Setting the Pace," *New York Sun*, 1933.
18. "Campaigner," American League Services Bureau, December 9, 1928.
19. Jeo Williams, "Today's Yankees Owe Spirit to Gay Old-Timers," *New York World-Telegram*, January 15, 1952.
20. *Ibid.*
21. Waite Hoyt, "Farm Boys in Baseball," *Farm Quarterly*, Spring, 1958.
22. Dick Reynolds, "Baseball: 'It Was My Whole Life,'" *Richmond (IN) Paladium-Item*, September 4, 1982.
23. "Hall of Famer Waite Hoyt Dies," *Associated Press*, August 26, 1984.

Chapter 4

1. Tot Holmes, *Brooklyn's Babe: The Life and Legend of Babe Herman* (Gothenberg, NE: Holmes Publishing, 1990), viii.
2. Mike Madden, "Other 'Babe' Was More than a Comedian," *The Sporting News*, December 15, 1979.
3. *Ibid.*
4. Harold Parrott, "French, Casey and Babe—Three Clowns with Clout," *The Sporting News*, December 2, 1972.
5. Jim Murray, "Babe's Version of Legend," *Los Angeles Times* (no date, Baseball Hall of Fame Library archives).
6. Arn Shein, "Mom & the Babe," *MM Magazine*, April–May 1990.
7. National League Service Bureau, citing Tom Meany, *Brooklyn Times-Union*.
8. National League Service Bureau, citing Tommy Holmes, *Brooklyn Eagle*.
9. National League Service Bureau, citing Tom Meany, *Brooklyn Times-Union*.
10. Tot Holmes, *Brooklyn's Babe: The Life and Legend of Babe Herman* Holmes, viii.
11. *Ibid.*
12. *Ibid.*, ix.
13. *Ibid.*, 3.
14. *Ibid.*, 27.
15. *Ibid.*, 67.
16. *Ibid.*, 68.
17. Bill Bryson, "From Confusion to Chaos," *Baseball Magazine*, July 1949.
18. Lewis Burton, "You Shake It and ... Oh, Babe," *New York Journal-American*, January 15, 1951.
19. *Ibid.*
20. Sidney Fields, "Babe's Son Scores," *New York Daily News*, June 16, 1967.
21. *Ibid.*
22. Maury Allen, "Babe Herman, Beloved Ex-Dodger, Dead at 84," *New York Post*, November 30, 1987.
23. Arthur Daley, "Babe Herman: Dodger-Met Link," *New York Times*, July 21, 1965.
24. Red Smith, "Holy Name in Brooklyn: The Babe," *New York Times*, November 7, 1979.
25. Holmes, 235.
26. *Ibid.*
27. Red Smith, "Holy Name in Brooklyn: The Babe."

Chapter 5

1. *Time*, January 18, 1954.
2. Bob Cooke, "Another Viewpoint,"

New York Herald-Tribune, January 24, 1954.
   3. Harry Jones, "No Sleeping after Midnight, First Order of Maranville," *Cincinnati Times-Star*, February 6, 1957.
   4. *Ibid.*
   5. Bob Cooke, "Another Viewpoint."
   6. George Vass, "Screwballs of Baseball: Rabbit Bouncy, Frolicsome Infielder Loved Pranks," *Chicago Daily News* (date missing, Baseball Hall of Fame Library archives).
   7. Thomas S. Rice, "Maranville's Odd Throwing One of Baseball's Puzzles," *Brooklyn Daily Eagle*, June 10, 1919.
   8. Harry T. Brundidge, "Rabbit Maranville, Preparing to Start 19th Season, Predicts One of His Biggest Years," *The Sporting News*, December 18, 1930.
   9. *Ibid.*
   10. William Braucher, "The Best Legs in Baseball," NEA Service (undated, Baseball Hall of Fame Library archives), 1931.
   11. J. Lloyd McGowan, "Maranville the Manager," (unidentified clipping, Baseball Hall of Fame Library Archives), November 1937.
   12. Rabbit Maranville, "Old or New, It's Baseball," *American Legion Monthly*, October 1935.
   13. *Ibid.*
   14. *Ibid.*
   15. Rabbit Maranville, "Hot Stove Stuff," *American Legion Monthly*, January 1936.
   16. Harry Jones, "Maranville Pranks Won Affection of Ball Fans," *Cincinnati Times-Star*, February 2, 1957.
   17. Vass, "Screwballs of Baseball: Rabbit Bouncy, Frolicsome Infielder Loved Pranks."
   18. Arthur Daley, "The Rabbit," *The New York Times*, January 7, 1954.

Chapter 6

   1. Bob Broeg, "Ol' Diz Sure Could Boast ... Then Back it Up!" *The Sporting News*, October 11, 1969.
   2. *Ibid.*
   3. *Ibid.*
   4. *Ibid.*
   5. Davis J. Walsh, "Maybe Ball Players Are People," *King Features Syndicate*, June 19, 1937.
   6. *Ibid.*
   7. David King, "No Average Utility Player," *San Antonio Express-News*, May 5, 2002.
   8. Bill Corum, "Chicago's Red Letter Day?" *New York Evening Journal*, July 18, 1938.
   9. Curt Smith, "Diz Slud Hard, Safely into Fame," *Associated Press/Cleveland Plain-Dealer*, July 20, 1975.
   10. Dizzy Dean, "Poppin' Off," Syndicated column, July 25, 1935.
   11. Dizzy Dean, "Poppin' Off," Syndicated column, July 10, 1935.
   12. "Reds' Manager Says He Can't See Where Dizzy Dean Is Swell-Headed," *Associated Press*, July 23, 1935.
   13. John Kieran, "Two Stitches in Jig-Time," *New York Times*, July 18, 1939.
   14. Curt Smith, "Diz Slud Hard, Safely into Fame."
   15. *Ibid.*
   16. *Ibid.*
   17. Francis J. Powers, "Dean Ascribes Comeback to Goose Grease," *Chicago Daily News*, July 19, 1938.
   18. Robert Gregory, *Diz: The Story of Dizzy Dean and Baseball During the Great Depression* (New York: Viking, 1992), 30.
   19. *Ibid.*, 31.
   20. *Ibid.*, 69.
   21. *Ibid.*, 54.
   22. *Ibid.*, 59.
   23. *Ibid.*, 364.
   24. *Ibid.*
   25. *Ibid.*, 371.
   26. *Ibid.*, 374.
   27. Melvin Durslag, "Dizzy Dean Last of Rare Breed," *Los Angeles Herald-Examiner*, July 18, 1974.
   28. *Ibid.*

Chapter 7

   1. Jim Murray, "The Beethoven of Baseball," *Los Angeles Times*, June 23, 1964.
   2. Joe Durso, "Satchel Paige, Black Pitching Star, Is Dead at 75," *New York Times*, June 9, 1982.
   3. Larry Tye, *Satchel: The Life and Times of an American Legend* (New York: Random House, 2009), 241–243.
   4. Durso, "Satchel Paige, Black Pitching Star, Is Dead at 75."

5. David Sterry and Arielle Eckstut, *Satchel Sez: The Wit, Wisdom And World of Leroy "Satchel" Paige* (New York: Three Rivers Press, 2001), 15.
6. *Ibid.*, 29.
7. *Ibid.*, 46.
8. *Ibid.*, 48.
9. *Ibid.*, 65.
10. John "Buck" O'Neil, "Unforgettable Satchel Paige," *Reader's Digest*, April 1984.
11. *Ibid.*
12. *Ibid.*
13. Satchel Paige and Hal Lebovitz, Hal, *Pitchin' Man: Satchel Paige's Own Story* (Westport, CT: Meckler Books, 1948/1992), 9.
14. Dave Anderson, "Satch Surveys Catfish and Ages," *New York Times*, October 12, 1976.
15. "Ageless Satch Ready to Snip More Batters' Buttons," *Associated Press*, September 7, 1968.
16. "Paige's '100-Year Career' Ends," *New York Times*, June 9, 1982.
17. *Ibid.* "Ageless..."
18. Wayne Minshew, "Satchel Comes to Grips with Pop Time, Hangs 'Em Up," *The Sporting News*, April 19, 1969.
19. *Ibid.*
20. Sterry and Eckstut, 69.
21. Bill Ford, "Looking Back, Paige Relates Good and Bad," *Cincinnati Enquirer*, June 24, 1981.
22. Bob Matthews, "Satch: Late-Arriving Legend," *Rochester Times-Union*, February 4, 1976.
23. Dennis Lustig, "Paige a Fond Memory to Many Former Indians," *Cleveland Press*, June 9, 1982.

Chapter 8

1. Max Patkin and Stan Hochman, *The Clown Prince of Baseball* (Waco, TX: WRS Publishing, 1994), xiv.
2. J. G. Taylor Spink, "Looping the Loops: Max's Ministry Makes Moola," *The Sporting News*, March 2, 1949.
3. *Ibid.*
4. Ron Shelton, Script for movie "Bull Durham." The Internet Movie Script Database, 1988.
5. Dave Newhouse and Tommy Carnes, "Max Patkin: Baseball's Lonely Clown Prince," *The Sporting News*, October 18, 1980.
6. *Ibid.*
7. *Ibid.*
8. James Warren, "Clown Prince: At 72, Ex–Minor League Pitcher Max Patkin Still Plays to the Crowd," *Chicago Tribune*, July 26, 1992.
9. Richard Hoffer, "Patkin Is Still out There Clownin' Around," *Los Angeles Times*, January 1, 1987.
10. George Rorrer, "Patkin, Chicken Go Head to Beak," *Louisville Times*, April 11, 1986.
11. Newhouse and Carnes.
12. Mark Winegardner, "Long Live the Clown Prince," *The Sporting News*, January 20, 1997.
13. *Ibid.*
14. *Ibid.*
15. "Veeck Knows a Clown, So He Hired Patkin," *Associated Press*, August 14, 1977.
16. Max Patkin advertising brochure, Baseball Hall of Fame Research Library Archives, undated.
17. Rich Westcott, "When Patkin Performs, Fans Laugh," *Phillies Report*, undated, Baseball Hall of Fame Research Librarchives.
18. Patkin and Hochman, x.
19. Dick Fenton, "Clown Price Still Going Strong," *Columbus Dispatch/Yankees Magazine*, August 30, 1982.
20. *Ibid.*

Chapter 9

1. Robert W. Creamer, *Stengel: His Life and Times* (New York: Simon & Schuster, 1984), 17.
2. *Ibid.*, 129.
3. *Ibid.*, 262.
4. *Ibid.*
5. *Ibid.*, 264.
6. *Ibid.*, 224.
7. Dave Condon, "Casey Stengel, Everybody's Pal," *Chicago Tribune*, March 31, 1957.
8. Bruce Nash and Allan Zullo, "Pranks for the Memory—Baseball's Funniest Moments," *National Enquirer*, undated, National Baseball Hall of Fame Library archives.

9. John McCallum, "Casey at the Bat," Newspaper Enterprise Association, undated, National Baseball Hall of Fame Library archives.
10. *Ibid.*
11. Congressional Record, Casey Stengel testimony, July 8, 1958.
12. *Ibid.*
13. www.BaseballAlamac.com, Mickey Mantle Congressional testimony, July 8, 1958.
14. Milton Richman, "The Loneliest Man in Baseball," *This Week Magazine*, February 10, 1957.
15. Creamer, 297.
16. *Ibid.*
17. *Ibid.*, 300.
18. George Vecsey, "There Is No Joy in Metsville," *New York Times*, August 31, 1965.

Chapter 10

1. Stephen Martini, *The Chattanooga Lookouts & 100 Seasons of Scenic City Baseball* (Cleveland, TN: Dry Ice Publishing, 2006).
2. "Obituaries: Joseph W. (Joe) Engel," *The Sporting News*, June 28, 1969.
3. *Ibid.*
4. *Ibid.*
5. *Ibid.*
6. *Ibid.*
7. Jack Miley, "It's Circus Day Summer 'Round with Lookouts," *Washington Post*, February 2, 1939.
8. *Ibid.*
9. Richard B. Leggitt, "Today's Sportrait," *Associated Press*, June 20, 1967.
10. James H. Street, "Joe Engel's Antics Have Given Dixie Loop Moguls Some New Ideas," *Birmingham News*, May 28, 1932.
11. Al Thomy, "Sad Engel Walks with Ghosts of Past," *Atlanta Journal and Constitution*, February 11, 1962.
12. *Ibid.*
13. *Ibid.*
14. Frederick G. Lieb, "Make 'Em Laugh, Lookout Chief's Slogan" (Part I), *The Sporting News*, October 29, 1952.
15. *Ibid.*
16. *Ibid.*
17. *Ibid.*
18. *Ibid.*

19. *Ibid.*
20. Frederick G. Lieb, "The P. T. Barnum of the Bushes" (Part III), *The Sporting News*, November 12, 1952.

Chapter 11

1. Arthur Daley, "Expert Opinion," *New York Times*, October 30, 1963.
2. Yogi Berra, *The Yogi Book* (New York: Workman, 1998), 9.
3. Bob Broeg, "Only One Yogi ... Pitchers Glad of That," *The Sporting News*, August 7, 1971.
4. *Ibid.*
5. *Ibid.*
6. Berra, 73.
7. *Ibid.*, 74.
8. *Ibid.*, 69.
9. John Vergar with Carmen Berra, "The Yogi I Know," *New York Daily News*, April 7, 1974.
10. Joe Reichler, "Don't Laugh at Yogi Berra," *Associated Press*, October 27, 1963.
11. *Ibid.*
12. *Ibid.*
13. Gordon Manning, "Yankee Yogi: 'I'm Human, Ain't I?'" *Collier's*, August 13, 1949.
14. *Ibid.*
15. Irv Goodman, "The Other Yogi Berra," *Sport*, May 1958.
16. *Ibid.*
17. *Ibid.*
18. *Ibid.*
19. Yogi Berra and Tom Horton, "Yogi ... It Ain't Over" (New York: McGraw-Hill, 1989), 5–6.
20. *Ibid.*, 6.
21. *Ibid.*, 16.
22. *Ibid.*, 30.
23. *Ibid.*, 48.
24. *Ibid.*, 9.
25. *Ibid.*, 11.
26. *Ibid.*
27. Leslie Lieber, "There's No Place Like Home Plate," *XXX*, March 25, 1956.
28. Dave Anderson, "Berra, 80, Transcends the Test of Time," *New York Times*, May 12, 2005.
29. Bruce Weber, "Yogi Berra, Hall of Fame Catcher For the Yankees, Dies At 90," *New York Times*, Sept. 23, 2015.

Chapter 12

1. Til Ferdenzi, "Garagiola ... A Funny Feeling," *New York Journal-American*, February 6, 1966.
2. Joe Garagiola, "Were the 1952 Pirates the Worst Ever? Maybe So," *New York Times*, February 20, 1977.
3. *Ibid.*
4. Fred Petrucelli, "'I'm Not Ex-Star, Just Finished Player' Garagiola Quips In Talk," *The Sporting News*, November 6, 1957.
5. Ed Wallace, "Joe G. Even Has the Ball in Stitches" (Undated clipping, Baseball Hall of Fame Library archives).
6. Joe Garagiola and Martin Quigley, *Baseball Is a Funny Game* (New York: J. P. Lippincott, 1960), 44.
7. *Ibid.*, 46.
8. *Ibid.*, 55.
9. *Ibid.*, 76.
10. *Ibid.*, 77–78.
11. Bob Broeg, "Garagiola a Hero to TV Fans," *The Sporting News*, April 19, 1975.
12. *Ibid.*
13. *Ibid.*
14. Kay Gardella, "Garagiola at Mike as New Voice of Yankees," *New York Daily News*, March 21, 1965.
15. *Ibid.*
16. Joe Garagiola, *It's Anybody's Ballgame* (New York: Jove Books, 1989), 1.
17. *Ibid.*, 5.
18. *Ibid.*, 12.
19. Matt Schudel, "A Career Bench Warmer with a Flair for Repartee," *Washington Post*, February 8, 2015.
20. Garagiola, 18.
21. Garagiola, 28.
22. Joe Garagiola, "Gags? Players' Wit Is Barbed," *The Sporting News*, April 5, 1969.
23. Jim Gintonia, "D-Backs Press Box Wing Named for Garagiola," *Arizona Republic*, September 20, 2009.
24. Steve Gilbert, "With Trademark Wit, Garagiola Ends Career," mlb.com, February 22, 2013.

Chapter 13

1. Verona Gomez and Lawrence Goldstone, *Lefty: An American Odyssey* (New York: Ballantine, 2012), 267.
2. Arthur Daley, "Fast Pitches and Fast Repartee," *New York Times*, September 3, 1971.
3. *Ibid.*
4. *Ibid.*
5. Gomez and Goldstone, 99.
6. Gomez and Goldstone, ix.
7. Gomez and Goldstone, 33.
8. Gomez and Goldstone, 101.
9. Gomez and Goldstone, 107.
10. "Yankee Star Lefty Gomez Dead at 80," *Wire Services/San Francisco Chronicle*, February 18, 1989.
11. "Hall Of Famer Gomez, 80," *The Sporting News*, February 27, 1989.
12. *Ibid.*
13. "Screwball Pioneer, That's Lefty Gomez," *Associated Press*, August 15, 1974.
14. Dick Young, "Spinning a Yarn at the Series," *New York Daily News*, October 13, 1977.
15. Tom Meany, "El Goofo Dispels El Gloom-o," Syndicated column, *Field Publications*, 1943.
16. *Ibid.*
17. Dan Daniel, "Daniel's Dope," *New York Telegram*, undated clipping, Baseball Hall of Fame Library archives.
18. Frank Graham, "Setting the Pace," *New York Sun*, January 28, 1943.
19. Frank Reil, "Hi There, Morpheus!" *Brooklyn Daily Eagle*, May 30, 1937.
20. *Ibid.*
21. Lefty Gomez, Hall of Fame acceptance speech, August 7, 1972.
22. Wells Twombly, "A Great Wit Enters the Hall of Fame," *San Francisco Chronicle*, February 19, 1972.
23. Harry Jupiter, "Lefty Gomez: One Yankee Whom Everyone Loved," *San Francisco Examiner*, February 19, 1989.
24. Gomez and Goldstone, 370.

Chapter 14

1. Gerald Eskenazi, *Bill Veeck: A Baseball Legend* (New York: McGraw-Hill, 1988), 93.
2. Bill Christine, "How Many Actually Saw Eddie Gaedel Bat?" name of newspaper missing from Baseball Hall of Fame Library clipping, August 15, 1981.
3. Jerome Holtzman, "Bill Veeck: 'Barnum of Baseball' Made Sure Fans Were

Entertained," *Chicago Tribune*, January 3, 1986.
  4. Paul Dickson, *Bill Veeck: Baseball's Greatest Maverick* (New York: Walker, 2012), 149.
  5. Arthur Daley, "Radical Realignment," *New York Times*, May 12, 1967.
  6. Dickson, 155.
  7. Dave Anderson, "Veeck: One of Baseball's Dying Breeds," *New York Times*, undated clipping in Baseball Hall of Fame Library archives.
  8. Bill Veeck and Ed Linn, *Veeck—As in Wreck* (Chicago: University of Chicago Press, 2001), 105.
  9. Bill Furlong, "Bill Veeck Glamorous Elf," *Chicago Daily News*, September 23, 1959.
  10. *Ibid.*
  11. Will Grimsley, "Veeck: It's Been Great," *Associated Press/Oneonta Daily Star*, February 3, 1981.
  12. *Ibid.*

Chapter 15

  1. Jim Bouton, "Books We Talked About Most," https://www.jimbouton.com, December 1999/January 2000.
  2. Lew Freedman, *Knuckleball: The History of the Unhittable Pitch* (New York: Skyhorse, 2015), 200.
  3. Jim Bouton, *Ball Four* (New York: Dell, 1970), 12.
  4. *Ibid.*
  5. *Ibid.*, 16.
  6. *Ibid.*, 18.
  7. *Ibid.*, 27.
  8. *Ibid.*
  9. Dick Young, *New York Daily News*, May 28, 1970.
  10. Jim Bouton, *I'm Glad You Didn't Take it Personally* (New York: Dell, 1971), 6.
  11. *Ibid.*, 24–25.
  12. *Ibid.*, 31.
  13. *Ibid.*, 43.
  14. *Ibid.*, 48.
  15. *Ibid.*, 57.
  16. Bouton, *Ball Four*, 52.
  17. *Ibid.*, 53–54.
  18. Jim Bouton, *I Managed Good, But Boy Did They Play Bad* (New York: Dell, 1973), 15.

  19. *Ibid.*, 28.
  20. *Ibid.*, 159.
  21. Jim Bouton, *Foul Ball* (Guilford, CT: Lyons Press, 2005), 1.
  22. Bouton, *Ball Four*, 298.

Chapter 16

  1. Wells Twombly, "Every Day Is Play Day for Bo," *San Francisco Chronicle*, June 30, 1973.
  2. Al Cartwright, "Pool Cue Saved Bo in Bush-Loop Days," *Delaware Evening Journal*, April 3, 1965.
  3. *Ibid.*
  4. Braven Dyer, "Belinsky, Ex–Pool Shark, Pockets Wins for Angels," *Los Angeles Times*, May 9, 1962.
  5. *Ibid.*
  6. Rick Sorci, "Much Mileage from 28 Victories," *The Sporting News*, November 16, 1987.
  7. *Ibid.*
  8. *Ibid.*
  9. Maury Allen, *Bo: Pitching and Wooing* (New York: Bantam, 1974), 102.
  10. *Ibid.*, 119.
  11. *Ibid.*
  12. Sorci, "Much Mileage from 28 Victories."
  13. *Ibid.*
  14. Allen, 121.
  15. *Ibid.*
  16. Allen, 131.
  17. Myron Cope, "Bo Belinsky's Dilemma: Baseball or Dames," *True*, October 1962.
  18. *Ibid.*
  19. *Ibid.*
  20. Myron Cope, "A Dialogue Between Baseball's Bigmouths," *True*, August 1965.
  21. *Ibid.*
  22. *Ibid.*
  23. *Ibid.*
  24. *Ibid.*
  25. Melvin Durslag, "Philly Is Bo's Kind of Town," *Los Angeles Herald-Examiner*, undated clipping at Baseball Hall of Fame Library archives.
  26. Melvin Durslag, "Hero Worship Tough on Bo, His Laundry and Landlady," *Los Angeles Herald-Examiner*, June 16, 1962.
  27. Richard Goldstein, "Bo Belinsky, the

Playboy Pitcher, Dies," *New York Times*, November 27, 2001.

28. Bud Furillo, "The Belinsky Re-Visited," *Los Angeles Herald-Examiner*, August 6, 1969.

29. Phil Pepe, "The Unbashful Bo," *New York Daily News*, March 22, 1965.

30. Sorci, "Much Mileage from 28 Victories."

Chapter 17

1. Paul Hagen, "Philadelphia Loses an Icon: McGraw Dead at 59," *Philadelphia Daily News*, January 6, 2004.

2. *Ibid.*

3. Jack Lang, "Pretty Wife Calms Flighty McGraw," *The Sporting News*, April 26, 1969.

4. *Ibid.*

5. Dave Anderson, "A Snooze, a Snack and a Save," *New York Times*, June 11, 1972.

6. *Ibid.*

7. Tug McGraw and Mike Witte, *Scroogie* (New York: Signet, 1975), 1.

8. *Ibid.*, 3.

9. *Ibid.*, 91.

10. Tug McGraw and Mike Witte, *Scroogie: Hello There Ball* (New York: Signet, 1976), introduction.

11. *Ibid.*, 66.

12. Melvin Durslag, "Nothing Personal about Trade," *The Sporting News*, March 8, 1975.

13. "Mets Ace Fireman McGraw Realizes His Ambition," *Boston Record-American*, May 18, 1972.

14. Joe Durso, "McGraw Becomes First Met to Sign for 1966," *New York Times*, January 19, 1966.

15. Tug McGraw and Don Yaeger, *You Gotta Believe* (New York: New American Library, 2004), 31, 49.

16. *Ibid.*, 65.

17. *Ibid.*, 66.

18. *Ibid.*, 67.

19. *Ibid.*, 69.

20. *Ibid.*, 134.

21. *Ibid.*, 146.

22. *Ibid.*, 149.

23. Frank Dolson, "Tug McGraw: He's Different," *San Francisco Chronicle*, May 17, 1981.

24. *Ibid.*

25. McGraw and Yaeger, 1.

Chapter 18

1. Paul Dickson, *Bill Veeck: Baseball's Greatest Maverick* (New York: Walker, 2012), 293.

2. John M. McGuire and Ellen Futterman, "It Might Be ... It Could Be ... It is! Harry Caray," *St. Louis Post-Dispatch*, April 20, 1983.

3. *Ibid.*

4. *Ibid.*

5. "Sounds Like Another Golden Year Ahead for Caray," *Associated Press/Albany Times-Union*, April 4, 1994.

6. *Ibid.*

7. Ian Thomsen, "The Master's Voice," *Boston Globe*, undated clipping, National Baseball Hall of Fame Library archives.

8. *Ibid.*

9. *Ibid.*

10. *Ibid.*

11. *Ibid.*

12. Tom Fitzpatrick, "Holy Cow! Baseball's Harry Caray Is Taking Over Scottsdale," *Arizona Republic*, February 3, 1982.

13. Mike Conklin, "Harry Caray Gets Roasted on a Low Flame," *Chicago Tribune*, October 21, 1988.

14. *Ibid.*

15. *Ibid.*

16. Jerome Holtzman, "He Had Many Loves: People, Baseball, Chicago—and Life," *Chicago Tribune*, February 19, 1998.

17. *Ibid.*

18. "Quoting Caray," *St. Louis Post-Dispatch*, February 19, 1998.

19. Holtzman.

20. Paul Sullivan, "A Last Interview: Speaking of Past, Looking to Future," *Chicago Tribune*, February 19, 1998.

21. *Ibid.*

22. Michael Hirsley and Mitch Martin, "It Was Harry's Kind of Funeral," *Chicago Tribune*, February 28, 1998.

23. *Ibid.*

24. Carrie Muskat, "Fans to Raise Glasses in Memory of Lovable Caray," *USA Today*, February 17, 2000.

Chapter 19

1. William Barry Furlong, "At Last, A Likeable Ump," *New York Times*, February 25, 1979.

2. Ron Luciano and David Fisher, *Baseball Lite* (New York: Bantam, 1990), 34.
3. *Ibid.*, 48.
4. Gene Duffey, "Hold the Mustard," *Albany Times-Union*, February 14, 1979.
5. *Ibid.*
6. Bill Dwyre, "Mum's the Word," *Referee*, October 1978.
7. *Ibid.*
8. *Ibid.*
9. Luciano and Fisher, 117.
10. Jim Henneman, "Slip of Tongue Embarrasses Ump, Irks Earl," *The Sporting News*, July 31, 1976.
11. Ron Luciano and David Fisher, *The Umpire Strikes Back* (New York: Bantam, 1982), back cover.
12. *Ibid.*, 3.
13. *Ibid.*, 4.
14. *Ibid.*, 26.
15. *Ibid.*, 27.
16. *Ibid.*, 79.
17. Robert L. Burnes, "The Bitter Feud," *St. Louis Globe Democrat*, March 14, 1979.
18. Tom Fitzpatrick, "1-2-3 Stupid Players, Home Plate and Weaver," *Chicago Sun-Times*, June 15, 1976.
19. Ira Berkow, "Secrets of a Fallible Umpire," *New York Times*, March 13, 1982.
20. *Ibid.*
21. Bill Gleason, "Ron's O-U-T of This World," *Chicago Sun-Times*, May 25, 1970.
22. Jack Craig, "Luciano Finds Job—Where He Fits In," *Boston Globe*, April 13, 1980.
23. Chuck Johnson, "Luciano Suicide Sparks Questions, Memories," *USA Today*, January 20, 1995.

Chapter 20

1. Ross Newhan, "Chesty Johnstone—He Backs up Puffs with Speedy Legs," *Los Angeles Times*, May 20, 1967.
2. Jay Johnstone and Rick Talley, *Temporary Insanity* (New York: Bantam, 1986), vi.
3. *Ibid.*
4. *Ibid.*, 5.
5. *Ibid.*, 10.
6. *Ibid.*
7. *Ibid.*, 12.
8. Ross Newhan, "The Moon Man," *Los Angeles Times*, August 25, 1976.
9. Ira Berkow, "Johnstone of Cubs: Durable Prankster," *New York Times*, August 14, 1982.
10. *Ibid.*
11. Jay Johnstone and Rick Talley, *Over The Edge* (New York: Bantam, 1987), 13.
12. *Ibid.*, 62–63.
13. Gary Stein, "Johnstone: Cubs' Outfielder Is No Joke," *Fort Lauderdale News and Sun-Sentinel*, March 27, 1983.
14. Johnstone and Tally, *Over the Edge*, 100.
15. Jonathan Rand, "The Morning Line," *Kansas City Star*, undated clipping, National Baseball Hall of Fame Library archives.
16. Ray Kelly, "There's a Method to Clownish Jay's Madness," *The Sporting News*, August 6, 1977.
17. Don Merry, "He's a Real Firecracker," *Los Angeles Times*, May 20, 1977.
18. *Ibid.*
19. Jay Johnstone and Rick Talley, *Some of My Best Friends Are Crazy* (New York: Macmillan, 1990), 8.
20. *Ibid.*, 28.
21. DD Eisenberg, "Johnstone: Jim Piersall Revisited," *Philadelphia Bulletin*, August 10, 1975.
22. *Ibid.*
23. Randy Schultz, "Jay Johnstone's Unique Career Was Littered with Many Base Hits and Even More Laughs," *Sports Collectors Digest*, November 3, 1995.
24. Johnstone and Talley, *Some of My Best Friends Are Crazy*, 30.
25. Johnstone and Talley, *Temporary Insanity*, 195.
26. Johnstone and Talley, *Some of My Best Friends Are Crazy*, 219.

Chapter 21

1. Steve Henson, "Bill Lee Wins Minor League Game at Age 63," yahoosports.com, September 5, 2010.
2. Gail Jennes, "Is He Baseball's Flake of Flakes? Montreal's Bill Lee Says Yes, No and Maybe," *People*, August 13, 1979.
3. *Ibid.*
4. Bill Lee and Dick Lally, *The Wrong Stuff* (New York: Penguin, 1985), 3.
5. *Ibid.*
6. *Ibid.*, 5.

7. *Ibid.*, 17.
8. *Ibid.*, 114.
9. *Ibid.*
10. *Ibid.*, 198.
11. *Ibid.*, 200.
12. Henson, "Bill Lee Wins Minor League Game at Age 63."
13. *Ibid.*
14. Lee and Lally, *The Wrong Stuff*. Bill Lee and Dick Lally, *Have Glove, Will Travel: Adventures of a Baseball Vagabond* (New York: Crown, 2005), p. 14.
15. *Ibid.*, 30.
16. *Ibid.*, 83.
17. *Ibid.*, 97.
18. *Ibid.*, 219.
19. Thom Loverro, "Spaceman Cometh with Odd Views on the Expos' Situation," *Washington Times*, March 6, 2002.
20. *Ibid.*
21. Jere Longman, "A Campaign Pitch for Spaceman," *Philadelphia Inquirer*, May 28, 1987.
22. *Ibid.*
23. *Ibid.*
24. *Ibid.*
25. *Ibid.*
26. Jim Hickey, "Bill Lee Hurls Verbal Curves for Big Hitters," *Vineyard Gazette*, July 10, 2009.

Chapter 22

1. Steve Lyons, *Psychoanalysis* (Champaign, IL: Sports Publishing, 1993), xi.
2. *Ibid.*, 143.
3. Dave Dyer, "Colorful Lyons Relishes the Ultimate Utility Role," *Haverhill (MA) Gazette*, June 18, 2001.
4. E. M. Swift, "Moon Man," *Sports Illustrated*, August 13, 1990.
5. Steve Lyons and Burton Rocks, *The Psycho 100* (Chicago: Triumph, 2009), 3.
6. *Ibid.*, 4.
7. Lyons, *Psychoanalysis*, 143.
8. Swift, "Moon Man."
9. Lyons, *Psychoanalysis*, 10.
10. *Ibid.*, 15.
11. *Ibid.*, 36.
12. *Ibid.*, 27.
13. *Ibid.*, 31.
14. Chaz Scoggins, "Steve Lyons: The Red Sox' Top Prospect Will Make It to the Big Leagues on Desire Alone," *Lowell (MA) Sun*, July 22, 1984.
15. *Ibid.*
16. Joe Giuliotti, "Entertaining Fans Is Lyons' Specialty," *The Sporting News*, June 17, 1985.
17. Joe Giuliotti, "Lyons' Share of Mistakes Considerable," *The Sporting News*, June 2, 1986.
18. *Ibid.*
19. Bill Doyle, "Marlboro's 'Voice of the Red Sox' Is on the Team," *Worcester (MA) Evening Gazette*, February 19, 1986.
20. Ed Bridges, "Chip off the Block," *Hudson (MA) Daily Sun*, April 17, 1985.
21. Lyons and Rocks, 94.
22. *Ibid.*

Chapter 23

1. Jerome Holtzman, "Sox's Hoyt-For-Guillen Deal Looks Much Better 13 Years Later," *Chicago Tribune*, April 23, 1997.
2. S. L. Price, "War of the Words," *Sports Illustrated*, February 20, 2006.
3. Teddy Greenstein, "Guillen Shoots from Hip in HBO Interview," *Chicago Tribune*, February 5, 2006.
4. *Ibid.*
5. Phil Rogers, "Guillen Won't Sell Himself Short," *Chicago Tribune*, March 2, 1997.
6. *Ibid.*
7. Teddy Greenstein, "White Sox Name Ozzie Guillen Their Latest Manager," *Chicago Tribune*, November 3, 2003.
8. *Ibid.*
9. Dave Van Dyck, "Guillen Grades Himself an 'A,'" *Chicago Tribune*, May 31, 2004.
10. Chris DeLuca, "Put an 'E' in Scoreboard for Entertainment," *Chicago Sun-Times*, May 19, 2006.
11. Brett Ballantini, *The Wit And Wisdom Of Ozzie Guillen* (Chicago: Triumph, 2006), 17.
12. *Ibid.*, 20.
13. *Ibid.*, 35.
14. *Ibid.*, 38.
15. *Ibid.*, 39.
16. Price, "War of the Words."
17. Lew Freedman and Billy Pierce, *Then Ozzie Said to Harold* (Chicago: Triumph, 2008), 207.

18. Josh Krocky, "Guillen: Cheating Is OK if it Helps Team Win," *Daily Southtown*, June 18, 2005.
19. Rick Morrissey, *Ozzie's School of Management* (New York: Henry Holt, 2012), 9.
20. *Ibid.*, 21.
21. *Ibid.*, 39.
22. *Ibid.*, 91.
23. Greenstein, "Guillen Shoots from Hip in HBO Interview."

Chapter 24

1. Drew Olson, "Uecker Celebrates Golden Anniversary," *Milwaukee Journal-Sentinel*, August 27, 2005.
2. Jeff Vella, "Side-Splitting Uecker Leaves 'Em Laughing," *Oneonta (NY) Star*, July 28, 2003.
3. *Ibid.*
4. *Ibid.*
5. *Ibid.*
6. Sandy Grady, "Uecker Clouts 'Only the Best,'" *Philadelphia Bulletin*, March 15, 1966.
7. Ray Kelly, "Uecker Keeps Braves Loose in New Role," *Philadelphia Bulletin*, July 14, 1967.
8. *Ibid.*
9. *Ibid.*
10. Bob Wolf, "Forgotten Braves Catcher Uecker in Series," *Milwaukee Journal*, October 10, 1964.
11. Bob Uecker and Mickey Herskowitz, *Catcher In The Wry* (New York: Jove, 1983), cover.
12. *Ibid.*, xi.
13. *Ibid.*, 4.
14. *Ibid.*, 5.
15. Lauren Simon, "Uecker to Star in New TV Sit-Com," *USA Today*, March 6, 1985.
16. Uecker and Herskowitz, 6.
17. "Uecker Has Seen This Scene Before," *Associated Press*, October 25, 1995.
18. "Uecker Glad to be Back in Front Row," *Associated Press*, March 6, 1989.
19. *Ibid.*
20. Anthony Witrado, "Uecker's Back, Despite Doctor's Orders," *Milwaukee Journal-Sentinel*, July 23, 2010.
21. *Ibid.*

22. Michael Hiestand, "Uecker Gets Front-Row Seat in WWE Hall of Fame," *USA Today*, March 26, 2010.
23. *Ibid.*
24. Uecker and Herskowitz, 164.
25. Uecker and Herskowitz, 193–194.
26. Adam McCalvy, "Brewers Celebrate Native Son Uecker," MLB.com, May 12, 2009.
27. Olson, "Uecker Celebrates Golden Anniversary."

Epilogue

1. Bill Adler, *Baseball Wit* (New York: Crown, 1986), 2.
2. Red Foley, "Bird Talks to Press, Too," *New York Daily News*, 1976. Baseball Hall of Fame Research Library archives.
3. *Ibid.*
4. *Ibid.*
5. Adler, 3.
6. Bill Ordine, "O's Series Hero Was a Prankster, Too," *Baltimore Sun*, June 11, 2006.
7. "Fan Says Baseball Needs 'More Nuts' Like Big Moe," *The Sporting News*, July 2, 1966.
8. Matts Fulks, "Coaching Helps Former Royal Drabowsky Cope with Incurable Cancer," *Kansas City Star*, April 16, 2006.
9. Adler, 78.
10. Mark Purdy, "With Pedro, Commentary Must Be Biting," *Cincinnati Enquirer*, June 26, 1979.
11. Alan Schwarz, "Fears of a Clown," *Baseball America*, April 17–30, 1995.
12. Rich Marazzi, "Chatting with the Always Entertaining, Frequently Over-The-Top and Occasionally Outrageous Jimmy Piersall," *Sports Collectors Digest*, January 21, 2000.
13. *Ibid.*
14. *Ibid.*
15. Joe King, "Me 'n' Case Mets' Answer to Broadway," *The Sporting News*, June 8, 1963.
16. *Ibid.*
17. Schwarz, "Fears of a Clown."
18. *Ibid.*
19. Adler, 79.

Bibliography

Books

Adler, Bill. *Baseball Wit.* New York: Crown, 1986.

Allen, Maury. *Bo: Pitching and Wooing.* New York: Bantam, 1974.

Ballantini, Brett. *The Wit and Wisdom of Ozzie Guillen.* Chicago: Triumph, 2006.

Berra, Yogi. *The Yogi Book.* New York: Workman, 1998.

Berra, Yogi, and Tom Horton. *Yogi ... It Ain't Over.* New York: McGraw-Hill, 1989.

Bouton, Jim. *Ball Four.* New York: Dell, 1970.

___. *Foul Ball.* Guilford, CT: Lyons Press, 2005.

___. *I'm Glad You Didn't Take It Personally.* New York: Dell, 1971.

___. *I Managed Good, but Boy Did They Play Bad.* New York: Dell, 1973.

Creamer, Robert W. *Stengel: His Life and Times.* New York: Simon & Schuster, 1984.

Dickson, Paul. *Bill Veeck: Baseball's Greatest Maverick.* New York: Walker, 2012.

Eskenazi, Gerald. *Bill Veeck: A Baseball Legend.* New York: McGraw-Hill, 1988.

Freedman, Lew. *Knuckleball: The History of the Unhittable Pitch.* New York: Skyhorse, 2015.

Freedman, Lew, and Billy Pierce. *Then Ozzie Said to Harold.* Chicago: Triumph, 2008.

Garagiola, Joe. *It's Anybody's Ballgame.* New York: Jove Books, 1989.

Garagiola, Joe, and Martin Quigley. *Baseball Is a Funny Game.* New York: J.P. Lippincott, 1960.

Gomez, Verona, and Lawrence Goldstone. *Lefty: An American Odyssey.* New York: Ballantine, 2012.

Gregory, Robert. *Diz: The Story of Dizzy Dean and Baseball During the Great Depression.* New York: Viking, 1992.

Handrinos, Peter. *The Funniest Baseball Book Ever.* Kansas City, MO: Andrews McNeel, 2006.

Holmes, Tot. *Brooklyn's Babe: The Life and Legend of Babe Herman.* Gothenberg, NE: self-published, 1990.

Johnstone, Jay, and Rick Talley. *Over the Edge.* New York: Bantam Books, 1987.

___. *Some of My Best Friends Are Crazy.* New York: Macmillan, 1990.

___. *Temporary Insanity.* New York: Bantam Books, 1986.

Lee, Bill, and Dick Lally. *Have Glove, Will Travel: Adventures of a Baseball Vagabond.* New York: Crown, 2005.

___. *The Wrong Stuff.* New York: Penguin, 1985.

Luciano, Ron, and David Fisher. *Baseball Lite.* New York: Bantam, 1990.

___. *The Umpire Strikes Back.* New York: Bantam, 1982.

Lyons, Steve. *Psychoanalysis.* Champaign, IL: Sports Publishing, 1993.

Lyons, Steve, and Burton Rocks. *The Psycho 100.* Chicago: Triumph, 2009.

Martini, Stephen. *The Chattanooga Lookouts and 100 Seasons of Scenic City Baseball.* Cleveland, TN: Dry Ice, 2006.

McGraw, Tug, and Mike Witte. *Scroogie.* New York: Signet, 1975.

___. *Scroogie: Hello There Ball.* New York: Signet, 1976.

Bibliography

McGraw, Tim, and Don Yaeger. *You Gotta Believe*. New York: New American Library, 2004.

Morrissey, Rick. *Ozzie's School of Management*. New York: Henry Holt, 2012.

Paige, Satchel, and Hal Lebovitz. *Pitchin' Man: Satchel Paige's Own Story*. Westport, CT: Meckler, 1992.

Patkin, Max, and Stan Hochman. *The Clown Prince of Baseball*. Waco, TX: WRS, 1994.

Schacht, Al, and Murray Goodman. *Clowning Through Baseball*. New York: Bantam, 1949.

___. *G I Had Fun*. New York: G.P. Putnam's Sons, 1945.

Smith, Curt. *The Storytellers*. New York: Macmillan, 1995.

Sterry, David, and Arielle Eckstut. *Satchel Sez: The Wit, Wisdom and World of Leroy "Satchel" Paige*. New York: Three Rivers, 2001.

Tye, Larry. *Satchel: The Life and Times of an American Legend*. New York: Random House, 2009.

Uecker, Bob, and Mickey Herskowitz. *Catcher in the Wry*. New York: Jove, 1983.

Veeck, Bill, and Ed Linn. *Veeck—as in Wreck*. Chicago: University of Chicago Press, 2001.

Zweig, Eric. *Home Plate Don't Move*. Richmond Hill, ON: Firefly, 2006.

Magazines

American Legion Monthly
Baseball America
Baseball Magazine
Collier's
Columbus Dispatch/Yankee Magazine
Farm Quarterly
MM
People
Reader's Digest
Referee
Sport
Sports Collectors Digest
Sports Illustrated
The Ohioans
The Sporting News
This Week
Time
True

Newspapers

Albany (NY) Times-Union
Arizona Republic
Atlanta Journal and Constitution
Baltimore Sun
Birmingham News
Boston Globe
Boston Record-American
Brooklyn Eagle
Brooklyn Times-Union
Chicago Daily News
Chicago Journal
Chicago Sun-Times
Chicago Tribune
Cincinnati Enquirer
Cincinnati Times-Star
Cleveland Plain-Dealer
Cleveland Press
Daily Illinois Southtown
Fort Lauderdale News and Sun-Sentinel
Haverhill (MA) Gazette
Hudson (MA) Daily Sun
Kansas City Star
Los Angeles Herald-Examiner
Los Angeles Times
Lowell (MA) Sun
Louisville Times
Milwaukee Journal
Milwaukee Journal-Sentinel
National Enquirer
New York Daily News
New York Evening Journal
New York Graphic
New York Herald-Tribune
New York Journal-American
New York Post
New York Sun
New York Times
New York World-Telegram
Oneonta (NY) Daily Star
Palladium-Item (Richmond, IN)
Philadelphia Bulletin
Philadelphia Daily News
Philadelphia Inquirer
Portland Phoenix
Rochester (NY) Times-Union
St. Louis Globe-Democrat
St. Louis Post-Dispatch
San Antonio Express-News
San Francisco Chronicle
San Francisco Examiner
USA Today
Vineyard (MA) Gazette

Washington Post
Washington Times
Wilmington (DE) Evening Journal
Worcester (MA) Evening Gazette

Wire Services

Associated Press
King Features Syndicate
NEA News Service
United Press International

Websites

BaseballAlmanac.com
Baseball-Reference.com
Jim Bouton.com
MLB.com
Yahoo!Sports.com

Other Sources

American League Service Bureau
Congressional Record/testimony
National Baseball Hall of Fame Library Archives
Bull Durham movie script

Index

Aaron, Hank 56
ABC 114, 182
Aberdeen, South Dakota 120
African American 51, 56, 105, 106
Alabama 54, 55, 76
Alabama-Florida League 119
Alaska 157, 158, 159
Alaska Baseball League 157, 162
Alaska Goldpanners 157, 159
Alexander, Grover Cleveland 34
Allen, Dick 152
All-Star Game 43, 53, 97, 142, 173, 186, 187, 190
Altrock, Nick 2, 5, 6, 7, 8, 9, 10, 11, 12, 15, 31
Amarillo, Texas 120
American Association 6
American League 6, 18, 20, 24, 75, 80, 83, 97, 98, 104, 106, 107, 131, 142, 144, 146, 154, 165, 173, 174, 176, 177, 186
American Legion 92
Anderson, Dave 55
Anderson, Sparky 1
André the Giant 184
Ann-Margret 120
Aparicio, Luis 104, 108, 173, 175
April Fool's Day 124
Arizona 95, 112, 138
Arizona Diamondbacks 94, 95, 170
Arkansas 21, 137
Armstrong, Neil 60
Army (U.S.) 17, 43, 45, 47, 49
Ashburn, Richie 71
Astors 23
AstroTurf 152
Atlanta 20
Atlanta Braves 56, 76, 115, 135, 137, 140, 180, 181, 185, 189

Atlanta Crackers 76
Attanasio, Mark 179
Automat 100
Autry, Gene 121

Bakersfield, California 33
Ball, Lucille 191
Ball Four 111, 112, 113, 114, 115, 116, 117
Bally's Casino 138
Baltimore 16, 69, 106, 145
Baltimore Orioles 17, 106, 119, 120, 144, 145, 146, 170, 188, 189
Baney, Dick 116
Barber, Red 46
Barber, Steve 120
Bard's Room 104
Barnett, William 48
Barnum, P.T. 73, 77, 105
Barrett, Marty 169
Bartell, Dick 45
Bartlett's Quotations 81
Baseball Assistance Team (BAT) 89
Baseball Hall of Fame 1, 3, 19, 20, 21, 22, 23, 26, 27, 30, 34, 35, 36, 38, 43, 45, 51, 57, 63, 65, 72, 75, 76, 79, 80, 85, 96, 97, 99, 101, 102, 103, 104, 108, 138, 139, 142, 169, 179, 180, 184, 187, 191
Baseball Is a Funny Game 90
Baseball Magazine 109
Baseball Writers Association of America 101
Bastrop, Louisiana 21
Beckham, Gordon 177
Bedrosian, Steve 153
Belinksy, Bo 118, 119, 120, 121, 122, 123, 124, 125, 153, 154
Bell, Cool Papa 57, 106
Bell, Gus 71

Belle, Albert 169
Berg, Moe 18
Berle, Milton 81
Berman, Chris 167
Berra, Carmen 81, 82, 84
Berra, Dale 82
Berra, Lawrence Peter "Yogi" 80, 81, 82, 83, 84, 85, 86, 87, 88, 95, 101
Big Bird 186
Bill Haley and the Comets 60
Binghamton, N.Y. 63
Birch, John 143
Bird, Larry 162
Bisher, Furman 20
Black Sox 109, 174, 175
Blair, Paul 188
Bloch, Maurice 78
Bluege, Ossie 75
Boggs, Wade 169
Bonds, Barry 163
Boot Hill 141
Borbon, Pedro 189
Boston 24, 169
Boston Braves 36, 37, 38, 39, 40, 67
Boston Celtics 191
Boston Globe 137, 157
Boston Herald 157
Boston Hobos 14
Boston Museum of Science 158
Boston Red Sox 9, 24, 75, 89, 155, 156, 157, 158, 159, 162, 164, 166, 167, 169, 170, 174, 175, 177, 190, 191
Boudreau, Lou 3, 59, 106
Bouton, Jim 111, 112, 113, 114, 115, 116, 117
Bozo the Clown 160
Breadon, Sam 49
Breslin, Jimmy 71
Brett, George 131, 186
Bridges, Rocky 85, 93
Brockton, Massachusetts 159
Brockton Rox 155
Broda, Lou 114
Broeg, Bob 81
Brooklyn 20, 30
Brooklyn Dodgers (Robins) 20, 23, 27, 28, 29, 31, 32, 33, 34, 38, 49, 65, 66, 67, 68, 70, 71, 90, 94, 106
Brooks, Mel 2
Brown, Bobby 83
Brown Derby 29
Bruce, Lenny 116
Brunswick, Georgia 119, 120
Buck, Jack 138
Buckingham Hotel 35

Budweiser/Annheuser-Busch 135, 136, 178
Buffalo 28
Buffalo Bills 142
Buffalo Heads 157
Buice, DeWayne 93
Bull Durham 58, 59, 61, 62, 91
Burbank, California 155
Bush, "Bullet" Joe 21
Bush, George H.W. (president) 86
Bush, George W. (president) 158

California 30, 70, 97, 126, 129, 154
California Angels 94, 153
"Camelot" 186
Campanella, Roy 90, 93
Canada 28, 31, 159, 160, 161, 162
Candlestick Park 192
Cape Cod League 162
Caray, Chip 140
Caray, Harry (Harry Christopher Carabina) 89, 134, 135, 136, 137, 138, 139, 140, 190
Caray, Skip 140
Carbo, Bernie 156, 157
Carew, Rod 187
Carlton, Steve 63
Carrasquel, Chico 173, 175
Carson, Johnny 92, 129, 179, 183
Casablanca 15
Castro, Fidel 178
Catcher in the Wry 181
CBS 45
Cerone, Rick 168
Chamberlain, Wilt 130
Chance, Dean 120, 121, 122, 154
Chattanooga, Tennessee 74, 77, 79
Chattanooga Lookouts 73, 75, 76, 77, 79, 105
Chicago 106, 109, 110, 135, 136, 138, 139, 140, 148, 156, 173, 177, 178, 191
Chicago Cubs 5, 8, 21, 36, 41, 43, 46, 48, 103, 105, 109, 110, 134, 135, 136, 138, 139, 140, 191
Chicago White Sox 5, 8, 9, 72, 103, 107, 109, 110, 134, 135, 146, 156, 164, 165, 167, 172, 173, 174, 175, 176, 177, 178
China 21
Churchill, Winston 182
Chylak, Nestor 143
CIA 142
Cincinnati 5, 20, 23, 25, 116
Cincinnati Reds 1, 5, 19, 20, 22, 25, 46, 73, 86, 124, 156, 189

Index

Clearwater, Florida 124, 125
Cleveland 107, 109, 116, 190
Cleveland Indians 3, 51, 53, 59, 60, 73, 103, 106, 107, 146, 176, 190
Clinton, Bill (president) 137
Clown Prince of Baseball 3, 11, 16, 18, 58, 59, 62, 63
Coast Guard (U.S.) 74
Cocoanut Grove 124
Coleman, Jerry 70
Collins, Jo 120, 124, 125
Colorado 158
Columbus Jets 116
Comiskey Park 104
Communism 161
Concepción, Dave 173
Congress 69
Congressional Record 69
Connecticut 18
Considine, Bob 45
Cooper, Gary 32
Cooperstown, N.Y. 26, 30, 36, 64, 79, 129, 138, 139, 180
Cosell, Howard 135
Costner, Kevin 59, 61
Courtney, Clint 85
Craig, Roger 71
Crockett, Davy 138
Cronin, Joe 75
Crosetti, Frank 99, 101
Cubbage, Mike 63
Cubs Convention 139
Curse of the Bambino 174
Cy Young Award 120

Dangerfield, Rodney 32
Danks, John 178
Dark, Alvin 188
Davis, Crash 59
Davis, Jody 138
Daytona Beach, Florida 68
Deadball Era 38, 39
Dean, Daffy (Paul) 42, 43, 45, 46
Dean, Dizzy (Jay Hanna) 42, 43, 44, 45, 46, 47, 48, 49, 50, 53, 54, 79, 186
Des Plaines, Illinois 138
Detroit 101
Detroit Lions 142
Detroit Tigers 2, 25, 33, 43, 45, 59, 84, 98, 108, 146, 165, 175, 186, 187
Dickey, Bill 21, 99
Dickson, Murray 91
Dietz Stadium 14
DiMaggio, Dom 43, 191

DiMaggio, Joe 43, 59, 67, 96, 97, 98, 101, 177
DiMaggio, Vince 43
Dixie Series 48
Doby, Larry 106
Dr. Phil 67
Dodger Stadium 150, 152
Dominican Republic 150
Dominican Winter League 189
Doyle, Harry 183
Drabowsky, Moe 187, 188, 189
Dressen, Charlie 46, 90
Dugan, Joe 19
Durante, Jimmy 20
Duren, Ryne 191
Durocher, Leo 92, 116, 117
Dylan, Bob 3

Earley, Joe 107
Ebbets Field 28, 31, 32
Einstein, Albert 98, 160
Eisenhower, Dwight D. 9, 44
The Empire Strikes Back 141
Endicott, New York 142, 147
Engel, Joe 73, 74, 75, 76, 77, 78, 79, 105
Engel Stadium 78, 79
Equal Rights Amendment 156
ESPN 158, 167
Europe 16
Evans, Darrell 153
Evans, Jim 165
Everett, Carl 169

F-16 173
Fairbanks, Alaska 157, 159
Falstaff Brewing Corporation 48
Faust, Nancy 107
Faust Charlie "Victory" 189
Fear Strikes Out 190
Federal League 8
Feller, Bob 17, 53, 54
Fenway Park 170, 190
Fidrych, Mark 2, 186, 187
Fielder, Cecil 165
Finley, Charlie 135, 188
First Holy Communion 156, 158
Fisher, David 147
Fitzpatrick, Eddie 40
Fletcher, Art 13
Florida 131, 144
Florida Marlins 173, 178
Forbes Field 37
Ford, Gerald (president) 89

Ford, Whitey 66
Ford Frick Award 139, 179
Fort Slocum 16
Foul Ball 113
Fox, Nellie 104, 108
Fox Sports 170
Foxx, Jimmie 40, 99, 102
Franks, Herman 93
Fregosi, Jim 145
Frick, Ford 45
Frisch, Frank(ie) 43, 50

Gaedel, Eddie 103, 104
"Game of the Week" 49, 89
Gammons, Peter 157
Garagiola, Joe 64, 80, 81, 85, 88, 89, 90, 91, 92, 93, 94, 95, 102
Garagiola, Mickey 88
Garbo, Greta 69
Gashouse Gang 27
Gehrig, Lou 32, 76
Gehringer, Charlie 98
Geisel, Harry 7
Gettysburg Address 52
Gibson, Bob 159, 184
Gibson, Josh 54, 57, 101, 105, 106
Giles, Bill 126
Glendale, California 28, 30, 65
Glenn, John 162
Gold Glove 173, 190
Golden Gloves 144
Goltz, Dave 149
Gomez, Gery 102
Gomez, Lefty 96, 97, 98, 99, 100, 101, 102
Goodyear Blimp 93
Goosen, Greg 112
Gorman, Tom 90
Goslin, Goose 75
Gowdy, Hank 40
GQ 61, 161, 166
Great Depression 21
Great Falls, Montana 60
Green Bay, Wisconsin 60
Greenberg, Hank 45, 59, 99, 108, 109
Gregg, Eric 141
Gregory, Dick 162
Gregory, Robert 49
Griffith, Clark 6, 17, 75, 78, 79
Grimm, Charlie 37
Grissom, Marv 119, 120
Groat, Dick 91
Guatemala 177
Guillen, Ozzie 172, 173, 174, 175, 176, 177, 178

Haller, Bill 143
Halloween 124
Hamey, Roy 83
Haney, Fred 94, 121
Harlem Globetrotters 2, 60, 61, 106
Harridge, Will 101, 104
Harris, Bucky 75, 83
Hartnett, Gabby 46
Have Glove, Will Travel 159
Hawaii 58
Hawaii (baseball team) 125
HBO 173
Henderson, Rickey 31
Herman, Babe (Floyd Caves Herman) 27, 28, 29, 30, 31, 32, 33, 34
Herman, Bobby 29
Hillerich & Bradsby 98
Hitchcock, Alfred 167
Hitchcock, Billy 180
Hoak, Don 116
Hodges, Gil 71, 127
Hodges, Russ 23
Hollywood (baseball team) 33
Hollywood, California 49, 118, 121, 122, 152, 181
Holtzman, Jerome 139
Holy Name Cathedral 140
Honolulu 21
Houk, Ralph 146
House of David 48
Houston (baseball team) 48
Houston Astros 71, 115, 124, 131, 174, 177
Houston Colt .45s 71
Howard, Frank 63
Howe, Steve 149
Hoyt, Ad 20
Hoyt, Waite 19, 20, 21, 22, 23, 24, 25, 26
Hudson, Massachusetts 170
Huggins, Miller 22, 24
Hunter, Jim "Catfish" 1
Huntsville, Alabama 116

I Managed Good, But Boy Did They Play Bad 113
Illinois 58
I'm Glad You Didn't Take It Personally 113
International League 13
Italy 17, 29

Jack the Ripper 115
Jackson, Andrew 119
Jackson, Bo 124

INDEX

Jackson, Reggie 1
Japanese language 29
Jenkins, Ferguson 157, 180
Jersey City, N.J. 13, 17
Johnson, Ban 6
Johnson, Walter 6, 17, 54, 73, 77
Johnstone, Jay 148, 149, 150, 151, 152, 153, 154, 164
Jordan, Michael 124
Judge, Joe 75

Kaat, Jim 162
Kaiser, Ken 147
Kansas 189
Kansas City 6, 65
Kansas City (minors team) 75
Kansas City Athletics 56, 188
Kansas City Monarchs 54
Kansas City Royals 63, 126, 131
Kaufman, Ewing 63
Kaze, Irving 118
Kelley, Emmett 160
Kelly, Joe 31
Kennedy, John 157
Kentucky Derby 75
Khrushchev, Nikita 113
Kilbane, Johnny 6
Kimball, George 157
King, Stephen 164
Kingdome 93
Kingston, N.Y. 14
Kingston Colonials 14
Klem, Bill 36, 68
Knoxville, Tennessee 120
Kobe, Japan 21
Koosman, Jerry 127, 132
Korea 21
Koufax, Sandy 101, 129, 180
Krause, Lew 188
Kuhn, Bowie 111, 112, 113, 158, 187, 188

Labine, Clem 71
Ladies Day 103
Lakewood, Ohio 107
Landis, Kenesaw Mountain 106
Landrith, Hobie 71
Larsen, Don 66
La Russa, Tony 138
Las Vegas 125, 137, 138
Lasorda, Tom 148, 150, 151, 152
Latham, Arlie 5
Laugh-In 149
Lazzeri, Tony 76, 99, 101
LeBatard, Dan 158

Lee, Annabelle 156
Lee, Bill (Spaceman) 155, 156, 157, 158, 159, 160, 161, 162, 163
Lee, Mary Lou 157
Leonard, Buck 101, 106
Lethbridge, Canada 62
Letterman, David 130, 131, 166
Leyva, Nick 153
Lieb, Fred 77, 78
LIFE magazine 57
Li'l Abner 44
Little Rock, Arkansas 120, 187
Longueuil, Canada 160
LOOK magazine 115
Lopes, Davey 153
López, Al 34
Los Angeles 28, 120, 121, 124
Los Angeles Angels 7, 118, 119, 121, 123, 145, 190
Los Angeles Dodgers 148, 150, 151, 153, 170, 188
Louis, Joe 85
Louise, Tina 120
Louisiana 75, 130
Louisville 62
Louisville Cardinals 62
Louisville Colonels 5
Louisville Slugger 98
Lucas, Arkansas 42
Luciano, Ron 141, 142, 143, 144, 145, 146, 147
The Lucy Show 191
Lyons, Dick 170
Lyons, Steve "Psycho" 164, 165, 166, 167, 168, 169, 170, 171

Mack, Connie 189
Macon, Georgia 32
Macy's Turkey Day Parade 164
Maine 63
Majestic Hotel 35
Major League Baseball 51, 53, 106, 144, 158, 160
Major League 179, 183
Major League II 183
Manchester, Connecticut 148
Manila, Philippines 21
Mann, Earl 78
Mantle, Mickey 4, 66, 69, 70, 82, 85, 129
Maranville, "Rabbit" Walter 35, 36, 37, 38, 39, 40, 41
Marines 105, 129, 151
Maris, Roger 85
Marlboro, Massachusetts 169

Marlboro Country Club 170
Marshall, Mike 113
Martin, Billy 142
Marx, Harpo 186
Maryville Academy 138
Massachusetts 117, 186, 187
Mathewson, Christy 12, 54
Mauch, Gene 143, 180
Mays, Willie 37, 129
McCarthy, Joe 101
McCarver, Tim 128, 129
McDonald, Ronald 160
McDowell, Jack 165
McDowell, Roger 153
McGinnity, Joe "Iron Man" 100
McGraw, Hank 129
McGraw, John J. 3, 13, 40, 189
McGraw, Tim 130
McGraw, Tug 126, 127, 128, 129, 130, 131, 132, 133
McKinley, William (president) 191
McNamara, John 169, 170
McQueen, Steve 82
Memphis 137
Men's Journal 158
Metkovich, George 91
Metropolitan Opera 32
Miami 63, 178
Milkes, Marvin 112
Miller, Bob (two pitchers) 71
Miller, Marvin 112
Miller Lite Beer 87, 182, 183
Miller Park 183, 185
Milwaukee 107, 184, 185
Milwaukee Braves 76, 94, 107, 137, 185
Milwaukee Brewers (majors) 111, 179, 182, 184, 185
Milwaukee Brewers (minor league team) 105
Mincher, Don 116
Minneapolis 78
Minoso, Minnie 5
"Mr. Baseball" 179
Mr. Belvedere 179, 182, 183
Mitchell, Jackie 76
Mobile, Alabama 21, 51, 56
Moncton, New Brunswick 160
Monroe, Marilyn 98
Montclair State University 87
Montreal 39, 161
Montreal Expos 155, 158, 159, 160, 161, 168
Moore, Wilcy 25
Moriarty, George 19

Moscow 161
Mount St. Mary's College 75
Mount Sinai Hospital 86
Municipal Stadium (Baltimore) 188
Municipal Stadium (Cleveland) 60, 109
Munson, Thurman 141
Murphy, Dale 189
Murphy, Johnny 96, 101, 127
Murray, Jim 51
Musial, Stan 85, 188
"My Way" 172

Napoleonic Era 32
NASA 99
Nash, Jim 188
National League 5, 23, 24, 27, 31, 33, 37, 43, 45, 70, 74, 88, 89, 94, 106, 126, 131, 150, 180
National League Championship Series 131
NBA 135
NBC 138
Neal, Charlie 71
Negro Leagues 51, 52, 53, 54, 57, 98, 101, 104
New Britain, Connecticut 167
New England 190
New Guinea 17
New Jersey 64, 82, 85, 87
New Jersey Turnpike 131
New York 9, 16, 20, 22, 49, 71, 81, 82, 86, 100, 114, 121, 127, 128, 131
New York Daily News 69, 113
New York Giants 3, 12, 13, 20, 23, 40, 43, 45, 70, 92, 99, 189
New York Knickerbockers 71
New York Mets 3, 33, 63, 65, 70, 71, 72, 81, 85, 87, 89, 126, 130, 131, 132, 156, 191
New York Post 69, 112
New York Times 19, 22, 41, 46, 55, 69
New York Yankees 12, 19, 20, 21, 22, 24, 25, 38, 49, 59, 65, 66, 67, 68, 70, 71, 76, 83, 84, 85, 87, 92, 93, 96, 97, 98, 99, 100, 101, 111, 141, 142, 154, 157, 170, 172, 174, 190
Newark 12
Niekro, Phil 179
Nixon, Richard (president) 158
North Africa 15, 17

Oakland Athletics 127, 134
O'Day, Hank 39
O'Dea, June 98, 100

INDEX

215

Oglethorpe Hotel 119
Ohio Valley 23
Oliver, Gene 181
O'Malley, Walter 33
O'Neal, Shaquille 183
O'Neil, Buck 54
Ordonez, Magglio 175
Ortiz, David 159
Ott, Mel 17, 99, 154
Over the Edge 148
Ozark, Danny 152

Pagliaroni, Jim 117
Paige, Satchel 51, 52, 53, 54, 55, 56, 57, 98, 101, 105, 106, 155
Palace Theatre 20, 22
Palm Beach, Florida 75
Patkin, Eddie 64
Patkin, Max 2, 58, 59, 60, 61, 62, 63, 64
Pawtucket Red Sox 166, 168
Pena, Hippolito 142
Pennsylvania 161
Pennsylvania Railroad 69
Pensacola, Florida 120
People magazine 162
Peoria, Illinois 138
Peoria Chiefs 140
Pep, Willie 182
Perry, Gaylord 180, 187
Petry, Dan 165
Philadelphia 35, 58, 59, 62, 123, 124, 126, 131, 132
Philadelphia Athletics 3, 25, 189
Philadelphia Phillies 63, 92, 105, 106, 123, 124, 126, 128, 130, 131, 132, 133, 151, 152, 153, 154, 180
Phoenix (baseball team) 93
Piersall, Jimmy 136, 148, 153, 190, 191
Pignatano, Joe 127
Piniella, Lou 170
Pittsburgh Pirates 1, 21, 24, 33, 36, 37, 40, 70, 75, 88, 89, 90, 91, 92, 94, 116, 119, 123, 124, 125, 130, 132
Playboy magazine 120, 124
Playgirl magazine 165
Poland 187
Poli's Theater 22
Polo Grounds 12
Presley, Elvis 137, 191
Price, Jackie 3, 59
The Pride of the Yankees 32
Prohibition 37
Psycho 167

PsychoAnalysis 164
Puerto Rico 167
Pulsipher, Bill 63
Puss'n Boots (cat food) 87

Quebec 160, 161
Quigley, Martin 90
Quisenberry, Dan 154

Ramirez, Alexei 177
Reagan, Ronald (president) 20, 138
Redford, Robert 60
Reese, Pee Wee 49, 108
Reggie Bar 1
Reinsdorf, Jerry 173, 174
Reuss, Jerry 149, 150, 152, 192
Rhinoceros Party 162
Rickey, Branch 33, 88, 89
Rickles, Don 152
Rigney, Bill 121, 122, 153
Rizzuto, Phil 93, 96, 108, 191
Roaring Twenties 23
Robinson, Brooks 2
Robinson, Frank 82
Robinson, Jackie 53, 106
Robinson, Wilbert 31, 65, 68
Rochester, N.Y. 39
Rodríguez, Pudge 173
Rogers, Roy 156
Rookie of Year 173, 186
Roosevelt, Franklin D. 29
Roosevelt, Teddy 73
Rose, Pete 111, 113, 168
Rowland, Pants 23
Royster, Jerry 189
Ruggeri's (restaurant) 85
Runnels, Tom 168
Ruppert, Jacob 21, 38
Rush Street (Mayor of Rush Street) 135, 139
Russia (Russians) 161, 162, 191
Ruth, Babe 17, 19, 21, 24, 25, 27, 29, 77, 85, 97, 103, 174, 175, 191
Ryan, Nolan 127

Sagan, Carl 162
St. Louis 35, 80, 81, 82, 88, 104, 106, 109, 134, 139, 189
St. Louis Browns 3, 5, 48, 49, 103, 104, 106, 109, 135
St. Louis Cardinals 27, 42, 43, 46, 48, 49, 85, 88, 89, 92, 100, 106, 134, 135, 136, 137, 180, 181, 184, 188
St. Louis Hawks 135

Index

St. Louis University 135
St. Mary's Mission (Alaska) 158
St. Paul, Minnesota 90, 98
St. Petersburg, Florida 92
Sale of the Century 92
San Diego Chicken 62, 64, 146
San Francisco Giants 94
San Francisco Seals 97
Saperstein, Abe 106
Sarandon, Susan 61
Saturday Evening Post 104
Sawyer, Carl 8
Sax, Steve 151
Schacht, Al 2, 5, 8, 9, 10, 11, 12, 13, 14, 15, 16, 17, 18
Schaefer, Germany 8
Schecter, Leonard 112
Schiltz beer 136
Schultz, Joe 112, 113
Scott, Jack 38
Scott, Rodney 158
"Scroogie" 128
Seattle 93, 112
Seattle Pilots 111, 112, 115, 116, 117
Seaver, Tom 127, 156, 157
Selig, Bud 179
Selkirk, George 101
Selma, Alabama 78
Sewell, Joe 99
Shakespeare 63, 111, 146
Shea, Frank 83
Shea Stadium 128
Sheen, Charlie 179
Shelton, Ron 58
Shibe Park 24
Showalter, Buck 170, 171, 175
Simmons, Al 24
Sinatra, Frank 152, 172
Smith, Harry 12
Smith, Red 34
Some of My Best Friends Are Crazy 148
South Boston 161
South Dakota 188
South Pacific 105
Southern Association 76, 77, 79
Spink, J.G. Taylor Spink 106
Splittorff, Paul 186
Sporthings 154
The Sporting News 58, 77, 106, 120
Sports Illustrated 172
Sportsman's Park 104
Springfield, Massachusetts 35
Stanhouse, Don 152
Star Wars 141

Stargell, Willie 1
Steinbrenner, George 85, 154
Stengel, Casey 27, 28, 33, 65, 66, 67, 68, 69, 70, 71, 72, 81, 83, 127, 191
Stevens, Connie 120
Stockton, California 120
Stone, Steve 136
Street, Gabby 42, 48
Stuart, Dick 123, 124
Stuckey's 162
Sullivan, Frank 4
Sullivan, Marc 167
Sullivan, Paul 139
Sutcliffe, Rick 138
Swoboda, Ron 81, 82
Syracuse University 142

Tacoma, Washington 164
"Take Me Out to the Ballgame" (song) 102, 134, 136, 139, 140
Talley, Rick 148
Tampa, Florida 79
Temporary Insanity 148, 150
Tennessee 76
Tennessee River 74
Terry, Bill 27
Texas League 48
Texas Rangers 169, 175
Thomas, Frank 71
Thompson, Hunter S. 162
Thomson, Bobby 23
Thorpe, Jim 39
Throneberry, Marv 72
Thurber, James 104
The Today Show 89, 92, 183
Toledo Mud Hens 68
The Tonight Show 92, 183
Torre, Joe 181
Travis, Cecil 75
Trenton, New Jersey 119, 122, 123
The Truth Hurts 191
Turley, Bob 66

Uecker, Bob 179, 180, 181, 182, 183, 184, 185
The Umpire Strikes Back 41, 144
Unger, Felix 151
United States 18, 162, 167, 172, 175
U.S. Cellular Field 104
U.S. Senate Anti-Trust and Monopoly Subcommittee 69
U.S. Supreme Court 128
University of Missouri 135
University of Southern California 156

Index

Vance, Dazzy 27, 32, 33
Vancouver, British Columbia 120
Van Cuyk, Chris 90
Van Doren, Mamie 118, 120, 121, 124
Van Slyke, Andy 2
Veeck, Bill 55, 57, 59, 64, 73, 74, 103, 104, 105, 106, 107, 108, 109, 110, 134, 135, 140
Veeck, William, Sr. 103
Venezuela 122, 172, 175, 176, 177
Verdun, Canada 160
Vermont 155, 158
Vero Beach, Florida 150
Veterans Committee (Baseball Hall of Fame) 101
Veterans Stadium 63, 131
Vonachen, Peter 140

"The Wabash Cannonball" (song) 44
Waddell, Rube 2, 3
Wagner, Honus 40
Wagner, Leon 123
Walker, Moses Fleetwood 105
Wallace, George (presidential candidate) 116
Walters, Barbara 89
Walters, Bucky 89
Waner, Lloyd 20
Waner, Paul 20
Waseda University 21
Washington, D.C. 9, 73, 75, 98, 161
Washington Monument 68
Washington Post 73
Washington Senators 5, 6, 7, 8, 9, 11, 17, 25, 31, 73, 75, 77, 100
Waterbury, Connecticut 190
Weaver, Earl 142, 144, 145, 146
Webb, Clifton 182
Weissmuller, Johnny 184
Wertz, Vic 86
West, Mae 55
Wetteland, John 143, 144
WGN 139
Wheat, Zach 23, 65
Wheaties 20
White House 1, 161

Whitehead, Burgess 44
Wilhelm II, Kaiser 29
Wilkes-Barre, Pennsylvania 60
William Morris Agency 20
Williams, Joe 9, 25
Williams, Kenny 173, 174
Williams, Ted 59, 191
Willoughby, Jim 157
Wilson, Mookie 3
Wilson, Willie 131
Wilson Sporting Goods 96
Winchell, Walter 121
Windsor, Canada 101
Wisconsin Rapids, Wisconsin 60
Wise, Rick 157
Witte, Mike 128
Wolff, Hoffman 155
Women's Semi-Pro Hardball League 156
World Series 5, 6, 8, 11, 15, 17, 19, 20, 21, 23, 31, 43, 44, 65, 66, 68, 70, 80, 86, 87, 89, 92, 94, 97, 99, 100, 103, 111, 116, 127, 130, 131, 140, 142, 166, 172, 173, 175, 177, 178, 188, 189
World War I 29
World War II 3, 15, 18, 29, 49, 58, 74, 91, 96, 105, 107
World Wrestling Entertainment Hall of Fame 184
Wrestlemania 184
Wrigley, Philip 105
Wrigley Family 103, 109
Wrigley Field 105, 134, 140
The Wrong Stuff 156
Wynn, Early 101, 188

Yankee Stadium 23, 100, 101, 191
Yellow Horse, Moses 37, 38
Yogi Bear 81
The Yogi Berra Museum and Learning Center 86
Yoo-Hoo (drink) 87
Young, Cy 54
Young, Dick 113, 114
Youngs, Ross 101

Zimmer, Don 71, 155, 157, 172

www.ingramcontent.com/pod-product-compliance
Ingram Content Group UK Ltd.
Pitfield, Milton Keynes, MK11 3LW, UK
UKHW041956140426
5217IPUK00015B/820

9 781476 663586